D1400177

Chapter 1

Official Story of Barry's Death

Barry Seal was packing his briefcase in Baton Rouge when three Colombian hitmen arrived at his hotel room ready to kill him.

Barry stood under a large chandelier in his living room and said "Debbie," gazing up at his wife.

Debbie wore a blue floral top and white pants with brown hair. "OK. "OK.

"Right after my jog?"
"You started jogging!"
Barry smiled. Barry smiled. Barry spoke slowly and with a pleasant Louisiana accent, "If I can't be rich I might as well be pretty.".
Debbie smiled, resting her elbows on a banister. "Well, you're pretty, rich or poor," Debbie said.

Barry exclaimed, "Whoo-whee!" He shook his shoulders and hips while yelling. His smile vanished as he checked his watch. "Oh,

I have to go. It's quarter-to six."
Debbie said.

"I love you too, Mrs Seal."

Debbie shouted at her husband, a hefty man with thick sideburns, as he walked out.

"Be careful!"
The Colombians concealed a machine gun in a hotel room by wrapping clothing around it. They walked quickly in light-coloured clothes and suits, and then got into a car. As they drove towards the Salvation Army halfwayhouse, the sun was almost gone from the skyline.

WITHDRAWN FROM
RAPIDES PARISH LIBRARY
Alexandria, Louisiana

Barry looked forward to his six-month sentence at Baton Rouge's halfway house, as he drove in a white Cadillac.

After his status as an informant was leaked to the media by the Reagan-Bush government, he was told by the Medellin Cartel that he had been placed under $500,000 by the Medellin Cartel. It is run by powerful Colombian drug lords like Pablo Escobar.

Barry arrived at the halfway home in darkness. He reversed his vehicle towards the two-storey, beige building. He was about to get out of his car when a shadowy figure caught him off guard. Barry stared at the man in front of his Cadillac. It was a thin Colombian male with a moustache. Barry was able to see the man leap forward and point a gun at him.

Peter Jennings, News Anchor reported that Seal used to smuggle drugs. He was caught and became one of the most valuable informants for the government in the fight against cocaine. Barry Seal was killed by his enemies in Louisiana last night. Three men are currently in detention tonight. Brian Ross of NBC reports that Seal was set to testify once more for the government.

"Authorities believe last night's gun-mashing," Brian Ross stated, "of top drug informant Barry Seal" was ordered by drug bosses from Medellin, Colombia who sent five men to Baton Rouge. Barry Jr., Seal's youngest son, was arrested by police. They claimed that the gunmen had waited for Seal at a Salvation Army shelter where Seal had been sentenced on a drug case to perform community service. Seal, a TWA pilot who was tough, was caught with cocaine smuggling and was one of the most prominent and daring undercover agents, infiltrating top Colombian drug operations. Seal stated that he knew he was putting his life at risk in a recent interview.

Barry was seen in sunglasses while in a cockpit. Barry stated, "If you can't handle the heat, don't work in your kitchen."

Brian Ross stated that Seal posed as a smuggler and flew into Nicaragua to take these photos showing Sandinista officials and Colombian drug dealers loading cocaine onto his plane.

Reagan-Bush claimed Pablo Escobar was in one of the grainy photos.

Seal discovered the Colombian connection to Turks and Caicos and set up a videotape payoff meeting that led to the conviction and arrest of the prime minister. Seal was to be the main witness against Jorge Ochoa (the top Colombian drug boss currently in Spain and about to be extradited) Authorities claim that the Ochoa drug organization was responsible for the bombing at the US Embassy in Bogota last January, as well as the assassination and murder of Colombia's attorney General.

All media reported that Barry was a government witness against drug dealers, Jorge Ochoa of the Medellin Carrtel and Pablo Escobar, who had authorized the hit. Barry, who refused to enter the Federal Witness Protection Program was ambushed at a Louisiana halfwayhouse and shot in the head. Later, the media reported that a Colombian hit squad of three men had been captured and convicted. They were sentenced to life imprisonment without parole. The case is closed.

The official Barry story was a mess as I began to research his life for my War on Drugs trilogy. Barry was involved in powerful people who were specialized in assassinations, and trafficked drugs and arms on an international level. He was a liability because of the information he had accumulated while working as a pilot for them. George HW Bush's phone number was still with him when he died. It is necessary to look at Barry's life beyond the Hollywood portrayal and the relationships he formed while working for CIA.

Chapter 2

A Young Pilot

Barry was born on July 16, 1939. He became obsessed with flying from a young age. Barry would ride his bicycle to the private airport close to his Baton Rouge home and watch the movements of small planes. He was already flying by age 15 and earning money towing banners. He spent $14 per lesson on flying lessons with the earnings from his paper round.

Mary Lou, his mother, was a domestic worker. BC was an alcoholic candy wholesaler. He also belonged to the Ku Klux Klan. This hate group's members wore white robes and hoods and danced with burning crosses. Although they hated blacks, they also had a lot of hatred for Jews and gays. Some of their members were responsible across the US for atrocities like hanging people, bombing black churches and setting them ablaze.

Barry was the oldest child of the three. The boys loved playing with cars and ball. Barry's mother asked Eddie Dufford, his flight instructor, if he would not teach him lessons. Eddie replied, "Ma'am! That boy of yours will find a way learn to fly, regardless of what." He needs to learn from someone." She trusted Eddie and agreed to give lessons.

Barry flew to the match, while his classmates took long bus rides. He landed a helicopter at one high school game. He even took girls up in the air for dates.

His skills as a pilot were evident, but so was his risk-taking nature which would land him in serious trouble. Barry took his friends to a small plane that he had stalled in order to scare them. When the plane refused to turn on, it was a prank that backfired. Barry concentrated all his attention to try and land the plane in a field after it lost its propelling power. The plane that was descending crashed into a field and smashed into trees. One passenger suffered a broken arm. Barry injured his ankle and it would continue to affect his entire life. Barry's skills in landing the plane were appreciated by the owner, but he was banned from flying.

Barry joined the Baton Rouge Civil Air Patrol in 1955. Barry met Lee Harvey Oswald, a trainee, while on a joint training exercise. Eight years later, Oswald would become the one who took the fall for President John F Kennedy's assassination. According to some records, Oswald joined Civil Air Patrol in mid-1950s. However, most of the records from the squadron were destroyed in 1960. Oswald was intelligent and spoke Russian and Spanish.

David Ferrie was the New Orleans Civil Air Patrol's commander. Jim Garrison, the New Orleans District Attorney, alleged that Ferrie was involved in the plot to assassinate JFK. Ferrie was diagnosed with alopecia wereata, which is a skin condition that makes him less hairy as he ages. He was an impressive sight with his reddish-colored home-made wig, and pasted-on eyebrows. Barry was impressed by Ferrie's discipline as he barks orders.

Ferrie, a former priest who couldn't control his sexual proclivities towards boys was defrocked. Ferrie had previously obtained a pilot's license and taught aeronautics in Cleveland's Benedictine High School. However, he was fired for numerous infractions including taking boys to a prostitution house. After being twice arrested on morals charges, he made the move to New Orleans in 1951 and became a pilot for Eastern Air Lines.

Ferrie was involved in Civil Air Patrol since 1947. He arranged for children from troubled families to be air cadets. Some of these kids were not allowed to give physicals. He guided cadets like Barry Seal and Lee Harvey Oswald to clandestine service. Ferrie was an ace pilot as well as a medical researcher and a linguist, who spoke Italian. He also worked as an armchair psychologist and a hypnotist. Ferrie was initially supportive of Fidel Castro's Cuban government, but he became hostile to Castro after he declared a Marxist. He flew to Cuba and bombed and sabotaged raids as well as rescued anti-Castro resistance fighters.

Barry Seal and David Ferrie had a few commonalities, including photographic memories and flying with the CIA. Barry was also able to read upside-down. Ferrie and Barry were referred to as CIA contract pilots in order to create the impression that they were rogue agents who were operating independently. They were eventually deemed liabilities and were removed from the service they were providing.

Ferrie and Oswald were killed after the media attacked them for their involvement in the JFK assassination. Chapter 5 examines this chapter to reveal clues about Barry's murderers.

Ferrie taught Barry how to transport weapons to Fidel Castro by 1958. Barry received a P51 Mustang, an American fighter-bomber and long-range fighter-bomber during World War II. Barry flew munitions for the Castro-opposing forces, as US weapon manufacturers made money from both sides of the Cuban Civil War.

Barry was trying to establish relationships with intelligence and military services, and was getting a taste for the international arms trade that would eventually lead him to his death. He was not prepared for the consequences. Barry purchased three planes as the money from arms trafficking began to roll in: a Champ Chief, an Arcana Chief, and a Comanche.

Chapter 3

CIA

Barry worked for the CIA for decades until his death. The nature of Barry's employer can provide clues to his murderers.

The CIA was established in 1947 and specialized in propaganda, economic warfare and regime changes. In later years, it also dealt with drug and weapon trafficking. Barry helped. The CIA had more than 3,000 employees involved in propaganda and controlled 25 newspapers and wire agencies by the 1950s. Members of The New York Times, Time Magazine and Newsweek were among those who promoted their views.

The CIA's Twitter account states that it is the Nation's first defense line. Over the years, the CIA has proven that it can accomplish what no one else can and goes where no one else will.

The 1954 CIA disapproval of President Arbenz of Guatemala was expressed by the agency. He had taken 240,000 acres from United Fruit, a company that had Allen Dulles as its director. 100,000 peasants were given the land. Although the CIA armed right-wing military officers, the uprising was unsuccessful. The CIA sent thirty aircraft that dropped leaflets, bombs, and fired machine guns. The uprising was successful this time and Walter Bedell, the CIA director, was rewarded with a seat on the board at United Fruit. Although the US provided almost $1 billion of aid to the new government, by 1957 the CIA had begun plotting regime change. The president was killed and shot at his table in July. Guatemalan violence continued for 40 years with around 150,000 deaths.

The CIA managed to place a bomb aboard a plane in 1955 that was meant to transport Chou Enlai (the Chinese Communist leader), who was due to fly from Hong Kong into Indonesia. Chou decided to change his mind and he avoided a flight that burst over the South China Sea killing all on board.

Political manipulation, torture, and murder are ways to get power

Rafael Trujillo was the Dominican Republic's president in 1930. He was an American ally until 1960 when US foreign policymakers turned against him. He was shot to death by assassins trained and armed by the CIA in 1961.

Despite using their most innovative methods, the CIA failed numerous times to assassinate Cuban dictator Fidel Castro over a twenty-five year period. Allan Robert Nye was an American contract killer who was found with a powerful rifle in a Cuban hotel near the presidential palace. Unfazed, a CIA agent hosted a meeting a month later between American mobsters with a former leader of the Cuban death squad. They discussed Castro's assassination outside the presidential palace.

The CIA devised several plans to drug Castro. They wanted to inject LSD by aerosol into Castro's radio studio. Castro was a fan of the cigars they used, so they added psychoactive drugs and lethal poisons to his favorite cigars.

The CIA had planned to poison Castro's shoes and his night table with poisonous thallium sodium salts to paralyze or kill him when Castro was due to appear in New York at the United Nations in 1960.

Johnny Rosselli, a mobster who was paid $150,000 by the CIA to arrange Castro's death, was the amount that the CIA paid in 1960. Rosselli met with two Mafia men: Sam Giancana, and Santos Trafficante. Giancana suggested that Castro be poisoned with poison pills. Six deadly botulinum pills were produced by the CIA laboratory and transported in a hollow pencil. To be safe, the CIA provided a box of botulinum-toxin-soaked cigars that could have been fatal to touch. Trafficante gave the cigars and pills to an insider of Castro who owed the Mafia money for gambling. But the insider refused to take them. Another batch of botulinum tablets ended up in a Castro-favorite restaurant, which Castro fortuitously stopped visiting before the pills arrived.

Castro managed to dodge various assassination attempts, strengthened ties with Russia, and committed the ultimate evil of expropriating land for the United Fruit Company. Both Barry and Ferrie would play their part as pilots.

In March 1960, President Eisenhower gave $13.1 million to CIA in order to overthrow Castro. Kennedy was only 12 weeks into his term when the invasion was scheduled. Members of the CIA who had inside information purchased shares in sugar companies, causing prices and stocks to soar. The US Mafia was ready to seize control of the casinos. The United Fruit Company was prepared to seize control of the banana plantations.

Over 1,400 paramilitaries were assembled in Guatemala, and they were divided into five infantry battalions, one paratrooper battalion. They then set out by boat for Cuba on April 13, 1961.

Eight CIA-supplied B26 bombers were used to attack Cuban airfields two days later, on April 15. The main invasion arrived at Playa Giron, a beach in the Bay of Pigs on April 16th. It overpowered a local militia.

With 25,000 soldiers, the Cuban Army launched an offensive to counter it. David Ferrie was trapped while on a weapons delivery mission. Legend has it that Ferrie managed to lift his plane from the ground using one hand and the other to fight off a soldier who had attacked him in the stomach. Ferrie was left with a large scar. Barry was a pilot and didn't have to deal with any death or life situations in Cuba.

Things quickly deteriorated with the exile force still at the beachhead. JFK refused to give up on the plan of the CIA. Over 1,000 invaders surrendered on April 20. A little over 100 had been killed. Most of the prisoners were interrogated publicly and taken to Cuban prisons.

JFK called the Bay of Pigs the most painful experience of his entire life. Kennedy previously stated, "First, let me say that there will be no intervention by the United States Armed Forces in Cuba under any circumstances." The government will do all it can and I believe it can fulfill its responsibilities to ensure that no Americans are involved in any actions." Kennedy was forced to accept responsibility for the unprovoked invasion by an enemy nation that had already failed. It was against several US laws and treaties. This was an embarrassment to the peace talks that had been made.

Kennedy wanted to shatter the CIA into a thousand pieces. Kennedy began by firing the CIA leaders. He shut down the camps in the US, where Cuban exiles had been trained by David Ferrie and Lee Harvey Oswald.

JFK made a bold move in June 1963 and ordered the issuance $4.2 billion worth of United States Notes instead of the regular Federal Reserve Notes. It was an interest- and debt-free currency that was backed by silver deposits in the US.

Treasury. The Federal Reserve System, owned by private banks and printing money for profit, was challenged. The Federal Reserve System's banks used ink and paper that were only a few thousand dollars each to print billions of dollar when the government needed it. They charged the government billions. Lincoln was the only president to issue interest- and debt-free currency. Lincoln was shot in the head after issuing Greenbacks.

Ferrie and other Barry associates called for JFK's assassination. It would not take long.

Castro was the victim of a CIA plot to rob him of his scuba diving gear. It was lined with a deadly mixture of Madura fungus, tubercle bacilli and implanted tubercle bacilli. High explosives were used to lure deep-sea lobsters into the area Castro dived. A ballpoint pen that doubled as an ink syringe was created with Blackleaf-40, an insecticide made up of forty percent nicotine sulphate. None of these methods worked, as usual.

Che Guevara, a South American revolutionary, was more easily captured by the CIA. This plot involved Felix Rodriguez, a Nazi war criminal and Klaus Barbie - a friend to George HW Bush - Barry Seal often received orders from the CIA. The third installment of this trilogy tells the story about Klaus Barbie: We Are Being Lying To: The War On Drugs.

Drug production soared in many of the countries America invaded. The CIA formed alliances and opium lords from Burma, Thailand, and Laos. This led to a high rate of drug addiction among US troops during the Vietnam War. Air America, a CIA front company flew opium from the mountains of Laos.

Tosh Plumlee (ex-CIA pilot) claims that Barry served with Air America from 1967 to 1968 in South Vietnam and Laos. He performed Search and Destroy and Special Ops. Plumlee noticed Barry's name on cables dating back to 1964.

Many South American countries were granted weapons by the US on CIA flights. The planes were loaded with drugs for the return trip - this was documented by Gary Webb, a journalist in his "Dark Alliance", series. Former DEA Agent Celerino Castillo, Powderburns: Cocaine Contras and Drug War: "The connections piled quickly. The planes of the Contra [Nicaraguan rebel organization] flew north loaded with cocaine and returned with cash. All were under the protection of the United States Government. My informants were well placed. One worked at the base with Contra pilots, and the other moved among the Salvadoran military officials responsible for the resupply operation. They gave me the names and addresses of Contra pilots. These names were repeatedly found in the DEA database as drug traffickers. My superiors advised me to continue my investigation into the case and to not be too aggressive.

Senator John F Kerry was appointed to head a committee that would investigate drug for weapon business. His Senate Committee Report on Drugs, Law Enforcement and Foreign Policy was found:

Individuals associated with the Contra movement are involved in drug trafficking.

Through business relationships with Contra organizations, participation of narcotics dealers in Contra supply operations.
Traffickers provide assistance to Contras with cash, weapons and planes.

The US State Department paid drug traffickers with funds authorized by Congress for humanitarian aid to the Contras. This was in certain cases after traffickers were indicted on drug charges by federal law enforcement agencies. In other cases, payments were made while the same agencies were investigating the traffickers.

It was ideal for financing covert, illegal activities such as assassination programmes. It was used to bribe politicians as well as to pay mercenaries, death squads, and other illegitimate activities. The US government has claimed to be fighting a War on Drugs for over 40 years while watching as the flow of drugs into America is increasing by design. Gary Webb's research revealed how the CIA protected traffickers while using drug laws against the competition to increase the US's power over South America.

After the rise of the CIA to power, the military-industrial complex was born - a network made up of individuals and institutions involved with the production and use of military technologies and lobbying for the lion's share of taxpayers' money.

The CIA operated the Phoenix Program, a counterterrorism operation that was conducted in rural South Vietnam from 1965 to 1972. According to William Colby, CIA Director, the program resulted in the deaths of 20,587 Vietnamese National Liberation Front activists between 1967 and 1971. According to the South Vietnamese, it was 41,000.

Barton Osborn was an intelligence officer with the Phoenix Program. He stated that "Quite often it was just a matter of expediency just for eliminate a person from the field rather than deal the paperwork." 29,000 suspects were also interrogated. In 1972, survivors testified before Congress that parts of their bodies were cut, including the fingers and ears. Some victims were given wooden dowels to insert into their brains. Others were fitted with electric probes to their rectums. Electroshock was a favorite.

The CIA takes power from governments, even democratically elected ones, that are not in line with US corporate interests. The majority of those killed when the bombs fall and death squads fire machine guns are civilians like schoolteachers, students and miners. Their crime was demanding better wages, more freedoms and better living conditions that the US dictators had often placed. When victims are identified as Communist sympathisers, activists or a threat to US security, it is much easier to cut the heads of village people and use electro-shocking needles and scrotums.

Barry was able to fly for the CIA because he needed excitement. But he was surrounded by killers and cutthroats who viewed those working below him as disposable. Barry would not be hurt while he was still in their good graces.

Barry was unable to serve time in prison due to their influence. According to Reggie Griffith who was a close friend of Barry, Barry was arrested in Longview, Texas with a plane filled with weapons that were destined for Cuba. Barry was released from prison without being charged. There is no record of his arrest. Barry's flight logs from most of 1959 and 1960, which Barry used to smuggle weapons to Cuba, are also missing.

In 1972, US Customs New Orleans arrested Barry for trying to smuggle seven tonnes of C-4 explosives to Mexico. The explosives were intended for a group of CIA-trained Cubans who wanted to overthrow the Cuban president. Barry, who was being held in handcuffs, said that he needed a group of Cubans to follow him. He was escorted into federal courthouse by armed guards and he smiled at the photographers.

Barry was released from jail and went to Plantation Chicken to purchase food. The young woman at the cash register was what drew him in. He held her hand for a few more seconds as she gave him the change. Debbie was impressed at the outfit of his TWA captain. Barry kept asking Debbie to come along, despite the C-4 case not making much progress in court every month.

One year after their first meeting, she finally gave in to her desire to be with Barry on Thanksgiving Day. Barry offered to take the entire family on a joyride in a plane. Debbie, who had never been on an airplane before, said yes.

Barry wrote to the lawyer representing him at the C-4 case, "Don't forget to volunteer for hazardous duty while working for TWA to fly TWA's US Military contracts into hot water areas in Vietnam. This I did with tons war material and explosives." TWA's youngest captain on Boeing 707's.

TWA did not fire him despite his arrest until 1974, when he was finally brought to trial.

Barry and his wife approached an undercover officer whom Barry knew from two years before.

Frank asked, "Frank was it hot when you were in
Veracruz?" Frank replied, "Very hot.".
Barry stated, "And I was wearing an outfit and sweating a lot.

"Yes, you were."
"And the bus stopped on its way back to Veracruz. Right?"

"I saw you standing there beside it as we drove past on our way back to town."

"Well, tell your wife. Barry laughed.

Prosecutors presented as evidence an automated weapon that had nothing whatsoever to do with the charges. The judge declared a mistrial on June 1974. These unusual events led congressional investigators suspect Barry had a special relationship to the US government. It was CIA intervention. They had instructed the US attorney's to close the trial in the national interest of national security.

Barry began flying full-time for the CIA in late 1974. He flew a Lockheed Lodestar at 300 mph. Barry, in his early twenties was making the equivalent of thousands per week and owned several successful businesses, including Seal Sky Service, Aerial Ad Associates, Helicopter Airways and Seal's Texaco.

Chapter 4

JFK Assassination

John F Kennedy's presidential delegation arrived at Dallas Love Field Airport on November 22, 1963. JFK was dressed in a dark grey suit and greeted the crowd. JFK and Mrs Kennedy spent several minutes chatting. The First Lady was dressed in pink and received a bouquet full of red roses. She carried the bouquet to her blue limousine with two flags at the front.

John Connally, Governor of Texas, was dressed in a dark suit and his wife, Mary Connally, was sitting behind him in an open convertible. The limo's plastic bubble top was missing. The motorcade also included Vice President LBJ's wife and another vehicle. The procession started at the airport and traveled ten miles through downtown Dallas to reach the Trade Mart, where JFK was scheduled to speak at luncheon. The Kennedys were greeted by a crowd of enthusiastic people who took photos and waved at them.

Around 12:30, the car left Main Street at Dealey Plaza. Gunfire erupted in various directions as the car passed the Texas School Book Depository. JFK pulled the hand that he was waving towards his neck with. His other hand ran to his throat. Alarmed, Mrs Kennedy looked at her husband and reached for her white-gloved hand. As he fell forward, she held him and shot in the back. JFK was behind him when the governor turned his body in his favor.

Mrs Kennedy was looking at her husband's throat when a bullet struck his forehead. It caused an explosion of blood and brains, as well as a skull. Both the governor and his wife ran, avoiding their eyes. JFK sank to the side. Mrs Kennedy climbed on the back of the car on all fours and reached for JFK's skull with her right arm.

An agent of the Secret Service climbed on the back of the car to tell Mrs Kennedy to get in. The skull fragment was still in her hand as she crawled back into car. The governor was hit in the chest and wrist, as well as her thigh. The limousine sped along a triple underpass to Parkland Memorial Hospital, which was only a few minutes away.

Numerous people raced up a grassy hill towards the spot where they had seen white smoke and gunshots. It was quickly crowded. Thirteen railroad workers claimed that shots were fired from behind a fence at the grassy knoll. The assassins may have been present for some time, as evidenced by the discovery of cigarette butts and muddy footprints.

Police encountered several men wearing Secret Service IDs. None of them were believed to be stationed at Dealey Plaza.

Jackie Kennedy presented a piece of her husband's skull at the hospital to the medical team. "Here, can this help?"

It was impossible to do much. The last rites were administered by a Catholic priest. JFK was declared dead at 1 pm. Although severely wounded, the governor was able to recover. The governor was left with a limp, but he recovered quickly.

JFK's remains were brought to Love Field, and then placed on Air Force One. Vice President LBJ, looking grim, stood in a crowded compartment before the plane took off and took the oath to office. It was administered by a judge. At 2:38 p.m., the brief ceremony was completed.

Everyone except LBJ was surprised by the shots that were fired that day. LBJ had ducked and huddled into his car before the first shot was fired. His car was three cars behind JFK's limousine.

LBJ gained a lot by taking over the presidency after JFK's death. He was in danger of political ruin and prosecution at that point, as Robert Kennedy - who wanted him to be removed from office - had a dossier about the bribes LBJ took. In the Bobby Baker Scandal, the US Senate was investigating Baker. Baker was involved with taking millions of dollars in bribes to LBJ. The main suspects in this hit - the CIA and organised crime, as well as the military-industrial complex, had special relationships to LBJ. He was responsible for budget control at the CIA. To protect illegal gambling operations, he accepted bribes from Mafia. JFK wanted to end the Oil Depletion Allowance which was worth millions to oil companies. JFK wanted to end Vietnam's war, while LBJ was buying suitcases from military companies. LBJ demanded that JFK visit Texas. LBJ also said that he quit his position as Senate Majority Leader for vice presidency, claiming that he calculated that JFK's death was one in four. Jackie Kennedy, who was not fond of or trusted LBJ, was informed by French intelligence that LBJ was a driving force behind this assassination plot. The KGB came to the same conclusion.

Barry's ex-comrade in air cadet and US military intelligence tip had led to the arrest of Lee Harvey Oswald by the police. Oswald had been hired two weeks prior to his arrest at the Texas School Book Depository. He was arrested for the assassination JFK and the shooting death of a Dallas policeman. Oswald was handcuffed and surrounded by police when he was approached by media around 7.55pm.

Oswald stated, "I would like legal representation." "These officers have not allowed my to have one. "In fact, I don't know what all this is about." A reporter asked.

"No sir, I didn't... I work at that building."

"Were your in the building at that time?"

"Naturally, sir, if you work in that building, yes."

"Did the president get killed?"

"No, they're taking you in because I lived in Soviet Union." Oswald argued that he was a fall man and that he was just a patsy.

Oswald was working at Texas School Book Depository when JFK's limousine passed at around 12:30. Oswald couldn't have shot JFK in his forehead. Oswald had to be in the building where the limo was approaching for a front shot. Due to the trees, it was impossible to see JFK from the sixth floor Texas School Book Depository. Oswald was not found with any gunpowder by the police. Oswald was portrayed as an expert sniper but he had failed his first Marines test. Oswald failed to qualify for the second test by just two points. He was the marksman category, below expert and sharpshooter, and only barely qualified for the third attempt. He claimed that the rifle he used cost $2, and had a $10 scope. It couldn't aim straight. According to the army's ballistic-test specialist, they had to place three pieces of metal underneath the telescopic scope to align it with rifle barrel before they could fire it for accuracy. The FBI was notified that all evidence, including the rifle and, was taken from the hands the state police. Although the FBI had all the evidence they needed to indict Oswald, they couldn't find Oswald's fingerprints on the gun.

Oswald was transferred from the police headquarters into the county jail on Sunday, November 24th. American viewers who were watching live television saw a man point a gun at Oswald, and then fire at point blank range. Jack Ruby, a local nightclub proprietor with Mafia ties was the assailant. Oswald was pronounced dead at Parkland Hospital two hours later.

Ruby was captured being taken from the court. When asked by media who was behind assassination JFK's, he replied, "When Adlai Stevenson was mentioned, if he were vice president, there wouldn't have been assassination. Our beloved President Kennedy."

Monday morning Oswald's hand was put on the rifle by his dead hand. The world was then told that Oswald had been able to locate his prints. J Edgar Hoover, the FBI's head and LBJ's neighbor, gave his approval to the Oswald story. Hoover had given LBJ a dossier about JFK's sex lives, which LBJ used to leverage over JFK. All of the evidence had been taken over by the FBI, who were unaccountable to anyone and had the power to destroy evidence and create fake documents. In the wake of Barry Seal's suicide, the FBI quickly removed all evidence from the state police and transferred it to federal authorities.

Oswald was dead. All that was left was to discredit witnesses who had reported that at least ten shots were fired from six locations. The Warren Commission, which was appointed by LBJ, achieved this. Allen Dulles, the ex-CIA director and long-serving member of the Warren Commission, was appointed to lead the operation. JFK had previously blamed him for the Bay of Pigs. He was fired.

According to the Warren Report (1964), three shots were fired by a single gunman during the assassination. There was no evidence that shots were fired from other locations than the Texas School Book Depository. JFK was killed by the first shot, which the Secret Service and FBI had reported to JFK. The second hit Texas Governor John Connally in his back, and JFK in his head. The Warren Report did not include any testimony from 51 witnesses who had seen or heard shots from the grassy knoll.

Later, it was revealed that the shot actually missed JFK and injures a bystander. The three-bullet theory was challenged by this revelation. The Warren Commission ignored this bystander for months. After being presented with photographic evidence of the bullet mark the Warren Commission changed the official story to include a magic bullet which defied gravity and physics by changing three directions while remaining pristine. The shot actually struck JFK's back, entered his throat and caused a non-lethal injury. It also entered Connally's back, broke Connally's right wrist bone, and damaged his fifth rib. It was anatomically impossible but it was accepted as the official account.

JFK's clothes, however, told a completely different story. His shirt and suit were damaged, indicating that the bullet entered between his shoulder blades. Not his back. An expert was called in to explain that JFK had rotated the body of the victim, which meant that his clothes had moved up his neck.

According to autopsy doctors, the photos that were shown to the public were not real ones they had taken.

The medical, ballistic, and eyewitness evidence of JFK's injuries has been meticulously examined. They were all four times. The shots didn't seem to have been fired from sixth floor of Texas School Book Depository. Three shots appear to have been fired from the Dal-Tex Building at 501 Elm Street, in the West End Historic District. The Dal-Tex's acoustics made the shots sound as though they were being fired from the Texas School Book Depository.

Many people were skeptical of the official story. Jim Garrison, a New Orleans district attorney, began an investigation into assassination after receiving tips that Barry's former flight instructor David Ferrie had been a coconspirator. Ferrie had no doubts about his situation, as so many people were killed in the assassination - nearly 100 died mysteriously. Joe Pesci played Ferrie brilliantly in Oliver Stone's JFK film. Ferrie claimed that he could not go home after his identity was revealed to the media. He met Garrison and his staff in a hotel room. Garrison asked him what he was afraid about.

"Me," Ferrie said, pacing around. "Everybody. Agency [CIA], mob and Cubans. That's it. Follow the Cubans. You can check them out. Here, Miami, Dallas Ferrie tried to get a notepad off of one of the staff. "Hey, hey! Don't write this down!" I'm not cooperating with anyone! What is the matter? I have a death warrant! Don't you get it? Damn! "Wait! "Agency plays with your hands. I knew Oswald. He was in my Civil Air Patrol Unit. He learned everything from me. He was a snitch. He was an egotist. But I treated him well." Garrison replied, "Did your ever work for CIA?".
It sounds like a distant fucking experience from ancient history. You can't leave the Agency. They have you for the rest of your life once you are in.

Garrison stated, "And Shaw?" Garrison was referring to another suspect in JFK's assassination.

"Shaw is untouchable. Highest clearance. Shaw, Oswald, and the Cubans: All

Agency."
Garrison asked, "What about Ruby?" Garrison was referring to Oswald's shooter.

Jack was a pimp. Bagman for the Dallas mob. When Castro was still on our side, he used to run guns to Castro. Castro was almost with us. We tried to beat him. Everyone is always flipping their sides. "Fun and games, man!"

"How does the mob fit into this?"

"They're Agency, too. Working together, the CIA and Mafia trying to whack the beard [Castro]. Mutual interest. They have been doing this for many years. You'd be surprised at the amount of things you can do with this. Operation Mongoose is a program. Government Pentagon stuff. They are in control. But who is the fuck pulling which chain? Who knows who the fuck is? Oh, how wonderful!

When we practice to deceive, we create a deadly web."

"Then, who killed the President?"

Ferrie raised his arms in protest. "Shit! You know this is too big! Who was the President? Fuck! It's a mystery. It's a mystery wrapped up in a riddle within an enigma. It's a mystery that the fucking shooters don't know! Don't you get it? Fuck, man! I can't keep talking

Like this! They'll fucking murder me! I'll fucking die..."

"Just speak to us on the recording. We will protect you.

They'll also get to you. They will destroy you. They're untouchable. I'm so fucking exhausted, I can't see straight."

Ferrie, along with two unsigned, undated suicide letters, was found dead in his apartment less than a week later, on February 22, 1967. An autopsy revealed that Ferrie died from massive cerebral hemorhage caused by a congenital intracranial brain berry aneurysm.

Garrison stated, "It could be just a strange coincidence that the night Ferrie wrote two suicide notes was also the day he died from natural causes.".

Debbie Seal claims that Barry flew a getaway aircraft as part of the JFK assassination. Ferrie and Oswald weren't the only ones to die from Barry's ties.

Chapter 5

Medellín Cartel

A small, twin-engine aircraft carrying marijuana flew fifteen feet above the Gulf of Mexico in 1977. It was trying to avoid radar detection and almost skimming the waters off Louisiana's coast. The plane was swept by the wind and rain poured onto the cockpit's windshield. Barry cursed the copilot for turning a face that was drained of colour toward his partner.

Barry smiled confidently as he steered the plane. "Relax, man. "Relax, man. My boys have been flying grass like this for four years and have never been touched."

The plane flew above a cemetery and dropped its cargo onto a river before arcing away. The bulky, plastic-wrapped box was retrieved by a barge with some cowboy hats-wearing men and they motored through the swampland. Their attention was drawn to a mechanical whirring sound. A helicopter dropped a wire with a hook toward the barge. The drugs were attached. The helicopter flew to remote rural areas where a van was parked. The van was loaded with the drugs that had been dropped. The van's windows fell on a bridge. Four cars pulled four packages over to the side of the bridge and ejected them. Each one took a package, and they drove off.

Doublecrossed (1991 TV movie) featured scenes of Barry's drug smuggling. However, it did not include his ongoing relationship with the CIA. David Ferrie in JFK pointed out that working for the CIA is a lifetime commitment. These lines are not crossed by most Hollywood directors.

Doublecrossed featured a scene from 1979 where Barry flew solo in his twin-engine aircraft over Honduras' green mountains, singing along to the music. He was flying in from Ecuador and was landing to refuel. Honduran soldiers wearing battle fatigues rushed onto the runway as his plane touched down at the National Airport. With a dozen guns pointed at the cockpit, his plane stopped.

Barry raised his hands high above his head. He chuckled. Honduran officials had been paid to facilitate Barry's smuggling. However, the government had just been replaced so the wrong people were bribed. Barry was charged with possessing an automatic weapon. The plane was taken into custody.

The movie did not show that Barry had previously dropped off a Moroccan Jewish passenger at a deserted runway in Honduras' Bay Islands. He left behind a briefcase containing cocaine and two duffel bags with cocaine. Barry waited for the passenger with 40 kilos of cocaine to return. He was finally caught in a hotel room, where he was accosted by three soldiers.

Twenty-three kilos were taken by the authorities, who then announced to the media that 17 kilos of cocaine worth $25 million had been seized. Because the Hondurans were supporting US interests in this area, the US didn't have any problem with them trafficking cocaine. Despite Honduras being awash in drugs, the DEA closed down its office there in 1983 for budgetary reasons as well as a lack of productivity.

Barry's passenger made the following statement on TV: "I arrived in Ecuador on business as an assistant producers for American television. I was invited to a bar by a man I did not know and we talked about many topics. I confessed to him that I would soon be leaving for Miami, where my wife was waiting. He promised to introduce me two friends who could transport me as far as Honduras and save me my airfare. I was then introduced to Mr. Stefan. Adler Barryman Seal, an American, arrived just a few minutes later and we headed for Honduras." He said that Barry had told him about problems in Honduran territory, and that he had insistent on dropping him off. Barry promised to pick him up the next morning. "At the Island...they forced me to leave my plane. They left their luggage to show me that they would be returning for me. I agreed. "I had no other choice." The passenger claimed that he didn't know anything about the cocaine.

Doublecrossed featured Barry being strip-searched. He was naked, and only a blanket covered him. Soldiers led him into a tunnel with flashlights.

Barry asked, "Have any of you ever seen Midnight Express?".
They put him in a cell-like dungeon and closed the iron-bar doors.

Barry yelled "Fuck!" He turned to face his cellmates, a dozen locals who were staring angrily and suspiciously at him. The door opened. The guard opened the door and threw his belongings onto the floor. His clothes were stolen by his cellmates. He yelled at them, "Get your hands off of my shit, Bayou swamp-rats!" and tried to wrestle his belongings away from them.

A white vest-clad cellmate stood tall over Barry, five feet seven. He reached out and grabbed a piece of Barry's clothing, and stood before Barry chest-to-face with an expression that asked, "What are you going to do about it?"?
Barry removed his blanket and urinated on the giant's legs.

Barry's clothes were taken by the giant, who then walked off with everyone laughing. The giant looked at Barry's leg and threw his clothes down. He then turned around to charge at Barry. As he was about tampering Barry, a man wearing a blue baseball hat emerged from darkness and struck Barry in the head with a workboot, knocking him out.

Barry stated, "Handy weapon that you have there.".
The American chewed gum and pointed at Barry's penis. He was square-faced with dark eyes and large sideburns.

Barry smiled and said "Well, thank you for your help.".
"Hey, you're right, I won't let a Louisiana boy get whooped."

Barry frowned and said, "How did you know that I'm from Louisiana?"
"Where are your origins?"

"Slidell."

"Slidell! Barry stated, "That's only eighty miles away from my home: Baton Rouge.".

"I have one question for you. What were you going to do after that monster realized he was pissed off?

"Sometimes I just let things happen." Barry said, "Make 'em up", while getting dressed.

"Well, you'd be damn glad that i was there."

"If you refuse to take the chance, the fun isn't yours." I had a great time pissing on him. I don't know what you are doing in that hole.

"I'm just like you, smuggling drugs."

"What. Barry said calmly, "You think I'm drug smuggler?".
"You kidding?"
Barry laughed. Barry laughed and said "My name's Barry Seal", shaking hands with the American.

The American smiled and said, "No, it is not." "But I'll still call you that, if you want me too," he smiled.

It's my real name. There is no room for lying here. They're going to tell me that I can go home for dinner anytime now." Barry looked out the window.

Emile asked, "What are you flying?".
"A Cessna 310. You?"
"I will do anything to get a job in flying. "I fly whatever God gives me with wings."

Emile sat beside Barry on a stone ledge. He said, "Camp, who do you work for?".
"Anyone that will give me a job."

"How about me?" I have five pilots who fly for me right now. I will hire you."

Emile looked down. "No, sorry."

"Why not? I pay one-hundred-and-fifty thou a run." "Nope,"
Emile said, getting off the ledge.

"Why the hell not?"

They laughed.

Barry and Emile became close while in prison. Barry also made many smuggling contacts that proved to be useful later, such as Roger Reeves (a New Orleans smuggler). Roger informed Barry that he had been doing business with Colombians.

Barry asked, "What's the name of this ol' boy down there in Miami?" Barry hoped Roger would link him with the Colombians.

"Lito. This guy is Jorge Ochoa, a business partner of Pablo Escobar. You know him, don't he? Barry stated that he plays third base for Cubs.

Roger said, "Listen to Barry," Roger said, "These boys down there have no sense or humor." You'll understand what I mean. None," they said.

Debbie Seal, who had given birth to three children quickly, were now six months, two, and three years old. She received a phone call informing her that Barry was being held. Barry finally called. Barry promised that he would be back in a few days. Six months later, he still made the same promises.

It was hard to get the right person in Honduras to take your money. Barry had already paid a lot to officials but elections had brought in new people. It was difficult to start from scratch. Barry devised a plan of escape that included outside help, and a helicopter. However, it was abandoned.

Barry lived lavishly while bribery negotiations were ongoing. He commissioned the construction of an air-conditioned house in La Ceiba prison with a movie projector and a screen. He ate at the finest restaurants in Port.

Debbie flew to visit the children on weekends. The guards gave her celebrity status because Barry was spreading so much money. She was not searched for contraband. Barry, fresh from showering, would hug her at the prison gates. The couple spent the night in a room that had a cot, candles, and bananas drying. From a nearby bar, country and western music were heard. Barry looked at Debbie and assured her that he was still her husband.

Barry was freed after nine months, and for $500,000 bribe. He celebrated his freedom in Baton Rouge by taking Debbie to a blues and jazz club.

Doublecrossed saw Barry fly to Miami to meet Carlos Bustamante (a Colombian man with a ponytail and a handlebar moustache) who oversees US cocaine distribution for Medellin Cartel. Barry introduced himself to the world as Mr Ellis MacKenzie.

Lito, who was walking along a beach crowded with children splashing in the water, said "We give one run." "Do good. Perhaps we can give more. Are you ready for that?"

Barry asked, "How can I find out who you really are?".
"You don't. You don't even know me. We pay $3,000 per kilo. You take that kind of money and you will be successful."

What happens if I loose a load?

Lito glowered. "We kill you."

Barry laughed. Barry laughed.

Barry was given three pager numbers by Lito to reach him.

Barry attended federal court trials and studied drug cases to avoid being arrested. His planes flew nightly in and out Louisiana with their lights off. The top equipment and night vision goggles cost $5,000 to his pilots. The Colombian military responsible for monitoring airspace was bribed. His pilots slowed down to 120 knots to return to the US. This allowed them to appear on radar as oil-rig helicopters. Duffel bags containing cocaine were parachuted from the planes over Louisiana marshland. Helicopters carried the cocaine to the men driving it to the main hubs:
Miami, Los Angeles, and New York.

Barry bought two condos, one on top of another, and dug a hole in the floor of the highest one. The hole was used to pass up money from Lito and cocaine down.

Barry sometimes ran into difficulties with honest law-enforcement officers who were not privy of his CIA protection. Barry saved up to $4million in Fort Lauderdale for his own smooth sailing. This amount allowed him to avoid jail in his early years of working for the Medellin Cartel.

Barry managed the drug operation as a mini intelligence agency. They used the most advanced CIA electronics and communication devices, including digital scramblers. Barry rented entire floors of hotels to keep their communications secret. Sometimes, people would fly from Mississippi to the engine room on a barge in order to attend meetings where the machinery noise was too loud to eavesdrop.

Barry was able to buy more houses and cars thanks to the trips with the Colombians. He was also a Little League baseball player, and took Debbie to dance and fancy restaurants when he wasn't flying cocaine. Barry told Debbie about the money when he said Seal Aviation was a top-notch company at buying and selling planes across North and South America.

Doublecrossed featured Barry driving a blue Mercedes convertible, with Emile as his passenger. They also saw an undercover car outside Barry's home.

Barry pulled up beside the police and said "Oh, look at these idiots." "Hello, lieutenant. You know that I'm coming over to my office. Next, I'll go to RJ's for lunch. Then, maybe I'll head over to Ascension. "I'm just telling you this in case you get lost."

"Go to hell Seal!" cried a corpulent lieutenant sporting a thick moustache.

Barry pointed at Barry and said "Don't get mad, lieutenant." "I hate it to see Louisiana state police waste tax payers gasoline following me. Barry drove off.

Emile replied, "I'm telling," "Maybe they shouldn't be baited like that."

"What right do they have to follow me around?" They have nothing on me, and they will never.

"You are the most dangerous and most-suspected bad man in Louisiana, and every cop wants to know how you got that money."

Barry said that he was referring to a rich televangelist. He lives in the big house over there. He's more wealthy than me, in fact.

Chapter 6

Mena

Barry relocated his business to Mena in 1982 after New Orleans authorities tried to impose their will on him. Mena is a charming town that lies within thick forests of the Ouachita Mountains in Western Arkansas. Mena was founded in 1896 and became a city on September 18, 1896. It was named after the Dutch who funded its railroad. In 1900, there were almost 3,500 residents. This number grew to more than 5,000 when Barry arrived. Timber, agriculture, and mineral extraction were the first industries. The surrounding wilderness was a refuge for many outcasts over the years. These included bandits, Civil War guerrillas, and smugglers of alcohol and marijuana.

Mena's Intermountain Regional Airport, despite being located in the backwoods was highly-tech. It was well-known for its ability to quickly repair and maintain aircraft and for hosting planes for those who needed secrecy. It was used by military agencies and other organizations.

Barry was wanted by the CIA because of his reputation as an airport where anything was possible, even if it was illegal. This included aircraft alterations which required Form 337 to file with the Federal Aviation Administration (FAA). Failure to file Form 337 could result in mechanics being imprisoned and losing their license. Because of safety concerns, modifications were strictly controlled. The Drug Enforcement Agency (DEA), which began using Form 337 to find traffickers and hone in on suspicious modifications, learned how to identify them. High demand was for mechanics who didn't file Form 3337. These mechanics were hired by the CIA to modify black ops aircraft. There was no paper trail. Barry had cargo doors that could be used to drop drugs or fuel bladders. His planes were equipped with the most advanced aviation electronics by the CIA. Barry owned a Learjet and helicopters as well as cargo and cargo planes. Many of these were purchased from entities that were not authorized by the CIA, such Southern Air and Air America.

Transport. The DEA eventually joined the Mena action because they didn't want a paper trace to reveal the modifications to Barry's aircraft that were being used in their missions. To avoid violating its laws, the US government paid for Barry's illegally modified aircraft.

Sally Denton and Dr. Roger Morris, in Partners in Power, cite coded records from the Pentagon's Defense Intelligence Agency(DIA) that show Barry Seal as a payroll employee starting in 1982. He was also part of Operation Seaspray at this time. Barry was selected as one of the most skilled pilots in the world. He flew four miles over the border of El Salvador, Honduras, and Nicaragua intercepting communications from political parties.

Arkansas Governor Bill Clinton was partly responsible for the favorable political climate that Arkansas enjoyed at that time. Larry Nichols, a Clinton aide, said that Barry and the CIA chose Arkansas for the guns-for drugs smuggling because the Clintons were open to it. The Clintons were assisted by Hillary Clinton's law office and made a handsome profit from money laundering.

Russell Welch is the Arkansas State Police Investigator responsible for the Mena investigation. He stated that Barry Seal said 1983 was the most lucrative year for cocaine smuggling. He had the planes placed at Mena airport... for cocaine smuggling.

Small clearings were also made in Arkansas for Mena. Each of Barry's planes brought home 200-500 kilos of cocaine every week. Parachuted down at odd hours of night were duffel bags containing cocaine. Truck drivers transported the drugs to New York, New Orleans and Miami hubs. The Mafia, South American supply companies, corrupt officials reaching the top offices of the US government, and opportunists looking to make quick cash were all part of the distribution network. The crime was so obvious that local authorities knew and were conducting criminal investigations. However, no indictments were ever filed because Governor Bill Clinton had integrated key individuals as judges, police officers, and other law enforcement.

Barry maximized his value to CIA as insurance against being prosecuted. The Reagan-Bush administration had one priority: to supply weapons and supplies to rebels in Nicaragua fighting a civil war. However, this was not allowed by Congress so it had to be done secretly. Barry's fleet in Mena was perfect. Weapons and cocaine were flown from America to Colombia. With

With CIA approval, Nicaraguan rebels were funded with drug money. The CIA stopped Barry's flights being intercepted or seized by US Customs. The US government was complicit in the Nicaraguan rebels using cocaine proceeds to finance war and buy arms from US weapon manufacturers. The drug was being sold on American streets at exactly the same time that the Reagan-Bush administration claimed to be fighting a War on Drugs.

The benefits of the CIA alliance were immediately apparent. US Customs stopped an investigation into one his pilots. One agent wrote to his bosses: "[name redacted] works with Seal and cannot be touched since Seal works for

CIA." A federal agent stated, "Look, we are told not to touch anything with Barry Seal's name on, just to let it pass."

The CIA funneled the majority of the income from cocaine smuggling – hundreds of millions per monthly - to the United States. Barry was so rich that he bought two Rolls-Royces in the UK. He decided they were too extravagant and donated them to Fort Lauderdale's Christmas Parade.

Chapter 7

Terry Reed

On August 23, 1983 Colonel Oliver North - a frontman of Vice President George HW Bush – called Terry Reed, a CIA asset who is an expert in machinery. North claimed that he knew of Terry's move to Arkansas by using a false name, John Cathey. "I can't talk about it on a secure line, but we have an exciting project down there and I believe there may be a spot for you. If you are interested, I will just introduce you to the man who's going on the operation. I will make the introduction, and have him check you out. He'll be impressed by my honesty and kindness." Terry replied.

"He will find you. Barry Seal is his name.

Terry arrived in Arkansas a few months later to work in the ultralight factory of Command-Aire Manufacturing.

"I'm Dan Lasater," declared a multimillionaire bond trader, with a square face and prey-like eyes. He was wearing a three piece suit and Gucci shoes. Roger Clinton is my driver," Lasater said, reaching out to Roger with his arm. Roger was a man with long dark hair and broad features, and a nose that had been enlarged by cocaine abuse. "He's his brother," Lasater was Bill Clinton's personal friend and one of his biggest political contributors.

Terry replied, "Oh, yeah," Lasater stated to Terry. "I suppose I should introduce a client. This is Mr Barry Seal.

Barry observed Terry: A man with sincere eyes and dark hair parted on one side, thick eyebrows, and a moustache. Barry shared with Terry that he had a friend who said Terry has the talent they need.

Terry asked, "Does this friend have a name?".

Barry spoke of Oliver North as John Cathey. "I'm a contractor. I specialize in transport. Anything that can be transported, I can do it. Certain connections are made within the government. You may be interested in a contract I currently have. I will speak to you privately later.

Barry was often seen in Little Rock, depositing money at Lasater's company. It was difficult to launder cash in such a small region. After many investigations, a secretary informed the IRS that Barry's flight had left behind "stacks of cash to be taken into the bank and laundered." In order to avoid reporting to the federal authorities, the launderers were instructed not to purchase cashier's checks in excess of $10,000. Witnesses said that Barry's bank officer "went down the teller lines, handed out stacks of $1,000 bills, and then got the cashier's checks.".

Barry and Terry spoke at a restaurant about their military flights in southeast Asia. Barry stated, "So, aside from being a flight instructor and knowing how to coordinate aircrews to get the shit on-target?".

Terry nodded.

Barry replied, "You're employed." "But I have a pressing problem right now. Can you please go to Mena with me?

Barry organized a December 1983 flight to assess Terry's abilities. Barry sat on the right, Terry on the back and his arm around Terry's neck as they took off in a Learjet. Barry said, increasing the pressure to Terry: "Now let's get some fun and release all the fucking brakes." You'll love this, relax.

Terry enjoyed the flight and was bonded with Barry. He kept laughing at his government handlers, calling them "Fucking GS suits" which means General Salary Schedule, while he accelerated the jet. "They have no brains and very little balls."

Terry suggested that maybe we could trade services. "I will teach you manufacturing if I'm trained to manage these GS bean counters so that I can have a plane similar to this."

Barry cancelled the flight plan, and gave the controls to Terry. It's your plane. Show me your true colors by grabbing this fetus.

Terry smiled and pulled off a pilot-fighter maneuver. He turned north and dived toward an airstrip at the top of a mountain. He flew up like a rocket and skimmed the runway.

Barry shouted, "Watch out for the compressor to stall!" Push it up and you can recover the thing. Barry stated, "Guess, I'm too old to do this." Terry stabilized the jet at 17,500ft. Let's go, hot dog. You have the right stuff.

Barry stated, "It is time I let you all know the truth about our mission." Let's get some coffee. Barry explained that the mission was to provide weapons for Nicaraguan Contra rebels. Mena would be a center for weapons and a training ground for Nicaraguan rebels. Barry may have guessed Terry was a straight shooter, and because of the compartmentalisations of different aspects of the operation Barry forgot the most important part: he was bringing back drugs on the return flights. "I will need to speak to Oliver North, our friend on this, but I need your help on this project. It's much more difficult than I was led to believe to make weapons parts.

Barry stated that Iver Johnson, a weapon company, was being moved by the CIA.

Arms from New Jersey to Arkansas, because Congress had prohibited the Defense Department's acquisition of weapons through the usual vendors for the Nicaragua war. Even if the war was not popular, the CIA would find a way to get around it, and everyone involved would make a tidy profit, even the arms suppliers. Arkansas Governor Bill Clinton claimed credit for Iver's Arms, a company that dates back to the American Revolution. He said that he had campaigned to move it there to create jobs. Barry knew better. The decision was made by the shadow government which included opaque organisations like the CIA that operate outside the law.

Otherwise, the US public could find out about the military parts that went to Nicaragua. Iver Johnson's Arms, Jacksonville, Arkansas was manufacturing sniper rifles under a classified contract with US Navy. This contract was subject to inspection. A plant at Mena was chosen to avoid detection of the production of untraceable components. The Mena plant was covered by Iver Johnson's Arms.

Barry stated, "So now you know what's up to," Barry added. "What machinery will it take to cast and machine lower receiver housings of the M-16?" An M-16 is fully automated with the lower receiver housing.

Terry stated, "I'll require blueprints and I'll have to know quantities.".

Chapter 8

DEA Trouble

Doublecrossed featured an airport scene that showed men wearing suits and guns marching down the runway towards Barry's cockpit. This was part of Operation Screamer. It happened after Barry had landed with 200,000 sedatives known as Quaaludes.

A middle agent raised a DEA badge. The agent shouted, "We have reason for believing you are transporting controlled substances aboard this aircraft!" "Will your agent please get out?"

Barry cursed as he pointed at them. He was taken to Broward County Jail in Florida. He was dressed in orange prison clothing after the strip-search.

Although the movie scene was amazing, it never happened. Barry was tipped off. He flew one of his pilots by helicopter to his suburban house. He landed the helicopter in his backyard and picked up his children and wife. Barry was waiting in a Learjet at a secret airport. Barry flew them all from Los Angeles to Las Vegas where they enjoyed an Easter vacation gambling. Barry surrendered after six weeks.

Operation Screamer was the culmination of a 18-month-long investigation into the drug trade in southern Florida. DEA agents recorded conversations at high-end hangouts used by drug traffickers like the Mutiny. Eighty-five people were arrested, including pilots and smugglers as well as money launderers. The arrests were made in Florida and North Carolina, Texas, Louisiana, Texas. Virginia, Texas, Florida and California in the early 1980s. One smuggler was able to open his door and show police a handgun, candle, and five-gallon cans of kerosene. After five hours of barricading his house, he lit the fire and set it ablaze.

Barry gave up after his Las Vegas stint. Doublecrossed took Barry to a cement-block-wall visitation room. He was greeted by Emile Camp and a lawyer. Barry spoke to Emile via a telephone from the other end of a Plexiglas windows, asking if Debbie knew that he was in prison.

Emile replied, "Not yet." "Debbie believes you're in Mexico, you know - buying planes and selling them like normal."

Barry went to his lawyer. Barry turned to his lawyer.

The lawyer said that they had caught a man in Lauderdale. He was a tall, slim, silver-haired man wearing a business suit and tie. To make a deal, he gave up everyone he knew.

An informant working for the DEA agent responsible for Operation Screamer led to Barry being indicted. After receiving information about Barry the informant contacted the DEA in Baton Rouge. "Hey, I found a guy. He is a pilot. He hails from Baton Rouge. He's called El Gordo, the Fat One.

"We know what you have and if we can get him, we will come down to you and kiss you. He's been with us for ten years, and we have never been able get him.

Barry's evidence was his testimony as an informant and wire-tapped telephone calls. In March 1983, a federal grand jury indicted Barry for smuggling 200,000 Quaaludes. Although his name was public and his name was published in the media, the Medellin Cartel was able to shield him from suspicion because they knew Ellis Mackenzie.

Barry stated in Doublecrossed that he was a lawyer. Barry grinned at Emile.

It's not easy. It's bad, Barry. It's bad, Barry.

Barry's face crimpled. "Sixty!"
"But that's not all. Baton Rouge jumped on board the bandwagon as soon as they heard that you had been arrested. There is a US attorney there.

His name's Thornton something."
"Thornton Biggs."
The lawyer stated, "That's him." "Says that he's going to file his own indictment on you, too."

Barry stated, "I went to highschool with him." Barry said, "Can you not talk to him?"

The lawyer frowned and said "Dammit Barry," "You're not very popular with Louisiana cops. They've been looking in the mirror for years.

This is their chance."

Barry smiled for a moment, but then his face turned to stone.

Emile asked, "What about Lito?".
Barry shrugged. "Lito doesn't know anything about this. This flight was side-by-side."

"Barry, you've been flying for Lito since 2005. Perhaps he will help." "Lito doesn't know anything about this. "If his organization finds out I've been arrested they'll drop my like a rock.".
The lawyer stated that the only way out was to become an informant.

"Bullshit!" Barry said.

The lawyer dropped the phone and leaning towards the Plexiglas, he hung up. "We will discuss strategy after I post my bond. In a few hours, you'll be gone.

Emile was told by Barry, "I'll keep your out of this.".
"I doubt if you can," Emile said.

"I won't give up on you."

"I don't care. "I don't care. I have been contemplating retiring for a while. Yes, I'd love to have a farm. Costa Rica maybe."

"Ha! "Ha!

They giggled briefly. They hung up the phones, their eyes misting.

Barry was released after posting a bond of $250,000. Barry approached Operation Screamer's DEA agent directly in the hope of negotiating a deal. Barry promised to deliver more cocaine than any DEA agent had seen before and he wanted to travel overseas without any DEA supervision. He also wanted the charges against two of his accomplices in Operation Screamer to be dropped. Barry's attempts to broker a deal with no lawyer was enough to put off the DEA agent. The offer was declined.

Doublecrossed featured Barry in a sky-blue, three-piece suit. He stormed out of the office at Stanford Bardwell who was his classmate and had been elected the US attorney in Baton Rouge.

Emile, who was waiting outside, threw down the newspaper and jumped up. "No dice, huh?"

Barry marched away, saying "I went high school with that bozo" Bardwell was aware that Barry was being investigated by the New Orleans state and federal task forces in Baton Rouge. He had also considered Barry's offer of becoming an informant but found it too obscure. Barry had spent $25,000 to broker the deal with Bardwell. The intermediary was paid $25,000 cash and became a judge.

Emile stated, "High school isn't exactly a lifetimelong bond you know.".
Barry grumbled, "He should give me ten more minutes in the office with his, don't ya think?".
"Well, what now?"
Barry stated, "I'm going Washington DC.".
"Washington DC! Yes, it makes sense. "Why don't we first talk to the governor?"

Barry threw his hands up and said "I don't know the governor.".
"Well, who do you think you might know in Washington DC?"

Barry stated, "Nobody," not disclosing his connections. He put on his reflective sunglasses and made his way out of the building. He was advised by his contacts at the CIA to contact Vice President George HW Bush's Drug Task Force. They made an appointment for him.

Chapter 9

Mena

Barry and Terry met at SOB's in January 1984. The food was Cajun, and the loud music made it difficult to listen. Barry wanted to find a remote area of Mena where they could secretly train Nicaraguan pilots.

Barry stated, "Christ, Cathey [Oliver North] did not tell me that we gotta teach them to fly." It was my first understanding that these men would be skilled pilots. All we had to do was teach them how the palletised loads of supplies hit the target. The truth is that the fucking Nicaraguans do not have any pilots. There are some fucking freedom fighters!

ReaganBush wanted Nicaraguans flying cargo planes in the event of any aircraft being shot down to prevent detection of illegal war supplies to

Nicaragua. The covert operation would be exposed if a US pilot was killed or captured on Nicaraguan soil.

Barry ate a salad and said "Tell me about the airport you opened in Oklahoma City." "Especially the FAA [Federal Aviation Administration] licensing you're near vector airways." Barry used Terry's information to figure out how to comply with FAA rules and avoid unwanted scrutiny of pilot training. Terry suggested, "Better still, why not just put you onboard officially as an aircraft consultant while I figure how you fit into all of this.".

Later, in a Learjet they flew around a remote area of Western Arkansas to see a field.

Barry stated, "Bank tighter for the left." "More! More! It's there, on my leftwing. What do you think?

"OK. Terry replied, "OK. It's certainly remote. The surrounding terrain is beautiful to me. But does it look like Nicaragua?" They were twelve miles north of Mena, over Nella.

Barry replied, "Yeah!" It will be a hit with the Nicaraguans. They will feel at home. Let's fly to Mena, then drive up here to check how it looks from above.

They met with the president of a metal casting company at Mena. They discussed computerized machine tools that are required to make weapon parts in the foundry.

They started from Mena but couldn't find Nella. This was a security advantage. They eventually arrived at Nella's dirt roads, which only four-wheel-drive vehicles were able to navigate. For the trainee pilots, the mountains added realism as well as danger.

Barry asked Terry to visit Nella again on another day in order to complete a thorough survey. He also wanted to make sure that the chosen location didn't interfere with commercial flights which could lead to FAA scrutiny.

Terry stated, while flying back to Little Rock that he was assessing the sites. He also said that he should consider the proficiency of the pilots using the field. The terrain surrounding the field could prove to be very dangerous, especially during bad weather. About half a dozen pilots from flatlanders still fly off Rich Mountain each year."

Barry laughed. "I received some good and some bad news. Cathey claims that Nicaraguans can fly single-engine planes. The bad news is that it's very difficult.

They arrived at Barry's headquarters at Rich Mountain Aviation, located in a new building located at the south-west corner of Mena's Inter-Mountain Regional Airport. Terry was able to meet some of Barry's associates over the next month, including Emile camp.

In February 1984, the Reagan-Bush administration was putting pressure on Barry to get Nella ready for pilot training. Barry met with Terry at SOB's. After consuming three dozen oysters, he took a napkin and began to take notes. "OK, you're the highly-skilled aviation consultant. We are going to build this airstrip. It is time to make a decision. Our friend Oliver North says that we must get online sooner than expected. What's your opinion? "Anchoring to the federal land to west or under the Hog-2 MoA?"

Because of its MOA (protected aviation space), and the ease with which it could be located from a cockpit equipped with a long-range receiver, Nella was a great site. Terry stated that security, training environments and logistics for bivouac should be our main concerns. Operation Jade Bridge was started at Nella, surrounded by thick forest. Boomerang was the call sign for aircraft. Prefabricated chicken houses were used as barracks by the Nicaraguans to camouflage. The headquarters was located in an old farmhouse. Construction began to improve a grass landing strip, which would be used as a landing area and drop zone. Operation Centaur Rose was the codename for the covert weapons transfer program. Its aircraft call sign, Dodger.

Barry saw Terry in hospital a few months later. Terry was injured in a crash into huge pine trees after his engine seized during flight. Eight hours of surgery were required to repair his right foot. He was now at high risk of losing his leg if circulation does not improve. Terry, a non-drug user, refused to take painkillers and was lying in bed in agony.

Barry replied, "Hey partner, you almost bought the fucking farmer, huh?" Your wife says that your heart is broken and almost lost. Did you take a decision or freeze?

Terry said that he had the opportunity to prove himself to Barry and was excited to tell his story. "Yeah. I thought all the way down all right. Most important for me was the fact that I flew all the way to ground, not freezing or praying to God. I was analyzing my options and executing them every step of the way to impact. My old instructor would have been proud to see this. Do not laugh, but I like the thought that I performed as though I had the right stuff.

Barry sat next to Barry on the bed and they spoke for hours about human death. They discovered that they both had the same birthday, July 16.

Terry stated, "Barry! I've made a decision." "I want to work full-time. Although it may sound absurd, this is what I want. He had bought into the Reagan-Bush media manipulation, which was used to manipulate him. Barry was considered expendable.

Barry stated, "You're employed." "Again."

Terry returned to work at Nella after a few months of rehabilitation. Terry was concerned about drainage and limped with Barry across a field to inspect it.

Barry took photos and said "You want to become an instructor." "I have hired a man from Tulsa and another from Nebraska. If you're willing to join the party, there will be four of them plus Camp. This is going to be dangerous, I swear. I was told by you that you like to fly at night. If you are interested, I can easily fit you into the night schedule. It's what you want?

Terry asked, "Does Pope shitin' in the woods?" "Is a bear Catholic?"

Barry stated that he would find you a plane, and that part of the deal was that you could keep it in Little Rock. It's your company car. Rich Mountain will provide all maintenance. Evans will have access to a secret source for bulk fuel, so you won't have to pay traceable fuel costs. Tulsa's guy will handle scheduling. The perfect cover has been created for all instructors. Ross Aviation, located 100 miles from Oklahoma, was a company that trained foreign students. "Have you left anything out?"

Terry asked, "What about communications?" Terry said, "Surely I don't use my home telephone for scheduling, or do I?"

"Oh, I was wrong. "Oh, I forgot.

Barry took Terry to Oversees International in Little Rock. This company specialized in Japanese business and provided cover for Aki's CIA activities. Barry and Terry entered a boring building near a pizzeria. Aki dressed in smart business attire quickly closed the door. Aki gave Terry an OSI card. OSI is an acronym for Office of Special Investigations in the intelligence community. It's a unit that functions similarly to the CIA, and falls under the Criminal Division of United States Department of Justice. They went to eat in order to avoid being eavesdropped on by Aki's workers.

Fu Lin's Chinese restaurant was visited by Aki, who explained that his company mainly shipped raw materials to Japan, and ships were returned with pulpwood and bauxite from Arkansas. They then got to work on the CIA business.

Barry stated that this was a sensitive matter because CIA agents are not supposed to be operating within the US. Aki is the agency's resident man. We all have an ally in Oliver North, who is our common friend. Terry sees Aki as your secure communication link. All the radio equipment is in his office. He will be our communication channel. Because he is local, there won't be any long-distance charges for you to Mena.

Phones aside, don't ever use the Mena payphones. They are all bugged," Terry stated.

"I had Aki bug the them for security reasons. Let's just say that we are looking for a mole. It's true. Barry was recording all his phone conversations and bugging payphones to try to identify a double agent.

Terry asked Aki, "What type of communication capability do you possess?" I mean, is it safe? Can you also talk on the frequencies of aircraft?

Barry stated, "Aki can communicate to God and the Devil can't jam him,".
Aki stated, "From an operational perspective, Terry," "I'll become your primary contact from now on." Mr Seal is often out of state, so you can consider me your boss. You are a great asset to our team. Mr Cathey highly recommends you.

Barry said to Terry after dropping Aki off: "Hey, Terry, I know that you're all very gung-ho about this." But if I were you, I'd go slow. This is not a guarantee of how long it will last. We don't know if Cathey will get his way, and the fucking Marines might invade Nicaragua tomorrow. The whole Mena thing could end before it gets started. Also, I don't want you and your wife to be financially hurt."

Terry asked Aki to work nights at Mena the next time they spoke. He preferred to fly in darkness so Mena agreed to take him to work. The other instructors agreed that it was the most dangerous time of the day to fly. He was able to conceal his activities at night by using machinery. Terry was also asked by Aki to watch over Barry. He suggested that they meet for lunch once per week to talk verbally, rather than write down anything.

Chapter 10

DEA Informant

Barry was convicted on February 17th 1984 of conspiracy and possession in intent to distribute Quaaludes. This sentence carried a ten year sentence. He was given the most severe sentencing judge in Southern District of Florida. He was also facing the possibility of another trial on additional charges in Operation Screamer, with a maximum sentence for forty-seven years.

Barry piloted for Medellin Cartel despite his difficulties. If he was able to become an informant, he hoped that this relationship would be turned into a card that allowed him to get out of jail. He was performing top-secret work for CIA and hoped that intervention by the federal government would eventually happen on his behalf.

Barry had flown three cocaine loads to Colombia since he was released from jail on the Quaaludes Charges. The less trafficking he did, the closer he was to his February 1984 court date. Barry was disappointed to hear that Lito's brother had shipped 3,000 kilos to the Medellin Cartel.

Barry was to do the exact same.

Barry said to Lito, "I'll just need to find a flight.".

Barry flew on his Learjet to Washington DC where he was able to present himself.

The Commission on Organized Crime Drugs Task Force is headed by Vice President George HW Bush. Barry complained to the Fort Lauderdale DEA that his offer of being an informant was declined for personal reasons. He sat on a sofa in a comfortable office and faced Jim Howell, a Bush staffer who used to work as a drug agent in US Customs. Barry claimed he could prove that Nicaragua's Sandinista government - the hated enemy of Reagan- had been a sponsor of his offer to be an informant.

Bush administration - drug trafficking. Kennedy later stated that Barry said exactly what Barry meant when he testified to a congressional committee: "Officials from Nicaraguan government are involved with smuggling cocaine to the United States, particularly the Sandinistas."

Barry offered to provide information about the Medellin Cartel. He claimed that they were importing three quarters the cocaine into the US.

"Three quarters!" Kenneth said. "And how much do you think comes into the US each and every year, Mr Seal?"

"Oh, it's about a hundred tons. Gentlemen, that's a surprise to you?

"Well, let me just say that if your estimate is accurate, then the DEA doesn't even touch the tip of this iceberg."

"That's right. You're not. You don't need me. I can provide you with names, dates and lab locations. We must have a deal. Are we able to make a deal?

"Er, well. I believe the first thing we would love for you to do it is to meet some field officers from the DEA in Miami."

"Why?"
"Mr Seal. We're Washington bureaucrats. To verify your claims, we need street experts. Men who are familiar with the territory.

"Well, they should be able to understand what they are doing. Do not waste my time.

"I'll call you and get it set up right away. Bob Joura is the best.

Barry, wearing dark glasses, hat and sunglasses, waited outside a shopping center until Joura, his partner, and Jake Jacobsen arrived in their car.

Jacobsen, a tall, muscular man with a moustache like a walrus, shouted "Hey Barry Seal!".

Barry was dismayed at their lack of professionalism and scanned the area before diving into the back seat of the car. He was told by the two DEA agents to "Drive out of there quickly!".

Joura, a tall, middle-aged man with dark circles under his eyes and a serious expression, replied "Yes sir.".

Barry sat sideways on the back of the car, keeping his head down below the window.

Jacobsen smiled, "Is someone watching?".

"Oh, no, probably, you know. Barry sat up. "I would rather not be seen getting in a four-door sedan equipped with Blackwall tires, if that's what you mean."

Joura displayed his badge and said, "I'm Bob Joura from the DEA." "This is Special Agent Jacobsen."

"You talked to Washington?"

Joura stated, "Yeah. They said they might help us out with our investigations into cocaine trafficking.".

"In exchange for what?"

Joura stated, "Well, they said that you have a problem in Lauderdale." "But, I'll tell ya something: unless we get something genuine, Mr Seal," Joura said.

Barry, who was a co-founder with Pablo Escobar of the Medellin Cartel, gave up Jorge Ochoa's name in Doublecrossed.

Joura asked, "Do you want us to tell you who Mr Ochoa thinks he is, Mr Seal?".

Barry smiled. "You're putting my on. Ochoa. Escobar. Gacha."

Jacobsen sat in the passenger seat and raised his head. "Why don't you tell us Mr Seal who they are?"

Barry looked at Barry. "Ochoa. Escobar. Gacha. Oh, shit. Amateurs. They send me fucking amateurs. Barry screamed, "How the fuck is it possible to make a deal.

"Hey, man, cool it," Jacobsen said.

"You morons! You are the number one man in this whole fucking cocaine industry! Joura shouted, "You assholes!" "Shut up!" "And you ..." Barry yelled.

Jacobsen pulled out a gun and pointed it towards Barry. "You settle the fuckdown."

Barry shouted, "Get that fucking pistol out of my face!".
Joura shouted, "Stop the fucking up!".
Jacobsen shouted "Fuck you!" and pushed the gun's barrel closer towards Barry.

"You two are such dumb fucking assholes!"

"Shut up!"
"What the fuck are I doing?" Stop this fucking car!

The car pulled off the roadway and sped to a stop. Barry leapt out. Jacobsen followed Barry and grabbed him by his neck. He pushed him against a chain link fence and placed a gun at the rear of Barry's skull. "You just stood there. I move you, and you just stand there. That's it?

Joura jumped from the car. Jake, put the gun down! Cool down! Do not do anything stupid!"

"OK. Barry replied, "OK. "Just take the gun out."

Jacobsen turned Barry around, grabbed his neck and shoved the barrel of his gun in Barry's nostril. He said, mispronouncing Ochoa to be okra: "You don't tell me what I should do. You don't call me an amateur because you know who Ochoa was.".

Barry smiled. "It's Ochoa. Jorge Ochoa. He is America's largest cocaine supplier. He is the head of Medellin Cartel. You're so good at your job, then why don't YOU know who he really is?

Jacobsen pointed out Barry. "Cause I've heard plenty more crap from scumbags such as you before Seal. Perhaps you are full of shit.

"And maybe, you're a fucking amateur."

Barry was pushed to the ground by Jacobsen. "Goddammit!"

Joura pulled Jacobsen behind her and stood in front Barry. "Cool it, Jake. Cool it.

Jacobsen promised to settle down, while Barry nodded and smiled behind Joura.

Barry turned to Joura. Seal, it's clear. Let's get in the car and talk.

"Talk about what?" "I came here to make an agreement."

Joura replied, "Fine." "Get in your car."

Barry stated, "I'll make some huge busts for your," and then you will go to bat in court for me. Deal?"

Joura raised his voice to say, "The more you get me," he said. "The more we vouchfor you." Seal, that's all you get.

"I want amnesty for all those who work for my company. They shouldn't be hurt.

Joura stated, "You want a lot,".
Barry stated, "I'm going to give you a lot." "I'll make you fucking a career."

"Huh!" Jacobsen laughed. Jacobsen walked towards the car and laughed.

Barry stated, "Why don't you grow up asshole?".

Jacobsen spun around.

Joura grasped Barry's chain-link fence on either side and pressed his body against Barry's chest. Seal, you need to be straight with me or you will get into more trouble than you have ever needed.

Barry stated, "This may surprise you," but Barry is an honest man. What if I set it up to fly 3,000 kilos cocaine from Colombia to Ochoa? Barry stated that he had flown more than 100 times, carried at least 300 kilos cocaine and earned $3,500 per kilo. He had flown in more than 30,000 kilos, earning him over $100 million.

Two Miami DEA agents, Steve LeClair (a US Justice Department attorney), and Barry agreed to use Barry for informant. He was given the DEA number SGI84-0028. The DEA would pay him $800,000 per year. His sentence for Quaaludes would be delayed.

Doublecrossed saw Barry and Lito meet in a booth at a dimly lit diner.

Lito stated, "I need to go to Colombia tonight.".

"Tonight?"

Before dropping his boss's number, Lito looked around the room. "Ochoa's plane is in Fort Lauderdale. It's what he needs."

"Why me?"

"It's what Ochoa wants."

Barry asked incredulously, "Ochoa wants me to meet him?" "Why?"

Lito looked around once more. "Maybe you do."

Barry wriggled his hands and said "Me, hell. I don't even know anything.".

"Vamonos," Lito stated, which means let's go.

"Sure, let's take a sex, then we can go."

Barry rang the outside agents using the payphone from the foyer. Barry bragged about his plans to visit Colombia in order to meet Ochoa. "When I hand Ochoa over to you, I'll march down to the Fort Lauderdale judge and tell him how good a boy I am."

Chapter 11

Medellín Cartel

Barry was a copilot and struggled through thick fog over Colombia's coast. He flew in darkness before dawn to avoid the air force. The Honduran pilot was a close friend of the Ochoa clan. "We'll be flying right over Jorge

Ochoa's farm and ranch. Barry asked Barry if he would like to see it.

Hacienda Veracruz was circled by the Cessna with its 5,400-foot runway. Pilots waved at someone on the ground. The Cessna flew south towards Medellin. Barry was awestruck by the dense green jungle and mountains. The plane touched down on a grassy jungle airstrip at 5,000 feet. Workers climbed ladders to paint over the US registration number after the engine was shut off. The Ochoas just lost a Cessna similar loaded with cocaine in the Bahamas. So that Barry could not deny knowing about the seized Cessna, the Colombian registration number was set to be transferred to Barry's plane.

Barry noticed the airstrip that was cut through the jungle. Barry was concerned about the potential for mud to make things hazardous and water from recent rains. The tractor pulled duffel bags of cocaine from the jungle and loaded them onto a small plane. It was refuelling for a trip to Andros Island, Bahamas.

Barry and the Honduran flew in a small plane to Jorge Ochoa's aircraft base. This complex of hangers is near Medellin was where a helicopter & jet were stored. They were then driven up the mountain to La Loma, where they found a driveway that led to the Ochoas' home. There, guards with fully-automatic guns protected them. The grounds were home to hippopotami, giraffes and flamingos.

They waited in a waiting room until five Colombian drug traffickers, including the Ochoa brothers Pablo Escobar, entered. Fabio, Juan David, and Jorge Ochoa were raised in a family that had a lot of money from restaurants and cattle breeding. Jorge was polite and strong on family values. He didn't take part in any drugs except for the occasional glass of wine. Pablo was a dark-skinned man with a short, curly hair that was parted to the side. Although he was well-mannered, he had a dangerous side that the Ochoas did not have. Pablo was the son of a teacher and a farmer. He had terrorized Colombia by bombing campaigns and offering rewards for anyone who killed members of the National Police. Although he didn't smoke or drink tobacco, he was a fan of marijuana.

Barry was greeted by the men in Spanish by the Honduran pilot.

Barry replied, "Yes, I am very glad that you met me after all these years."

Jorge Ochoa stated, "So, tell us, Mr MacKenzie how is Miami?" "I lived there for many years."

Barry stated, "Well, you should come back for another visit.".
Ochoa laughed. Ochoa laughed.

Barry stated that he was happy to have been asked, as Reeves had previously told Barry that Ochoa owed him $5 million.

Ochoa stated, "Oh, don't worry about that money Roger," Roger gave it to me. It's all taken care of." Barry told him that he could supply unlimited amounts of cocaine but had experienced some setbacks including confiscations in Bahamas and the loss of Land of Tranquility, a large Colombian cocaine processing laboratory in the jungle of Caqueta. This lab had nineteen labs and an independent water and electricity system as well as dormitories for its workers. The processing supplies were flown in, and the cocaine was then flown out via eight different airstrips. The Land of Tranquility was raided by units of the Colombian National Police and the DEA on March 10, 1984. They destroyed the complex, and claimed that they had disposed of 13.8 metric tonnes of cocaine worth $1.2 billion. Documents with the names of the Ochoas were found during the raid.

Jorge Ochoa's brother in law said that "things are really tight for us now." "People are looking into this large laboratory down in the Llanos valley that Mr

Lehder was running to us," Barry
    stated.

"Yes," Lehder was forced to move their labs. However, Lehder had kept their cocaine hidden in underground bunkers all over Colombia.

Barry may have relayed the next part of his conversation to the DEA outlandishly to get the Reagan-Bush administration to help him with his legal problems. Barry claimed that traffickers approached him and said that they had made a deal with Nicaraguan ministers. Reagan-Bush wanted to make a link between the Nicaraguan government and drug trafficking in order to gain support for continuing funding, arming, and training the Nicaraguan rebels. Reagan-Bush knew that the rebels were involved in drug trafficking with the assistance of the CIA. The Nicaraguan government would be accused of trafficking in order to cover their own complicity.

Barry later stated that the agreement between Medellin Cartel (the Nicaraguan government) was still in its infancy. He was sworn to blood secretion and refused to use the name Nicaraguan again. "Even in meetings thereafter, it was going be called Costa Rica." Barry claimed that Nicaraguans had made an airstrip to refuel drug planes so they could transport less fuel from Colombia and more cocaine.

Barry was shocked that the Medellin Carttel was in bed the Communist government Nicaragua. They claimed that they weren't Communists, but the traffickers disagreed. "We don't share the same political philosophy as them, but they serve their ends and we serve ours."

Barry stated, "Well, I don't really know if an American would be welcomed in Nicaragua smuggling Cocaine.".
"There is nothing to be worried about."

Jorge Ochoa stated that Barry was needed to land at Medellin's jungle airstrip and take 1,500 kilos cocaine. The cocaine was to be flown to the USA. Half of the cocaine was headed for Miami and the other half to LA. They were stockpiling cocaine for the 1984 summer Olympic Games. Barry had to deliver the 1,500 kilos to the Nicaraguan government. The Medellin Cartel was preparing another 2,000. He asked Barry to fly in ten days.

Barry met Lito in Miami a week later at Auto World. Lito and Pablo Escobar co-owned the luxury car dealership. Auto World was a front company that moved 500 kilos per week of cocaine. Barry was told that six aircraft belonging to the Medellin Cartel were recently lost in the Bahamas. Ex-Venezuelan Naval Officer Lizardo Marquez perez was reorganizing the Miami distribution network. He was wanted by the authorities for smuggling 667 kilograms of cocaine and calling for the overthrow the Venezuelan government. He had earned an electricalengineering degree from Georgia Tech in 1967. He enjoyed horses, just like the Ochoas.

Lizardo confided to Barry in private that Ochoas were worried about Lito's complacency and laxity. Instead of using payphones Lito had lazyly used home phones. Lizardo stated, "I need to improve security.".
Lizardo also showed Barry a draft he had created for a security manual. It was ten pages long and detailed the benefits and drawbacks of renting safe houses under false names. "Notes To Meditate On (Ponder)" contained the following: "The opportunity for credit is lost...which makes it difficult in future to obtain new residence." But fake names allow "the one who lives at the house" to "appear to be the butler of that house." To any question, he could reply, "The owners are traveling." He also said that cocaine is "the foods".

There would be no connection between "butler" and "food", "butler and company", and "company and food." It is important to always use gloves.

Lizardo had specific criteria when it came to houses: "Residence location, preferably on a low-traffic street; lots of greenspace; garage for two cars; garage possibly not within the neighbour's view." He also instructed that the residents "live a normal lifestyle... You can try to imitate an American in all of his habits like mow the lawn and wash the car. The resident must not host extravagant social events, but may invite trusted family members to a barbecue.

Both Lizardo and Barry bonded because they valued security very highly. Barry then gave Lizardo his beeper number and bonded with him. Barry took Lizardo's daily report to the Medellin Carrtel. The Medellin Cartel leaders were temporarily in Panama while they waited for things to settle down in Colombia after the assassination.

Barry was under pressure to fly 1,500 kilos cocaine and told the cartel that it was his intention to first inspect the Nicaraguan airstrip. He bought a recreational vehicle in Miami to transport the cocaine.

Barry told his Honduran copilot that Lito had cheated him on $100,000 for a cocaine shipment that he had flown to Bahamas. Or, two. One for you, one for your spouse. Give me one, while you're at the same time."

"Well, it's not that I thought of it that way."

Barry and his wife went to Auto World to shop for a Mercedes 500 SEL four-door sedan, which was priced at $63,585.

Barry received it as a down payment from Lito.

Barry had planned to fly 1,500 kilos cocaine in just two days. However, during a test flight his Learstar blew its engine. The repair cost $30,000 and took a week.

Barry met the Panama cartel in May 1984. Pablo Escobar claimed that the cartel had not ordered the assassination the justice minister. He claimed it was a CIA plot to get the Colombian government to extradite traffickers from America to trial. He claimed that the cocaine labs of the Colombian government had been demolished in order to allow them to be relocated to Nicaragua. The mountains had been cleared of cocaine. They needed Barry to transport 1,500 kilograms as quickly as possible. They would instruct Barry from their new headquarters, Panama.

Barry and Federico Vaughan met again in Panama on May 20, 1984 in the basement of a white stucco home. Federico Vaughan was claimed to be a Nicaraguan official by the cartel who introduced Barry. Vaughan, a slicked-back gray haired, was dressed in a business suit and tie, a watch, sunglasses, and cufflinks. Vaughan would accompany Barry on his visit to Nicaragua's airfield so that he could inspect it. Barry had to follow Vaughan's instructions in order to avoid any damage in Nicaragua. Barry was introduced to Vaughan by Vaughan as the Nicaraguan Sandinista interior minister. They were available to process cocaine paste with ether from Germany for the Medellin Cartel.

Barry, his Honduran copilot, and Vaughan boarded a commercial flight to Managua (Nicaragua) that same day. They sat separately so they weren't associated. Vaughan helped them get through immigration without their passports being stamped. Vaughan's wife took them to their home, where they stayed the night.

Vaughan advised them to not worry about security checkpoints or guards as they were only a formality. They stopped at an oil refinery in a rural area five miles from Managua.

"This is the only refinery in the country. Vaughan pointed out the anti-aircraft batteries at the perimeter. Vaughan said, "Any aircraft flying over the refinery will be shot down immediately." He led them to a huge sunken lake, which is a volcanic crater filled with clear blue water. This is the best water in the country. Managua's only source of unpolluted water. It is as important as the oil refinery in its own right. You will be shot at if you fly close to it."

They traveled around a mountain and then crossed a railroad track to reach Los Brasiles, an airport with one runway. Vaughan was stopped at roadblocks and checked in by AK-47-wielding guards. He led them to a hanger that was designated for their purpose. Pablo Escobar owned a Piper Cheyenne.

Barry inquired about the runway's length, foundation, and texture. Vaughan led them down the runway, which measures 3,500 feet.

Vaughan shouted "Stop!" as Barry and his copilot walked on the grass to inspect a drainage ditch. It is contaminated with landmines. Avoid veering to the west if you are having trouble landing your plane. You'll get killed.

They ate at a steakhouse afterwards. Vaughan marked the entry and exit points of the smuggling missions with arrows on a Nicaraguan map. You will need a code to enter Nicaraguan airspace. Call the Sandino tower at a specific frequency and identify yourself as Yankee November Whisky, X-ray Yankee. You will then be rerouted to Los Brasiles by the tower. Anti-aircraft guns are used to cover all approaches to Managua to prevent night attacks by Contra rebels.

Barry created circles on the map around Vaughan's house, Vaughan's gun emplacements and Sandinista People's Army Headquarters.

Barry explained to the cartel back in Panama City that the runway was perfect, but the hangar was too small to accommodate the plane he was envisioning.

Pablo stated that Barry's mission has changed. Barry was not able to pick up another shipment from Nicaragua, weighing 2,000 kilos. Instead, Barry had to travel to Bolivia to obtain 6,000 kilos cocaine base to build new labs in Nicaragua.

Barry flew to Florida from New York and immediately went to Fort Lauderdale Federal Courthouse to receive his sentence.

Grey-haired Judge Roettger, dressed in a black robe entered the courtroom. He sat down on a leather seat next to the American flag, and looked down from his podium unaware of Barry's role, a highly valued DEA informant. "Mr Seal. Today's proceeding is to hear your sentence on the one count of Possession with Intent To Sale An Unlawful Narcotic. You will not be sentenced for the other charges that you are facing before this court. Before I give you a sentence, Mr Seal. You are a death dealer and have no regard for the lives of others. You don't care about where the deadly substance you smuggle is going or who it hurts. This is why I am imposing the maximum sentence possible on you for this offense. This is a ten-year sentence in federal prison. "You will immediately begin serving your sentence." The gavel rang.

Barry stood up and yelled "Where is the goddam DEA?"

His lawyer grabbed him. "I don't know, Barry. They said they would be there.

Barry was taken away by a guard who placed him in handcuffs. He was taken to Broward County Jail.

Two days later, DEA agents visited Barry.

Barry shouted at a guard, "Don't open the fucking doors!" "You let these assholes into here, I might even kill them!"

Joura stated, "I understand how you feel Barry.".
Barry shouted from behind the bars, "How in hell do you know what I feel?" "You've been double-crossed lately?"

Jacobsen stated, "I know that we weren't there. But we're going to take care of it.".
Joura stated, "I know that this won't help. But it was a mistake." "The judge didn't get the word on me."

"Ten years!" Barry yelled.

Joura stated that they are trying to get a hearing.

Jacobsen stated, "We want to stay in business together Barry.".
"Why should you do this to me?" It's what it gets me! Go!"

Barry was held for two days before Jacobson and Joura convinced him to be released on bail. Barry was released from jail after he got into the car of the agents. Joura apologized.

Jacobsen stated, "The judge released your to us." Jacobsen said, "You can continue working with us if necessary." In about five months, he'll reexamine your sentence.

Barry said, with a sombre expression, "I owe to you an apology, Bob. Jake." "I'm sorry that I blew up in here. It's been a long time since I thought about it. It's not clear if you know, but I don't use drugs. Everyone was using them when I started my business. It was known as recreational. It was not addictive. Nobody was dying. Bad guys didn't kill bad guys. It was all peace, love, and that kinda thing. But then. It was so hard to believe. It turned out that I was wrong. I even believed that I was making up the bad things I had done by working with you guys, but I was mistaken. The judge was correct. I hadn't paid. It wasn't enough. But now I will. I will prove my worth to you. But I just want you to know what I think. Now, I'm going to call Lito. He will be curious about where I have been. I'm going to tell him a story so that we can get back in business. Okay.

Chapter 12

Carlos Lehder

Barry, fresh out of prison, called his Honduran pilot, who asked Barry where he was. Barry replied that he was busy. They had to transport 1,500 kilos the next day so they didn't have time to waste.

The co-pilot stated that she believed her wife had become a government informant. This was paranoid, he said. She was arrested for cocaine while she was in Panama. But, when I returned home, she had been released. She was a frequent travel companion on my trips to Panama. She might have spoken. I won't go unless she comes along with us. "I need to keep an eye out for her."

Barry tried to convince him that he would bring his wife but it was futile. So he gave in. Barry waited in Louisiana for two days to see the copilot. He kept promising that he would get on the next flight but never showed up. Barry finally asked Emile Camp for help.

They flew a Learstar over Colombian jungle from Arkansas to Medellin on May 28, 1984.

Barry shouted, "That strip looks very wet!".
Emile replied, "So." Emile said, "So, you gonna try it?"

"I didn't fly all the way to turn around."

"That mountain is very close to the river. You should not go into that banana grove. It will take your wings. It's too wet. It's going to be hell getting out there, I'll tell ya that." Barry replied.

It's easy to say, "It's a piece cake."

The plane glided towards land, its propellers roaring. As it skidded onto the landing strip, water and mud splashed from the wheels.

Barry was speaking to ground crew when a man with long hair and a mischievous, boyish face galloped toward the plane riding a white Arabian horse stallion. He brandished a machine gun as well as barking orders.

Barry asked, "Who the hell are YOU?".
He yelled, "Carlos Lehder!" Barry knew of Lehder's cofounder of Medellin Cartel, who worshipped Adolf Hitler, John Lennon and was known for his militaristic behavior. He was of German and Colombian descent and had taken control of a Bahamian Island through the purchase of his neighbours and terrorizing the rest with Dobermans and automatic

weapons-wielding neo Nazis. His island, Norman's Cay was the Caribbean's main hub for drug smuggling from 1978 to 1982.

"Now, you will do as I tell you. Immediately. Before anyone sees your plane in the air!"

A tractor pulled over a ton cocaine.

Emile exclaimed, "Holy shit!" "They expect us all to fly out this swamp with all that shit."

Barry replied, "No, ofcourse not,".
"We can't lift that much weight."

"Don't you worry. Barry laughed. "Hey, it's impossible to lift this muddy strip with all that weight.

Barry's attempts at reasoning led to him being pinned against the tractor, and Lehder inserting a gun into his chin. "I don't care what your words are. Just like you agreed to, I will fly every gram out of this place. If you refuse to do so, I will kill you and your copilot will do it. We'll load the plane, and then you'll get out. You start loading fuel."

Barry accepted the offer with a defeated expression. Within fifteen minutes, 1,500 kilograms of cocaine were loaded in duffel bags into burlap sacks. Barry was the pilot. Emile asked, "Are you ready?".
"I knew that I could count upon you."

The plane picked up speed as it accelerated on the muddy runway. However, it failed to rise.

"C'mon, baby," Emile said.
Lehder galloped along, shooting at the ground, while his workers lined up at a periphery in the jungle cheering for the plane. The cheering grew to a crescendo, but the plane crashed and skidded. The right wheel fell into the

mud, and was then ripped from its undercarriage. Barry lost control. The plane crashed due to a mechanical crunch.

"Get out, man! Barry yelled, "The fuel's going to blow!" Barry ran for his life and rushed to get out. Lehder appeared and exploded with more gunfire. "Gringos! Maricones!" In anticipation of an explosion, Emile and Barry dived into the jungle.

Lehder directed his workers to save the cocaine from the plane on fire.

Emile clutched a tree and said, "That crazy bastard's forcing them to go to the plane." They'll be barbecued.

Barry and Emile jumped from the jungle to try and stop two dozen workers running towards the plane. They were unsuccessful.

Lehder shouted, "Help them now!" and shot his gun at the dirt under their feet.

Barry and Emile joined the men as they seized large quantities of cocaine from the plane. The plane exploded as they ran, knocking them over. Fireballs erupted a distance of dozens of yards. Two workers were burned.

The tractor eventually returned the cocaine to its storage location, where it was inventoried.

Lehder shouted, "Cabrones! We have another plane!".
Barry, with a muddy face, said that he didn't care what type of plane he had. We can't fly with that load. We have to wait for the field to dry.

Barry and Emile were flown from Medellin. After spending the night in the home of a cartel member they were taken around the grounds. They were able to admire a waterfall, a tropical plant, and an Olympic-sized cycling track.

A Titan 404 was chosen as the replacement plane. "Certainly, you won't be able carry the 1,500 kilos you tried to transport with the larger plane. Is it possible to carry only half?

Barry replied, "No sir," he was concerned about the plane's descent over the Gulf of Mexico.

Mexico. "Because then, I wouldn't have any fuel to add."

"And with a stop at Nicaragua?" What can you take?

"Well, with an stop in Nicaragua we can probably take 700 - 750 kilos." Barry had already played the crash because the Reagan Bush administration would be more satisfied with the drug link the faster he could get to Nicaragua. The more favorable it would be to his legal situation.

Barry called Joura from Gulfport to discuss the new flight schedule at the Hotel Intercontinental, Medellin. Joura and Jacobsen waited for the 1,500 kilos in Gulfport.

Barry and Emile returned to their jungle airstrip the next day. The Learstar's burned remains were climbed by one of them while the other took photos. They spent three days in the jungle with Lehder, who guarded the cocaine.

He showed them 3,000 kilos and claimed that there were 6,000 kilos in Bolivian cocaine base waiting to be shipped to Nicaragua.

Barry informed the DEA on June 2, 1984 that he would be flying to Nicaragua the following day. Jacobsen was contacted in Miami by one of Barry's associates on June 3rd, at 10:30 PM. He informed Jacobsen that Barry had received a radio transmission and that Barry was returning home to Nicaragua due to engine problems. Jacobsen was informed by Barry that he had landed in Nicaragua three hours later. Jacobsen is concerned about legal issues. There was no further contact.

Barry arrived in the US three days later without any cocaine. He told the DEA at a debriefing that he had flown the Titan 404 from Colombia on June 3 with 700 kilos. It took longer than anticipated to stop in Los Brasiles (Nicaragu) for fuel. Barry took off in darkness and flew over a mountainous area without lights. The plane was illuminated north of Managua by anti-aircraft trackers. The plane began to descend quickly after his left engine was struck. Barry returned to Los Brasiles in order to avoid crashing. He was unable to land at the dark airport so he scrambled for radio Vaughan. But he had returned home.

Barry radioed an urgent broadcast to Sandino International Airport, Managua. He used a Vaughan code. The plane was immediately surrounded by soldiers upon landing. Barry insistently called Vaughan. Vaughan refused to answer the phone, even though he was granted one.

Vaughan was known to a sergeant, who had Barry's cocaine loaded from his plane. He instructed Emile and Barry to remain calm and accept whatever happened. "Everything will work out fine."

Barry and Emile were held in The Bunker, a military base in downtown Managua. They were released to Vaughan the next day and taken to a large landed property. Pablo Escobar welcomed them. Pablo Escobar had moved to oversee the cocaine-processing operation.

Vaughan returned with El Nuevo Diario a few days later. "This is why we asked you to keep your mouth closed at the airport because we had to keep the whole incident quiet in the newspapers. Barry was shown a two-paragraph article stating that anti-aircraft gunners had fired at an Agrarian reform Air Transport Company plane at Sandino Airport because it couldn't signal its location:
"The DAA [Anti-Aircraft Defense] had signalled and fired warning shots to incite it to land at the runway - which was done without any untoward consequences."

Vaughan claimed that the accident happened because he wasn't ready for a smuggling flight at night. Barry hadn't been seen by the gunners. They heard Barry and fired at the noise. Next time, communication was better. Barry was upset that Vaughan hadn't been able reach him from the plane and suggested they buy walkie talkies.

Pablo stated that Pablo had told him that the new lab for cocaine was located at a Ranch south of Managua. It was ready to go in just two weeks. Lehder owned almost fifteen tons cocaine base. This would make approximately one-fifth of America's cocaine consumption each year.

Barry stated, "Well that's going take a really large plane." "You should purchase a military cargo aircraft like the one I saw advertised in the aviation trade magazine."

Pablo asked Barry to get such a plane for him and then pick up the 700 kilos.

Barry asked, "Is this cocaine safe?".
Vaughan stated, "We haven't lost one gram.".
Pablo's Piper Cheyenne needed maintenance in America so Barry and Emile flew home with it.

Barry gave Lito Escobar his shopping list. It included night-vision glasses and 12 high-frequency radios, each costing $12,000.

Chapter 13

The Fat Lady

Barry was connected to the CIA and obtained a Fairchild C-123K Provider. This massive camouflage-green twin-engine military cargo aircraft was used in Vietnam War. It was nicknamed the Fat Lady by Barry. Barry flew the Fat Lady from Rickenbacker Air Force Base in Columbus, Ohio, on June 18, 1984. Air Force personnel worked round the clock to repair and retrofit the plane. Repairs totaling $40,000 were made by the military at taxpayers' cost.

Barry was told to photograph Nicaraguan officials who were associated with cocaine. The CIA asked Barry to explain the situation. There will be many men down there with guns. Nervous men who won't exactly say cheese to a gringo pilot with his camera.

Five days later, it landed at Homestead Air Force Base in Miami. The DEA installed a transponder to track the plane's flight. The CIA installed a hidden 35mm camera in its nosecone. Another was placed in a fake electronics box in rear cargo hold. The box contained a pinhole lens that would allow the camera film the cocaine being loaded into the plane's back. Barry received a radio-controlled trigger with an antenna attached that could be used to record the cocaine being loaded into the back of his plane.

"What! "What! Barry looked at the antenna and said "Stick it up my arse!". "You can keep it in your pocket."

"All of it?

"Put it into your pocket and let the antenna slide down to your leg."

Barry did this and pressed the remote button. He was furious at the clicking sound the camera made and cursed the CIA men wearing suits. "I am tired of spending my time with your scumbags. I will get your fucking photos. Autographed!

What are you going to do for me?

"We have a deal Mr Seal."

"The judge. "Speak it, dammit!"

"We will speak on your behalf to the judge."

Barry called Vaughan in a Miami hotel room. The conversation was recorded by Barry for the DEA. Barry used code for the cocaine shipment to say, "I was going see my grandmother at noon Saturday." Barry, referring to the Fat Lady, was worried about being shot again. Barry stated, "It is a big

Cadillac... Very large, big car... I wanted to make sure my grandmother would tell the landlord that it was very large, so that they wouldn't get excited when they see it."

Vaughan stated, "No, no. No," "Everything is okay about that."

Barry informed Vaughan on June 24, 1984 that he was going to a party at his grandmother's tomorrow. This meant that the cocaine would be arriving the next day. "It's all coming to the party, and you've notified these boys in green." He was still worried about being shot.

"Right," Vaughan said.
Barry stated, "They're all notified?".
"Yes," Vaughan said.
"Excellent. OK. Just wanted to be sure. "I don't want any problems."

"Yes, everyone is going to be there."

"OK, good. Is Pedro coming? Barry replied, referring specifically to Pablo and his shopping list.

Vaughan stated, "Yes, yes he's coming.".
"I'm leaving at midnight for the party. Barry asked, "Has it been raining in the yard where the cars are parked at the party?".
"It's dry, hard and only a bit muddy in a small area.

"I cannot stay at the party for too long." Barry stated that he must leave the party as quickly as possible, in order to get enough fuel to last him.

"Yeah, that's what we're going be doing."

"OK. "OK.

Vaughan laughed. "No, that's perfect."

Barry, a pilot from Los Brasiles near Managua, landed at 1pm on June 25, 1984 and opened the back of his plane. Pablo received $454,000 from him. Later, he claimed that Vaughan, Pablo and another cartel leader Gacha were on the ground. Barry shouted, "How do I like the plane?" Barry said over the engine noise. "I call her Fat Lady."

Soldiers began to load duffel bags full of cocaine into the cargo holds. Barry was constantly pressing his remote control to take pictures. The camera clicked so loudly outside that the Fat Lady could hear it. Barry turned on the generators to drown out the sound. An American spy plane captured high-resolution images above.

Pablo shouted, "Stop your engines!".
"I can't. "We gotta keep them warm," Barry stated, keeping the sound low to mask the camera noise.

A gun-wielding, overweight bodyguard entered the plane. He began to look around the plane as if he could see the camera noise. Emile turned the propellers so that the noise could be disguised. After checking around, the bodyguard left. The plane took off after being loaded with 700 kilos cocaine and 2,000 gallons fuel. This took approximately an hour.

The Fat Lady landed at Homestead Air Force Base the next morning. 700 kilos cocaine were seized by the DEA and the CIA took the film. It was a successful mission. Photos showed Barry, Pablo and Vaughan loading twenty-five-kilo duffel bag bags.

Barry organized a meeting at Dadeland Mall with Lito the night before his return. Barry met Lito at his car and he parked it just before 10 p.m.

Lito asked, "Where's my load?".
Barry stated, "It's right there in Winnebago.".
Lito was upset. The Winnebago was left exposed by the cars that were leaving the lot. Barry and Lito left the Winnebago.

The DEA observed a white-t-shirted man get out of a Chevy truck and get into a Winnebago. The man was followed by several cars, as well as a helicopter. It was also followed closely by cartel workers in a Chevy truck, and a grey Mercedes-Benz.

A DEA agent driving an old car collided with the Winnebago at a specific moment. Next came the Florida Highway Patrol. Barry was not aware that the accident had been planned. The trooper was instructed to let the Winnebago driver escape.

The trooper stated, "Please license and register.".
The young Colombian presented his license, but not for registration. "Can I cross the street to make a phone call?"

The trooper answered, "Yes", and allowed him to flee.

The Colombian ran across the street to Wendy's, then rushed behind the building as he fled. A pedestrian witnessed the Colombian run away after witnessing the incident. The pedestrian chased down the Colombian and grabbed his hand. The two were fighting when police arrived and the trooper was forced to take the Colombian into custody.

Barry's phone rang at 2 AM. An employee at Lito asked, "Have your heard the news?" "The load got busted."

Barry was summoned by Lito to meet him. He asked Jacobsen for surveillance to prepare him for danger.

Tony Roma's restaurant was visited by Lito, who told Barry that Jota, the Spanish word for letter J, was the highest-ranking Medellin Cartel member in Miami and wanted to meet everyone immediately. "One of our people was following Winnebago. He claimed he saw a car deliberately smash into the side. He said it was a setup.

Barry was taken by Lito to a South Miami luxury condo. Inside were a group of Colombians. Jota stated that he was investigating the seizure. According to the young Colombian man who followed the Winnebago, he saw a driver cause the accident.

Lito said that Lito didn't know what he was talking about and would be held responsible if the deal wasn't accidental. Barry was asked by Lito for his thoughts.

Barry stated that Jota should be notified immediately if she believes something is wrong.

The Colombians conferred Spanish. Jota asked Barry for his driver's license and he said that he would return to him. To avoid being followed, everyone had to stay in the condominium until Jota left.

Lito called back the next day in good spirits. All was settled. Barry was asked to buy more cocaine from Nicaragua. Barry agreed to call Vaughan in Managua.

Vaughan stated, "My friend said that everything was okay.".
Barry stated, "Yeah there is only one person in hospital and he seems fine," referring to the one arrested person who wasn't speaking to police. Barry was furious at the arrest and demanded senior officials make some changes.

Vaughan stated that Barry would be heard by the cartel. They have a special and very kind consideration for you. Our common friend Pablo wants a favor. Sometimes, my English isn't so great. A small water vessel for having fun... Water boat

Barry was able to decipher that Pablo wanted a rubber boat with an outboard engine. It was added to his shopping list that included plane parts and video recorders. Pablo also requested $1.5 million cash to pay Nicaragua for landing rights.

Lito lied about getting the money.

Barry called Pablo in Miami's Omni International Hotel. A translator was with him. He attached a small suction cup made from a Sony Walkman to his receiver, without the translator being aware. This allowed him to record the call for future reference.

DEA.

"It's MacKenzie calling Pedro," said the translator in Spanish to the man who answered.

Barry said to the translator, "Tell them that they're jacking him around." "That MacKenzie and you are about to leave tomorrow night, and that we have all the parts for the plane, and that the bill is approximately $150,000. They won't give it to us."

Pablo stated, "The gentleman with whom the he works didn't deliver anything?".
"No."
Pablo stated that he would call his friends. Pablo was told the $1.5 million had not arrived and he said, "Oh, yes, I see. Pablo said, "Oh, I see.

Soon after, an angry Lito called Barry. "I am vacationing in the Keys. Just got informed that you require this million-and-a half dollars. Pablo Escobar, his associates gave it to me. Pablo Escobar is not my employer. Jorge is my boss and I don't like being called out at night to bring you the million dollar.

Lito shipped $1.5 million to the DEA in three suitcases with a cardboard box and two more. To document the cash, the DEA sent a photographer.

Barry flew the Fat Lady from Chicago to Las Brasiles on July 7, 1984. He told Vaughan that he received a radio message in Mississippi telling him that the offloading location was under surveillance. Vaughan did not know that Barry wanted the cocaine to be left on Nicaraguan soil. The DEA would have it confiscated if he brought it home. Barry would have been suspect if two loads were taken at once, which could have led to the end of the largest investigation by DEA in history.

Barry was brought to Pablo who thanked Barry for being cautious and suggested Barry find underground hiding places near his landing strips. This is similar to what had been done in Colombia. Nicaragua would keep nine-hundred kilos.

Barry was requested by the DEA to fly the cocaine base in South America. This would allow them to identify the locations of the Nicaraguan labs and map the supply network for the cartel in Bolivia. Barry was authorized by the cartel to establish a radio communications center in Managua that would guide coca paste flights between the Andes and Los Brasiles. The DEA would have the ability to trace the drug source with this huge opportunity. Barry was also requested by the DEA to lure Jorge Ochoa, and Pablo to a country with an extradition treaty to America so that they could be deported to face trial in the US.

Pablo brought up the issue of the cocaine base before Barry left Nicaragua. Pablo wanted the Fat Lady, Gacha's West Coast distributor, to transport the cocaine from Nicaragua to a northern Mexico airstrip. The cocaine would be transported by small planes to the US, Georgia included. Pablo asked Barry to inspect the Mexican and Georgian airstrips. Barry agreed. Barry agreed.

Chapter 14

Oliver North

One day after Barry had shipped 700 kilos to Florida on June 26, 1984, Oliver North - George HW Bush's frontman – wrote in his notebook: nic Drug operation C-123 was acquired by DEA source and installed two cameras Miami plane t/o landed Los Brasiles Freddie Vaughan works at Tomas Borge Photos showing Vaughan + Nic Troops 750 lbs cocaine.
    The rolls of film that Barry had taken from Fat Lady were quickly flung to Washington.

David Westrate was the DEA's assistant administrator for operations and met with Oliver North (a CIA agent) and Duane Clarridge (a DEA deputy assistant administrator). In the hopes of encouraging support for Nicaraguan rebels, they discussed the possibility of Barry's photos being released.

Ron Caffery was the head of the DEA's Washington DC cocaine desk and he visited the Old Executive Office Building next to the White House to show Oliver North enlarged photos of Vaughan, Pablo, and other grainy photos.

North was wearing a military uniform, with many medals and decorations. A large American flag was visible behind him. These pictures are well-known around the world. The White House is interested in everything that comes out Nicaragua," North stated, "Now, this is Federico Vaughan right?"

Dewey Clarridge said that he was a Sandinista official and had a dossier about Vaughan. He said that he was an "assistant to Tomas Borge," Nicaragua Interior Minister, and that he was a co-founder the Sandinista National Liberation Front in Nicaragua.

Caffery stated, "Sandinista." "I was not told that."

"Oh. It's true." Clarridge pointed at a photo and said, "And that is your undercover guy." What is his name?

"Seal. Barry Seal is his name," Caffery stated.

They sent Barry home with $1.5 million in DEA cash to buy more cocaine and gifts for Pablo, Vaughan, and Vaughan. North wanted the sting operation not to take place in Nicaragua so that the $1.5million could be sent to Nicaraguan rebels for arms purchases. Caffery stated that the US Attorney's Office wouldn't approve of such an arrangement.

North asked, referring to the photos.

"It won't," Caffery said.
"Why not?" North said.
"Well, it would stop a vitally important inquiry for one thing. It would also seriously threaten Barry Seal's health for another reason."

North stated that the public is entitled to information about Nicaragua's drug activities, "Mr Caffery.".

"Colonel North Barry Seal is in the largest drug operation in the entire world. For the sake of God, the Medellin Cartel leaders trust him. We believe he may actually be able to lure one of the Medellin Cartel leaders to the USA, so that we can arrest him.

We can't afford to lose this kind of chance."

North spoke out about Nicaraguan rebels, saying, "Listen Ron, there is an important vote in Congress on an Appropriations Bill to Fund the Contras." "Sandinista participation in drugs will make an important difference."

Caffery stated that "I'm certain the US Attorney's Office would make it public at a proper time.".

"So tell me about the Seal. Clarridge asked, "What kind of man is he?".

It all depends on whom you speak to. He can be either a genius, or he can be a scummer of the earth.

Despite Caffery warnings about the dangers associated with releasing this information, the Reagan-Bush administration immediately released it.

General Paul Gorman, head of the Pentagon's Southern Command, gave a speech at the American Chamber of Commerce, El Salvador, on June 27, 1984. General Gorman stated that he had evidence that the Sandinista government was involved with drug trafficking.

Barry was present at a meeting with DEA officials and other officials in light of the leaks. The meeting decided whether Barry should be sent back for more cocaine. There was much disagreement over the source of the leaks. One official protested, stating that Barry's case against Jorge Ochoa would be thrown out if Barry was killed. Barry was opposed to being sent back.

Barry stood in a navy suit and wore his signature gold-rimmed Aviator sunglasses. "If I don't go, it's all gone."

Jacobsen stated, "Yeah but if they do, they might make you." "If I don't go, the entire investigation's over."

Jacobsen stated, "But if it does, you might die.".
Barry replied, "If you feel sorry for me Jacobsen," and he held his hand.

Joura stated that Jacobsen was correct. Barry, it may all fall on you.

"Or may not. We've gotta play it out."

Joura stated, "It's enough." "What you have will make your sentence lighter.

Trust me."
Barry replied, "Wait, a minute." It's not about a lighter sentence anymore.

It's all right. It's all about going to that court with Ochoa Escobar and Gacha. Barry pointed at himself and said, "I can do it." They don't have me. They haven't got me. It's my certainty."

Jacobsen shook his head and said, "There's no way that you can be certain of that,".
"In my guts. Barry shook his fists and said "OK. That's what this is all bout." "I can do it. My gut tells me that I can. I am the best. Don't try to stop me!

"It's just not worth taking the chance on one more run."

"One more run!" They want me haul 30,000 pounds from Colombia to Nicaragua. It cannot all be taken to the same place. Then, I will be able to find the labs as well as the new labs in Nicaragua. What's the Sandinista involvement? What is the value of that information to the DEA or the Justice Department?" Barry continued to harp on Nicaraguan connections, but the room became more relaxed as officials began to consider sending Barry back. "I might even manage to bring Mr Ochoa right here into the USA."

"On the pretense that his organization is in decline here."

"Do you really believe you can do that, Mr Seal?"

Barry said, "I'm the best." He approached an official and squatted. "And it wouldn't hurt your career too much for me to do that, would it?" The men laughed.

Barry asked, "What do YOU think about that Joura?".
Joura laughed more, "I think we just turned the corner in the War on Drugs," Joura stated.

"Alright then. "I'll just go one more time. I'm convinced by you."

Barry informed Emile Camp after the meeting that he was flying alone. Emile returned to Joura, Jacobsen's hangar with a strained expression. Their stress increased as they waited for Barry to return. The next morning, a radio signal arrived in the hangar. It read: "Fat Lady." It's all fine. Do you read me? Jorge [Ochoa] wouldn't come along. This trip is not for you.

Joura discovered on July 8, 1984 that Barry had left Nicaragua with 900 kilos. Joura was shocked to discover that the Washington Times was going to publish a story about Barry's undercover work. Joura realized that the White House was leaked information via Oliver North, a Reagan-Bush favorite paper. The DEA contacted Joura to inform her that the paper had agreed to delay publishing the story for at most a week.

The Washington Times published the story on July 17, 1984 as Barry flew to Mexico to meet with cartel members. Barry returned to Miami after receiving a radio transmission in frantic.

The DEA was concerned that Florida would soon expose its cover due to the White House's Washington Times. Therefore, it quickly obtained search warrants for Florida and indictments.

Barry lured Lito into the Skyways Motel in Miami where he was joined by an accomplice. Lito claimed he was Jorge Negrete, a car washer. He also showed a driver's license with the same name. The DEA discovered that Carlos Bustamante was his real name.

The Medellin Cartel's heads were all out of the US so they were free. Vaughan, a Nicaraguan trade official of low rank who had quit his job long before Barry's undercover work, denied any involvement in trafficking.

Frank Monastero (head of DEA) lambasted Oliver North over the leak. North denied all. North claimed that the inaccuracies of the story showed that he was not involved in it. Monastero replied that he did not believe North, as North planted inaccuracies into a story to hide his tracks.

This story did not generate any support for Nicaraguan rebels. Congress refused to provide aid to the rebels for months.

Barry's covert work had been destroyed by the leak. After enduring some trouble, the Medellin Cartel's heads returned to Colombia. It was then business as usual. They were surrounded by bodyguards and officials who served as their payroll. Pablo lived in Medellin, and was a regular attendee of bullfights and soccer matches. The American wholesale price for cocaine fell to $14,000.

Chapter 15

Mena

Twenty Nicaraguans arrived at Mena on a C130 military cargo plane, flown by Bill Cooper (an older pilot). They carried their bags to a hangar wearing Ray-Bans and a mix of civilian clothes. They dropped their bags to see if a Cessna was nearby.

Diego, a Panamanian, yelled, "Take those fucking glasses off, soldiers!" Cessna 414 manuals were given to the trainees. "You must memorise them!"

Terry Reid and Emile camp thought it would be difficult to get the Nicaraguans up-to-speed so that they could fly missions in their country within four months.

Barry flew in a new commander of the Nicaraguan camp. Ramon Medina, real name Luis Posada Cariles, was a Cuban terrorist and mercenary who was believed to be in Venezuela for bombing a Cuban plane in 1976. The attack killed all on board. He had been aided by the CIA to escape.

Barry and Terry met in Little Rock at the SOB's for dinner. Barry said that his plans had changed. "I won't be staying the night here. You need to be kind and do me a favor in the morning. I have a briefcase in my car with some money that I can give to Dan Lasater. He's referring me to a guaranteed investment deal. I need someone I can trust, and I mean really trust. Aki knows I am being watched. Isn't it a wonderful business? Everyone's watching everyone else. Terry, at some point you will have to decide who your true trust is. So it's time to decide. You or me?

Aki? Terry stopped to think.

Barry stated, "Look, Barry, you told me long ago that you wanted to learn how the suits work." Although I am willing to learn from you, I need to know that you are on my side. Aki will be using you forever, so play it his way.

Terry asked Barry about the information Barry previously suggested he had about Vice President George HW Bush.

"Oh, that's something you probably shouldn't say." Let's just say that I was given sensitive information about the Bush family during my last trip to Central America.

"OK, but this relationship is built on trust. First, what have your been doing in Central America?"

"Lots and lots of things. Some of these I cannot tell you about. It's not necessary to know and you won't be a liability if you don't. If you are in, the main topic I want to discuss tonight is guns and money. You sure you're in?"

"Barry, it's not completely stupid. I have a pretty good idea of how you fly weapons down south. It seems that you are doing this with the blessings of the CIA, and the White House. This operation is too big and well-equipped to go unnoticed. It is possible that you are motivated by something other than patriotism. Barry, I served in a war where I received no compensation. It would be great to win a war, not only to heal old wounds but also to serve my country and get paid. If that's what your talking about, I'm all for it.

Barry claimed that he was flying weapons from Mena, El Salvador, and other countries. He was so overwhelmed by the volume of the shipments that he received the C-123, a.k.a. The Fat Lady. Barry had two identical C123s down to the same tail number. Barry claimed that he could access two copies of every item, even Seneca and Navajo aircrafts as the CIA had planes all over the country. For various reasons, such as human or mechanical error, duplicates were necessary. To divert attention from a plane used in covert activities, to send pursuers on wild goose chases, or to make it appear that two places are being held simultaneously.

Barry stated that the US Army had donated parts of weapons to the Nicaraguan rebels. Terry was not allowed to tell Aki that Barry had disclosed that. Barry claimed that the CIA was selling M16A1s – guns that jammed when exposed in Vietnam to sand - to Nicaraguan rebels. The CIA kept the profits, and there was no documentation to prove that anything had happened. The guns were made from parts taken from stock and parts cast at CIA's foundry to circumvent the laws governing the sale of fully-automatic weapons.

He claimed that key players were profiting from the weapons deals by pretending to be patriotism. Barry flew so much money to Arkansas to help them, that he didn't want to be caught. "The Agency has me bring large amounts of cash from abroad to invest here. Lasater is part of this operation. When we sell weapons, I fly there. Cash profits are returned to the Agency for depositing. The problem is that the Agency doesn't want anyone to know the profits. If I'm being tracked out of Central America and someone discovers I have the cash, there's a way for me to get them off my tail.

Terry was asked to fly a duplicate aircraft as part of a technique that the CIA taught, which was used for entering foreign airspace. This helped him avoid detection. Barry showed how two planes could be piggyback by drawing a napkin. The two aircraft would appear as one radar blip, fooling air traffic controllers. Air-traffic control could not notice that the main aircraft had been switched and it could disappear on a covert mission. Barry owned two identical Senecas, November 8658 Echo (and November 8049 Zulu). Terry would meet him at Little Rock Air Center. "You'll be following me on my tail. I don't mean my fucking tail. You should be able count the rivets on the tail hook. Make use of your night-vision system. After that, you will be able to see clearly at night.

You can just go up to Mena or land. It's so simple." Terry stated,
    "Let's go outside and practice in the daytime.".
    "Sounds good. Emile will be with me. He is also on board. You know what's even more amazing? You and he look very similar. You are sitting in an airplane and I can see that you have misunderstood me for him."

Barry took his Mercedes' locked briefcase outside and retrieved it from the Mercedes. Do me a favor, bring this to Dan Lasater's house first thing in the AM and make sure it is well-guarded. Uncle Sam has given us a large deposit.

"Can you tell me where you are going?" "I thought you were going to spend the night with me."

"So did I. The Fat Lady and I have an appointment down south. Piggyback, see you later."

The White House and Oliver North had leaked information to discredit the Nicaraguan government. Barry's life was at risk from the Medellin Cartel who knew that the pilot for the Fat Lady was an informant. The

New York Times: "US accuses Managua Of Role in Cocaine"

Traffic."

Barry had brought their largest drug case to the attention of the DEA. While the DEA in Florida had been protecting Barry, now the DEA of Louisiana was pursuing him for drug charges. The Louisiana federal prosecutor wanted to bring Barry down, and make headlines. He was unaware of Barry's covert work for Mena. Oliver North could not intervene in the Louisiana justice system, as Barry's covert work for the CIA at Mena was known to the Reagan-Bush government. This was a government that was locking up drug users from the most vulnerable areas at record levels and using the proceeds of illegal drugs to fund its wars.

Barry chose to fight back. Barry decided to fight back, with federal agencies against him. He had the information he had about Bush's involvement in drug trafficking.

Barry was seen flying over Nella in a Fairchild C-123 camouflaged Fairchild C-123 in late September 1984. The massive plane glided through a forest and almost cut off the trees, enchanting Nicaraguan trainee pilots. Barry landed at Mena. Each week, two privileged students were allowed to take a seat in the cockpit and dream about flying a C-123. Barry grimacingly stated to his staff that the White House wanted students to fly missions as soon possible.

Barry was suffering from his problems. The DEA in Florida appeared to abandon Barry just as he was most in need of them to testify in court. He planned to release certain conversations he had secretly recorded while working for the DEA and FBI, CIA, and US Customs.

Bad weather arrived from Oklahoma the day Barry left Nella. It was a cold front with thunderstorms, tornadoes and thunderstorms. Training for pilots ended quickly. They were transported by a one-ton truck of gas to Mena, where Barry had been stranded because of the storm. He seemed preoccupied and apprehensive, which was unusual for him.

Chapter 16

Uncle Sam Wants You

Barry decided to document himself in September 1984 after realising the government was cheating him. He was beaten by the DEA and the Louisiana justice system, and he set out to televise evidence of his relationship with DEA agents that would stop them from denying his relationship.

John Camp, an investigative journalist at WBRZ TV Channel 2 in Baton Rouge was the one he spoke to about his work with the CIA/DEA. He supported his claims with videotapes of news clips that corroborated parts of his story. Camp was allowed to secretly film a meeting in Miami during which one his DEA handlers gave him $10,000. Barry's claims made Camp's skeptical melt away.

Barry submitted documents that revealed the overzealousness of federal prosecutors. He complained about how the US Attorney's Office in Baton Rouge made a deal for Kenneth Webb, an ex-classmate of Barry who was paid to do odd jobs. Prosecutors had offered to end Webb's legal troubles, including an auto theft charge, in order to get him to cooperate with Barry. Webb was prone to mental instability and had been arrested for minor offenses. A federal grand jury heard Webb tell that he delivered a shoebox containing cocaine to Barry. John Camp interviewed Webb. Webb confessed to fabricating the story about cocaine under pressure from drug agents. Webb's lawyer requested that Stanford Bardwell, the US Attorney, allow Webb to correct the perjured grand jury testimony. This request was turned down.

Meanwhile, Barry was being investigated by prosecutors in Louisiana and Miami.

According to a Justice Department prosecutor, Miami thinks that the man is the greatest thing since sliced toast, which is normal because he's helping them. Baton Rouge believes that he is the worst dealer in Louisiana history, which he was."

Barry met two of his lawyers over breakfast at Hyatt Regency Miami Hotel.

Scalfani stated, "We shouldn't be sitting next Barry at this public eatery.".
"Why?" Unglesby said.
Scalfani asked, "What do YOU mean? Why?" "Don't know there's an agreement on him?"

"You're kidding," Unglesby said.
"Don't worry. "He's closer to me than to you,"

They then walked to the US attorney's office near the Miami River. It took many hours to reach a plea bargain. Barry would plead guilty in Baton Rouge to the charges and receive the same sentence in Florida for the Quaaludes case. Prosecutors expected Barry to serve at most three years. Barry and his lawyers were happy to leave and are ready for some assassination jokes.

Scalfani walked towards a parking garage in downtown Miami and turned to Unglesby. "Gee Lewis, this is a great spot for a hit.

The Organized Crime Strike Force in New Orleans signed the plea-bargain on November 19, 1985. Barry had pleaded guilty in the conspiracy to possess 462 kilos cocaine with intent to distribute and failing to file currency transactions reports for $51,006.04 that were deposited at four Baton Rouge bank branches. The Florida sentence would be the same sentence as the one that Barry received for the first count.

The judge will be allowed to determine the probation conditions. "As regards count two of this instant indictment the defendant will be given a period for probation to be determined and imposed by the court."

Barry spoke to John Camp, an investigative reporter, about the plea deal at home that night. Camp published an article about the meeting on his website on January 27, 2015. "In contrast with past braggadocio he [Barry] was humble and polite in disclosing that, in Baton Rouge, he had agreed to plead guilty. I was given a copy and asked to keep it secret until the official announcement. He was confident that his Florida agreement would keep him out prison. Seal stated that he doesn't know much about the load and has hauled in as much cocaine into Louisiana. He said that he accepted the deal because of mounting legal costs. It was difficult to believe his explanation. It seemed that he was apologizing for my guilty plea. This was not relevant to the issues in my documentary.

Channel 2 in Baton Rouge aired Barry's documentary Uncle Sam Wants you, on November 20, 1985. It began with Barry meeting Jake Jacobsen, a DEA agent.

John Camp reported that Barry Seal was an "enigma". He has worked closely with federal drug agents in Miami as well as the Central Intelligence Agency. He was a key witness in one the largest drug investigations in South Florida. The veteran pilot was also a victim of an intense and unfair investigation in Baton Rouge.

Barry, who was wearing sunglasses and a combat flightsuit, said that he wasn't a drug smuggler. "I say prove. Barry's smile seemed to be a challenge for his prosecutors.

"A gun smuggler?" Camp said.

"No. "No. Why is Ryan Airport's paper not featuring me? You know that they are such great agents and I am the largest in the world. "The biggest people in the world can't get away with the law and justice, you know that," he said. "The bottom line was: 'How about we make a bust. What about setting up someone? Give us a load. Give us a chance.

John Camp claimed that the Baton Rouge detectives went to "extreme lengths to prove Barry was an international drug smuggler". Camp dissected Camp's Louisiana investigation.

Barry stated that he believed the current investigation headed by Mr. Stanford Bardwell had failed. "I don't believe they, in fact I'm positive that they have no evidence. They have threatened grand jury witnesses, threatened attorneys, and local attorneys. These are not things that can be done. I am not involved in a dispute between two government agencies. As I said before, I believe we are caught up in a feud between two government agencies. Now Mr Bardwell is in the middle of an elaborate cover-up.

Barry claimed that the prosecutors forced witnesses to lie on their behalf. Ken Webb claimed that the federal government pressured him into nipping Barry. Webb claimed that Barry was libelous because he was forced to do so under such circumstances.

Barry stated that "the federal authorities are," but that they were "mostly good people." While I believe there are some bad eggs in every nest of birds, I don't think there is any real mystery about me. My activities are most public. I don't hide what I do. When government agencies ask me to keep my conversations secret, I comply. I follow the instructions and move according to the way they tell me. It may appear to some that it's sometimes on the board for criminalism or sometimes not. The overzealousness and incompetence of the federal authorities in the Middle District Louisiana have led them to walk too far between right-and-wrong.

Barry described himself as an aviation consultant and stated that it was expensive to live an exciting life. It's impossible to live an exciting life in Baton Rouge if you don't work Monday through Friday from 9 to 5. It may be exciting for ninety-nine per cent of the population, but it's not to me. To me, the most exciting thing about life is getting into a life-threatening position. That's exciting... It's my way of living. Camp wanted to know more about his contract.

John, all covert-operations work is risky. Everything you do in this field of work is risky. This is why the pay is so great... "If you can't handle the heat, don't work in the cooking area.".
The contract is not a concern of mine. It will happen, Camp
said.

"No. If they indict you, it means I have to go to court. This means I can tell my side. This and many other things that you are hearing from me will all be made public. This is unacceptable to the Justice Department. They can't indict me.

Camp stated at the end of the documentary that Barry Seal was not innocent of any crime. Certain Seal chose a lifestyle that invites suspicion. Seal's association with Colombian cocaine sellers and his participation in exotic plots hatched at the CIA/DEA has given him a certain mystique. This mystique, he claims, is what has made him a target for overzealous investigators.

"We have repeatedly asked for comment from US Attorney Bardwell, and other officials regarding the allegations of prosecutorial and investigative misconduct. They refused to interview Seal and expressed a great deal of resentment at not being given an opportunity to voice their grievances. Barry Seal and others have also made claims that go far beyond their personal issues with the prosecutors. Questions about the integrity and fairness of our justice system were raised by the targeting of individuals, the pressure on witnesses, and the abuse of grand jury processes. These questions, no matter who they are asked, deserve to be answered.

"I'm John Camp from Channel 2, Eyewitness News."

The documentary incensed and embarrassed the Baton Rouge prosecutors. Unglesby Barry's lawyer said it was "a declaration war on the federal government." It's not possible to spit in the eye a hurricane and not plan to evacuate.

Chapter 17

Mena

Barry appeared to have come out of a funk by November 1984 when he was eating at SOB's with Terry. The Baton Rouge prosecutor had reached a plea deal that Barry accepted, meaning he would not serve any prison time. The deal was made without the intervention of the CIA, which allowed him to continue his involvement in black ops. It seemed that his problems were over.

Barry, Terry, and Aki celebrated at SOB's the plans to graduate the trainee pilots. This was scheduled for December.

Barry made a joke about taking them all on a ride in The Fat Lady. That should get their rocks moving. Barry laughed.

Barry's implication that illegal weapon sales were being funneled back to Arkansas government officials at the State Capitol was disturbing for Aki.

Terry remained silent, realizing that the money Barry was laundering through Dan Lasater was a payment to Clinton for allowing CIA operations to run through Arkansas, Mena. He realized that their covert operation couldn't have been continued without the support of the Arkansas government officials and the state police.

Terry asked Terry about four students he considered unsafe. "They're dangerous, and they will most likely get someone killed," Terry said as a flight instructor.

Barry stated, "That's the whole point, Terry," and added, "to get somebody killed!" Aki, tell him. He has a need to learn. He understands that aviation is serious business. I can sympathise with his inability to trust these four men flying around Central America in an aircraft. If you don't tell him, I'm going to.

Aki looked up. He pulled out a book from his briefcase - Assassination Handbook - and pushed the document across the table. "Terry! You were in a battle. If the right people are killed, many lives can be saved. The Agency must place pilots in a position that will allow them to reduce the conflict. These four men have been chosen for a special mission to kill Sandinista leaders. They must have the right credentials to enter the Nicaraguan aviation community.

Terry was shocked by the detail and said nothing for a few second. "I understand. Thank you for your understanding. They will be signed off. Washington will be informed that there will be ten graduating pilots. There will be four ground controllers and four transfers, as well as two washouts. This is the 1984 graduation class.

Barry stated that Aki had left and that he would make another deposit to Dan Lasater. He also had something to tell Terry.

Barry tipped a waiter after 7 pm to get his favorite table in the corner.

Terry asked Terry, "Do I keep [CIA] the Company airplane this winter while school is in mothballs?".
"Sure. Uncle Sam is responsible for all of this. Rule number one: Get as much water as you can. However, I would like you to trade around the beginning of the year to a Seneca. You will need to be with me for security reasons as I have a very special project.

"What's the project?"
"Right now Emile and me are piggybacking the money I told you about, as it comes in down south. Two identical Senecas are used. "I think a third one would confuse any overly curious controller of airtraffic control if the going gets difficult." Terry North described a scheme where the Senecas' owners would surrender them to the CIA and report that they were stolen. The insurance money would then be claimed by the Senecas. Barry described two Senecas that had vanished from Dallas and Florida airfields.

"Sure, that's fine. "Sure, Emile. Do you want to talk to me about specific instructions?"

"Talk to Emile. "Talk to Emile. He will give you the Seneca around the first day of the year."

"Why the first?"

"The January 1st increase in tithing will really be a big deal."

"Tithing?"

"The state is working to provide the money necessary for the Agency's operation. It's hard to believe that something this large could be happening without paying for it. You were in Southeast Asia. You didn't tell me that we had to pay a fucking prince from Laos for every bomb dropped by the Air Force there. It's all one thing. It's just one fucking banana republic after the other." Senior Arkansas state officials charged the CIA ten per cent with allowing illegal plane modifications, covert training for Nicaraguan rebels, and laundering money through local financial institutions including Bill Clinton's Arkansas Development Finance Authority.

Chapter 18

The Clinton Brothers

Many witnesses have told of Bill Clinton getting high over the years. According to the Sunday Telegraph, Roger Clinton stayed at his apartment for two months in 1984. According to the Sunday Telegraph, Bill was "a frequent visitor... there was drug use at these gatherings... she [the manager] could clearly discern Bill's voice while he talked with his brother about quality of marijuana they were using." She claimed she could hear them discussing the cocaine while they were passing it around.

Sally Perdue (ex-Miss Arkansas 1958) claimed that she witnessed Bill Clinton use cocaine frequently during their 1983 affair. He smoked joint joints in her living room and then he would snort cocaine from a table. She said that Bill had the entire [cocaine snorting] equipment set up like a pro.

Sharlene Wilson, grand jury witness, stated that she lived in Little Rock, Arkansas. She worked at Le Bistros and met Roger Clinton, Governor Bill Clinton. He also took along a few of his state troopers. Roger Clinton approached me and asked me if I could give him some coke. He also asked for my one-hitter... A small silver device that you stick into your nose, then you snort cocaine from there. Roger handed me the coke to Governor Clinton. He just sort of turned his back and walked away.

She was able to party on cocaine with the Clinton brothers at Governor Clinton's mansion, and attend toga parties. The attorney general and other members of the Arkansas State Police were present at the parties that turned into cocaine-fueled orgies.

Sharlene stated that they began to dance around, and "do cocaine in one room and have sex the next room." She said this because the Coachman's Inn rooms were adjacent. To be honest, you can end up with someone in particular and nine out of ten times you end up having sex. It was there, I know. I was the one who made sure it was there. I saw Bill Clinton lean against a brick wall. He must have had an acute problem with his nose. He casually stuck his toe up at me. He was so upset that he just slid the wall into a garbage bag and sat there as an idiot.

Sharlene confessed to having had sex with Roger Clinton. She partied until the very early hours of the morning in the governor's mansion with the Clinton brothers. "I thought it was cool that we had a governor who got up," she said.

The investigation was stopped by Charles Banks, the Republican-appointed US attorney. Sharlene had testified before a grand jury. Jean Duffy, a deputy prosecuting lawyer and head of a drug taskforce, reported Sharlene that her home was being monitored and that she was worried about the "powers That Be" because she had "for three to four months unloading bags at Mena airport with cocaine."

Sharlene was detained at her home with less that $100 of methamphetamines and marijuana for speaking up. She was convicted by her ex-boyfriend for trafficking through Mena. Her prosecutor was ultimately arrested for operating his Seventh Judicial District procuring attorney's office in a criminal enterprise. A jury found him guilty in 1997 of five counts each of racketeering and extortion as well as drug dealing. He received an 11-year sentence, which is a far better punishment than Sharlene's.

Gennifer Flowers, a former model, had a 12-year-long relationship with Clinton. Gennifer shared secretly recorded phone conversations that she had with Bill, which proved the existence of a sexual relationship. Bill Clinton lied under oath in January 1998 to admit that he had sex on the phone with Gennifer. She stated that Bill had smoked pot while she was present. "I was shocked that he would carry marijuana around. But it was typical of his bulletproof attitude."

Gennifer was told by Bill about the side effects of cocaine use. "He told Gennifer about the party he went to and said, "I got so fucked-up on cocaine at that party." He also said that he felt conspicuously because he was talking to people who weren't aware that drugs were present at the party and that all he wanted was to scratch his head.

Bill's cocaine addiction led to him needing medical treatment. He also had multiple stays in a drug rehabilitation according to Betsey, Governor Clinton's chief-of-staff for seven years.

A YouTube video shows Dr Sam Houston, the father of Hillary Clinton, stating that Bill Clinton was treated by Dr. Suen at Little Rock's medical centre for sinus problems. These sinus problems may be drug-related due to cocaine abuse and overdosage. Governor Bill Clinton was admitted to the hospital (I believe it was the medical center on at least one occasion) for cocaine abuse and overdosage

Clinton arrived at the University of Arkansas Medicine Centre for emergency cocaine treatment with a state trooper. Hillary was informed via phone. Hillary was unimpressed by Bill's addiction to cocaine and showed up.

"When Mrs Clinton arrived she told the two resident doctors on duty that night that they would not be able to practice medicine in the United States again if the word about Clinton's drug problem spread," Christopher Ruddy, CEO of Newsmax Media, wrote a 1999 article: Did Bill Clinton overdose with cocaine. "Reportedly, Hillary pushed one of the doctors against a wall with both hands against his shoulders as she gave her severe warning.

R. Emmett Tyrrell, a columnist, phoned one of the nurses on duty that night Bill was admitted to the hospital. Tyrrell claims that the nurse did not deny the story but stated that she could not risk losing her job if she spoke about it.

John Brown, a former Saline County criminal investigation officer, said that he had interviewed many people who saw Bill Clinton use drugs but that they were too scared to talk.

Someone who worked for the Clintons ten years revealed the extent of Bill's involvement with the cocaine flowing through Mena. Larry Nichols was eventually promoted to Director of Marketing at the Arkansas Development Finance Authority, which Clinton presented as a means to create jobs and assist churches and schools.

Larry stated that he had been there for about a month and realized that he was at the epicenter of everything I've heard all my life... He was literally sitting in the middle Bill Clinton's political machine. It was the place he made payments, and where he repaid favors to people for their campaign support." Millions were funnelled into Clinton's campaign, his circle of friends, and Hillary Clinton's law office.

Larry began to be suspicious two months into his job and started to copy documents. "I watched accounts accumulate money for about two months and then they went zero at the end. They were laundering drug money. Mena, Arkansas was receiving a hundred million dollars a month of cocaine."

Larry Nichols claimed that Clinton had hired Lasater to launder the proceeds of cocaine: "Dan Lasater was Bill Clinton's best friend... He didn't sell cocaine." Nope. They were giving it away. His office was filled with huge quantities of cocaine. They'd throw it at young girls and ashtray upon ashtray.

Larry Douglas Brown, a.k.a. state policeman assigned for bodyguard duty was known as Larry Douglas Brown. LD was Bill Clinton's fair-haired son. LD's fiancee, Chelsea Clinton, was his nanny. His future mother-in law was the administrator at Governor Clinton's mansion. LD was a trooper Clinton trusted to assist him in procuring women for sex. LD was so close with the Clintons, he and Hillary even shared their problems.

Bill Clinton, April Fools Day 1984. He said this in reference to an ad in The New York Times ad offering CIA employment.

LD was able to complete an application with Clinton's assistance. Clinton advised LD that he would study Russian to help him with his application. LD began to do so. He shared his knowledge of the Cyrillic alphabet with the CIA.

Clinton called the CIA to vouch on LD. He didn't use the official channels but he picked up a telephone and spoke to someone at CIA who he knew personally. This impressed LD.

An essay was required to be submitted as part of the application. "We agreed that I would write an essay on Marxism and Central America. "Governor Clinton and I," LD stated.

LD wrote 800 words about the rising threat of Marxism within South America and the need to help the rebels of Nicaragua at Governor Clinton's house. Clinton edited it.

LD passed the entrance exam after his application was accepted. He met a CIA recruiter named Magruder four months later in Dallas. This was towards the end 1984's summer. LD later identified Magruder as a member on Vice President George HW Bush's staff. Magruder asked him if he was interested working in security, paramilitary, and narcotics. LD accepted all of them. He signed a secrecy contract and was informed that someone would call him.

He was officially informed of his employment nomination on September 5, 1984. His home phone rang a month later. Barry Seal, the caller, had extensive knowledge about Barry. Barry organized a meeting at Cajun's Wharf in Little Rock, which is a bar/restaurant.

LD later described meeting Barry: "Big guy. He wore one of those shirts that falls down... outside your pants... He knew everything about me and the essay, so there was absolutely no doubt in my mind... He had been flying for the Agency. That was all I knew.

Barry spoke with LD over the next few weeks as if he had met Bill Clinton. Barry called Clinton "the guv" and asked LD to accompany Barry on a Mena operation scheduled for before sunrise on Oct 23, 1984.

Bill Clinton was the only person LD spoke of Barry's meetings.

"[Barry] was a kind of devil may-care."

Bill advised, "Don't worry about it." It's possible to handle it. It'll be fun.

LD expected to board a small plane. Instead, Barry met LD at Mena where the Fat Lady was waiting. LD was shocked to see a large plane in dark charcoal, with very few tail markings. Barry advised LD to forget his keys, ID and jewelry. Three unidentified men were found inside the plane: a copilot and two kickers. LD claimed that the engine made a loud noise. "[It] scared me just taking off."

The Fat Lady stopped in New Orleans to get fuel and then headed to Central America. It dipped below radar, climbed again and fell again to let the two kickers roll out tarp-covered pallets with M-16 rifles. These were then parachuted over a mountainous region to be captured by Nicaraguan rebels. The crew collected green canvas duffel bags from Honduras as they returned to Mena.

Barry presented $2,500 to LD in Mena and said he would be in touch regarding the next operation. LD gave the cash to Barry without any questions. Later, he stated that Barry knew exactly what he was doing. He was working for the Agency and knew this.

Everything about me was so I wasn't going to be too curious."

Clinton congratulated LD when he showed up at the governor's mansion for his next shift. "Are you having any fun yet?"

LD smiled. "Yeah but this is scary stuff," he said.

You can do it. Do not worry about it.

Surprised at the governor's casual demeanour, LD later testified to Clinton knowing everything about Mena and that it had been approved and sanctioned on behalf of the United States. "Well, he [Clinton] understood what I was doing. He was the one who helped me and guided me through this.

Barry called LD. "How's the Guv?" A second mission was set up for Christmas Eve 1984.

The situation was exactly the same as before except Barry only took home two duffel bags from Honduras. LD received $2,500 in Mena. Barry took a duffel bag and a kilo cocaine to LD's car in the parking lot. LD later described it as a brick-shaped, "waxene wrapped" package.

LD panicked and said "I don't want any part of what is happening." He then rushed back to Little Rock thinking, Well, this must be an official operation. Clinton got me into it. It's not as sinister as it seems... After telling his brother about it, LD decided that he would confront Clinton.

Clinton smiled as usual when LD arrived, but then he realized how mad LD was.

"Do you know what they're bringing back aboard that plane?" LD asked.

Clinton replied, "Wait! Whoa, whoa? What's the matter?".
"Well, they're basically bringing back coke."

Over a decade later, LD testified about Clinton's response. It wasn't surprising to him. He didn't try and say, "What?" He didn't deny that I was mad. He thought we were going on a cordial conversation. He didn't deny it wasn't returning, that I wasn't telling the truth, or that he didn't know anything about it.

LD was shocked by Clinton's complicity and said that he would not have any other choice but to end the affair. Put a fork in my mouth, I'm done."

"Settle down," Clinton said. Clinton stated, "That's not a problem." Clinton attempted to minimize the CIA's involvement in cocaine trafficking by saying, "That's Lasater's deal."

LD then withdrew his application to the CIA.

LD knew that Lasater was a Clinton donor and that Clinton met with Lasater several times a month at Lasater's company or at the mansion where Lasater had privileged entry through the back door. Lasater also hosted parties where silver platters laden with cocaine were distributed. LD had urged Clinton to avoid such parties in order to protect him.

Roger Clinton has a history of cover-ups and arrests. Roger Clinton was arrested in 1981 for not paying speeding tickets. Governor Bill Clinton made arrangements for Roger to be released into the care of a relative who was the chairperson of the state's Crime Commission. Roger was charged with drunk driving and possessing narcotics in March 1982. All charges were dropped as Bill was about to run for re-election.

Journalist: "The sheriff's Office and the Prosecutor succumbed under political pressure.".
A lawyer familiar with the matter said that "they leaned until they cracked".

Roger was a cocaine addict in the late 1970s according to his own testimony to investigators. Roger smoked up to four grams of cocaine per day. According to his therapist, he was "close to a fatal dose" of cocaine. He also paid for it by selling drugs. He was connected to drug dealers in New York and Medellin.

His suppliers offered him credit after he learned that he was Bill Clinton's brother. He smuggled in thousands of dollars worth of cocaine through Little Rock's airport. Roger brought so many women to Little Rock's governor's mansion for cocaine partying that a narcotics investigator stated, "They used Governor's home as a whorehotel."

Roger said to a police informant that he could get him a quarter pound while negotiating a $10,000 transaction. If you have the cash, I can get you whatever you want."

Roger's addiction spiraled out of control by 1984 and was ravaging his physical health. The thief took $8,000. worth of cocaine from Roger's convertible car by ripping open its top. His mother was not allowed to report the incident to police. Roger was threatened by his drug creditors and his family.

An FBI report states that Bill Clinton had a solution: Dan Lasater would house Roger on a Florida thoroughbred farm of a thousand acres. According to an FBI summary, Clinton asked Lasater to give Roger, his half-brother, a job.

"Mr Lasater made a comment at that point that the governor owed him a lot of favors," said the manager of the farm.

Roger accepted the job at Lasater for $8,000 to repay his drug debt.

Lasater stated to the FBI that "[Dealer] were] putting the heat upon him and something might happen his brother and mom.".
Roger lived a life of excess, with drug money being laundered through Lasater Ranch and constant cocaine parties there.

According to the book Partners in Power, a senior farm worker said that Roger Clinton could be seen as really stressed out while at the farm. I just recall him using and always saying that he was on the phone with his brother, the governor. Not worth a damn as hired labor. He was being kept in the house for Mr Lasater, a politician.

Roger was filmed by narcotics officers in 1983-84. Hot Springs police recorded Roger selling cocaine. Roger told an informant that he had four to five uniformed men who kept an eye on him. He was dealing with a Colombian linked to the cartels.

Roger would have been saved by Bill, as usual. "Roger Clinton was about be swept under a rug," a federal prosecutor stated, "by both US attorney and local boys, there is no question about that."

Some of the evidence was made public by brave state police officers. An investigator stated that some troopers had put the evidence out on the streets so it could not be ignored. They took a real chance."

Roger was being investigated by a federal grand jury in the spring 1984. Hillary informed Bill, as details were leaked to his wife and the governor, that intervening in the case of his brother would be detrimental politically. Roger Morris, author of Partners in Power claims that Bill was told not to warn Roger or prevent Roger from being arrested because such an action could be used against him in his campaign for re-election and later.

"I don't believe she [Hillary] knew how much coke Bill had snorted and Roger," stated a state policeman. "But we knew she'd tell Roger to the feds for his career, and that's exactly what he did."

Bill read to the media after Roger's federal conviction: "My brother is apparently involved with drugs. A curse which has reached epidemic proportions has plagued millions of families in this nation, including many here in the state." Clinton did not answer any questions. One reporter described Bill's condition as "visibly shaken".

The state police chief addressed the media. According to him, Bill Clinton had instructed him to handle the case as any other when he notified the governor about his brother's arrest. Bill Clinton used the arrest of his brother to show that the Clintons are not above the law.

Travis Bunn, a former military intelligence officer, was an undercover cop who filmed Roger on April 1, 1984. Roger informed Bunn that he needed "cocaine" for his brother Bill. His nose is like a vacuum cleaner.

Bunn suspected Roger was part in a larger criminal organization and wanted to "nab" him to "roll him over and go on the up the line" to catch the bigger players. After an Arkansas State Police officer in Hot Springs informed his superiors, Bunn's plan was stopped. The investigation was taken over by the state police. Dunn discovered the truth after having been on the case for over a year. He told a colleague who was investigating Roger that "We've been screwed."

Dunn stated that the investigation was a damage control operation. The federal government was given the case by the state police. Dunn never testified at Roger's trial or the grand jury, despite being familiar with Rogers' crimes. Dunn stated that the only reason this case reached this point was because they knew he had Roger. "They knew I had Roger before I got involved in this case." They couldn't undo that."

Roger was a victim of the strongest evidence, and the original officers involved in the case were removed from the investigation.

An officer familiar with the case said that they had more than Roger. Lasater, who owned whom in Springdale and other buys that included state police were just a few examples. Roger complies and our narcs are taken out. The case is over.

Roger was brought before a federal judge on August 14, 1984. He was partially deaf, and is well-known for his sleepiness during long testimony. Roger was released on $5,000 bail after pleading not guilty. Roger's trial was scheduled for slightly later than the general election so as to not disrupt Bill's reelection campaign.

A spokesman for Governor Clinton stated that he didn't know that he (Roger) had ever tried drugs or that he was addicted to cocaine after the hearing.

Roger reached a plea deal. Roger agreed to plead guilty to the election and to testify against low-level accomplices in exchange for a lower sentence. Roger and his family attended counselling sessions about drug addiction and codependency to help reduce the sentence.

Judith Warner, Hillary Clinton's biographer, said that Hillary took a leadership role in the sessions and was able to point out patterns and weaknesses to the family. Warner also stated that her participation did not always make her feel comfortable with her husband.

Friends of Roger and Bill's mother Virginia say that some of Hillary's questions regarding denial and irresponsibility brought Virginia to tears. This led to Bill getting into his next sexy and drug binge.

Roger pleaded guilty on November 9, 1984 to one count of drug distribution and conspiracy, just three days after Bill had won the election.

Asa Hutchinson, a Republican US attorney stated that Roger was "one tentacle of cocaine distribution" in Arkansas.

None of the larger players were investigated by design. Roger testified instead against Sam Anderson Jr., a boyhood friend.

Anderson stated, "I guess Roger's time is up for me,".
Roger drank cocaine with women in the governor's residence right up until his sentencing.

Roger, who was extremely alert, appeared in court on January 28, 1985. Bill, Hillary, and Virginia were also present. Roger was sentenced to two years federal prison for conspiracy. The judge suspended Roger's distribution charge. Roger's family witnessed him being handcuffed and taken away by marshals.

Roger's videotape describing Bill's use of drugs never appeared.

Bill declared outside the courtroom that he felt more committed than ever to fighting illegal drugs in his state. Roger spent thirteen months in federal prison.

Bill gave Roger a presidential pardon in 2001. This expunged his conviction. Roger was not subject to the difficulties of reintegration into society that hundreds of thousands of drug offenders were sent to prison during Clinton's presidency. This was due to the increased spending on the War on Drugs. These offenders, unlike Roger, had criminal records that prevented them from getting employment, education, or housing.

Roger was given the code name Headache by the Secret Service while his brother was at office.

Roger was arrested in 2003 by Dan Lasater, his ex-boss. He pleaded guilty federal drug charges for cocaine possession and distribution.

Bill Clinton responded to Lasater's indictment by saying, "I feel very sick about that." A journalist asked, "Have your ever used cocaine?".
Clinton replied, "No." Clinton said, "I don't know what it looked like if it was mine."

Doc DeLaughter was the police investigator who investigated Dan Lasater's cocaine case. He said that she was a fourteen-year-old cheerleader from North Little Rock. She was a virgin, and he [Lasater] eventually sent her to a doctor of his. She was put on birth-control pills by the doctor. She lost her virginity after he used cocaine. She became addicted to cocaine and, according to federal grand juries, she was still a Lake Tahoe hooker. I began to be harassed by my Arkansas State Police department after Lasater was indicted. It was due to the association with the state police, the governor's office and Dan Lasater's business associates that I realized the reason for it.

Lasater was sentenced in December 1986 to two and a half years. According to FBI documents, Lasater admitted to federal investigators that his cocaine use was documented and that he gave the drug away to friends, family, and business associates.

Lasater was sentenced to six months imprisonment, four months in a halfwayhouse, and two months house arrest before being released on parole. In November 1990, Clinton granted Lasater a state pardon.

Larry Nichols stated, "If you think that he's [Bill Cinton] tough on crime, then think about a man pardoning a man with cocaine to children." Clinton went to Washington with the rest of those involved in money laundering. His election campaign was boosted by the hot money.

Larry claims Barry Seal moved to Arkansas to escape the sleazy Governor Clinton. In private, he had no qualms about using cocaine. He rejected the recommendation of the US Sentencing Commission to eliminate the disparity in crack and powder - cocaine sentences. This tactic was used to mass imprisone blacks for non-violent drug offenses. He opposed the lifting of the federal ban on funding syringe accessibility programs. This increased the spread and severity of AIDS. He provided more federal funding to states that constructed prisons or housed people who were sentenced for longer periods of time. Under his presidency, the federal three strikes law mandated long sentences for repeat offenders. The US prison population grew by 487,000 under Clinton's presidency. This was due to non-violent drug offenders. He had 235,000 more prisoners than Ronald Reagan, his predecessor.

Chapter 19

Contract on Barry

Jorge Ochoa was one of Barry's top undercover targets. He was captured in Spain on November 15, 1984. This raised hopes that he would be extradited to America to drug trafficking. Barry was the principal witness against Ochoa and his value was increased by the DEA.

A Baton Rouge private investigator, who had seen Uncle Sam Wants You, sent Fabio Ochoa a videotape. Fabio sent Cano, an employee to Miami, with a copy the documentary and instructions on how to resolve the Ellis MacKenzie matter. An American and a group of Colombians watched the video in an office located in north Miami. They discovered that MacKenzie was actually Barry Seal.

Cano, who had flown with Barry during smuggling flights in Colombia, described Barry's routines while Rafa, a Colombian, took notes. Rafa was able to identify Barry's home address and the cars Barry and his wife drove. He also noted his preferences for restaurants and hangouts.

They would be able to capture Barry alive for $1 million, so Cano preferred kidnapping. However, Barry could still be killed and $500,000 would still be collected from Pablo Escobar or Fabio Ochoa who ran the Ochoa business while Jorge was in Spain.

Rafa warned Max, an American Jewish engineer who was overweight, that the Colombians would be visible in Baton Rouge. They wanted Barry to die looking like a Mafia hit if he had to.

Max, who had married a Colombian woman, fell into crime when he established a route through the Bahamas for Colombians to enter America. He managed Ochoa's accounting and distribution, and coordinated cocaine flights for Jorge Ochoa. His annual salary was $500,000 Max was afraid that Barry would kill him if Max refused to sign the contract. Max was afraid of Rafa who kept two handgrenades under his front seat and smoked cocaine all the time while carrying a gun. Rafa also kept $1 million of cash in a bag in case of emergency. Max tried to retire from Ochoa before Rafa replied, "There are only two ways out, going to jail and getting killed."

Max was given a phone. Fabio Ochoa thanked Max and wished him luck. Fabio would prefer a kidnapping. Pablo Escobar was his caller. Pablo thanked Max for his help and returned the phone to Fabio who asked if Pablo needed any expense money. Max agreed and advised them to follow their own discretion.

Cano revealed that Barry was married with small children. Max stated that he would not kill children or women. Rafa stated that it was possible to complete the contract if necessary.

Max was told by Rafa that he wanted Lito to be taken out of South Dade's federal Metropolitan Correctional Center.

Max didn't kill anyone and called Roberts, his friend, a drug dealer who had previously told Max that people could be eliminated. Roberts accepted the challenge after watching Barry's documentary.

A young Colombian sent Max a box with $100,000 inside from Fabio Ochoa.

Four Colombians were expelled to America on January 5, 1985. One of them was connected to Jorge Ochoa. The Medellin Cartel wanted Barry to be freed quickly, as extradition was imminent.

Max and Roberts' associate flew to Louisiana in January to find Barry. Max stayed in New Orleans in a hotel room and was paid $28,000 by Roberts' associate to locate Barry. Max was forced to join the search for Barry in Baton Rouge because his associate found places Barry used. They found everything on Cano's List, except Barry's helicopter company. They returned to Miami after the mission was abandoned.

Max asked Cano to return from Colombia in order to help them. They set out from Florida in Max's Jaguar. Max wanted to know if Jorge Ochoa knew about the situation. Cano confirmed that Jorge Ochoa, while in Spain, had authorized Barry's assassination.

To avoid driving around Baton Rouge in Florida with Florida plates, they used a rental car. They found Barry's white Cadillac and his home, as well as his preferred restaurants, offices, and helicopter business. Barry was still elusive. They relayed the bad news at a Holiday Inn to Fabio Ochoa, Colombia, and Rafa, Miami. Cano returned home to Miami. Max continued to search for Barry in Baton Rouge but was unsuccessful. So he decided to return home to Miami.

Rafa arrived at Max's place, an import shoe shop at the Four Ambassadors Hotel. Cumbamba, a notorious and strange-looking hitman, was accompanied by Rafa. He wore thick black-rimmed glasses with curly black hair and had a large chin. Max knew Cumbamba almost three years. Rafa was under pressure from Pablo Escobar, the Ochoas and wanted to know the reason the hit took so long. Max scolded them and said that it would take longer and they needed to be patient.

Cumbamba was furious at not being given the hit and stayed in Miami. He was furious to learn how much Max was paid and scolded Max.

Max stated that Seal lives in a remote area. There is only one way in and out. This road leads to a dead stop. It is impossible to do it without everyone in the house being taken out. I don't want to kill children and women.

Cumbamba stated, "That doesn't bother me at any,".
"I do not have the authority to give over the contract. Rafa is the best person to speak to.

Fabio Ochoa, Pablo Escobar

"I will."
Max returned to Baton Rouge. He followed Max to Baton Rouge after he saw a blue Chevrolet leave Barry's driveway. This was the car Barry knew from Cano's List. He was stuck at a red light as she turned into an industrial park. She ended up following him as he tried to catch up. He gave up and went home.

Max was driving along a quiet suburban road twenty miles west from Fort Lauderdale on June 5, 1985 when he was stopped by agents in cars. He surrendered and appeared relieved. The car's glove box contained a loaded gun. They found five additional weapons at his ranch house. $73,000 cash was in a wall safe, and $200,000 under his mattress.

Max agreed to cooperate after being snitched by an informant. He was facing life imprisonment on charges of continuing criminal activity. The agents took four weeks to get Max to confess to the crime against Barry. Agents from many jurisdictions were impressed by Max's insider knowledge of the Medellin Cartel's workings and his photographic memory for dates, names, and places. He described murders, kidnappings, and how cocaine was shipped.

Chapter 20

Legal Trouble

Barry woke up one morning while he was sleeping next to his wife and received a call. He answered the phone and jumped out of bed to gather his clothes before telling Debbie that he had to hurry to Miami.

In the coming days, there will be a lot of things."

"What stuff?"
He touched his wife's forehead. "You're just going to have to stay by me, baby. Barry left to go get the rest of his clothes.

His wife looked at him sadly and said, "Are they trying kill you Barry?"

Barry turned around. "Who?"
"The drug dealers. Barry, I'm not fool.

"How much do I know?"

"Nothing, just the things a wife knows." Please tell me.

Barry nodded and said, "I've been working with the government, Debbie." "For the CIA."

Debbie jumped out of bed wearing a white negligee. "Don't treat my like an idiot Barry!" She jumped out of bed in a white negligee and ran out of the room. Barry followed her, and opened the door. "The CIA! The CIA! Jesus, Barry! You can fly drugs and lie to your wife, but it's another thing.

It's the truth. The CIA. They have been my employer. "I've been photographing some very powerful drug dealers down Nicaragua." Debbie went back to her bedroom with Barry following. "I couldn't tell you."

"Oh, no! It's impossible to reveal the secrets of the CIA. Standing at the foot of the bed, she stated, "They hang you for that.".
Barry stated, "I couldn't tell you,".
"Then, why are you telling us now?"

"It might be over now."

Debbie sat down on the bed, unsteady on her feet. She looked at Barry with glazed eyes and said, "Oh, God Barry, what have I done?" "What have I done?"

Barry, Joura and Jacobsen were in an office together. He read from a newspaper that Barry was referring to: "Sandinistas connected to cocaine smuggling schemes involving three Colombia's biggest cocaine traffickers." Officials cited photos taken in Managua, Colombia, by the pilot. This was a DEA informant. Barry ripped the paper. "What are we going to do?"

Joura stated, "Bringing Lito into the house is all I can think of.".
Jacobsen stated, "The Miami paper's going to have that by afternoon edition.".
Barry threw his hands up and said "Now Ochoa, Escobar." "If only I could get them here to America."

Jacobsen stated, "Hey man, that newspaper practically gives you your name.".
Barry was on the verge to weep. "The bastards, man. They'll be killed."

Ron Caffery, Washington DC's head of the DEA's drug desk, called Colonel Oliver North to explain about the leaked photos. "I'm mad and crazy as hell."

North asked, "What's the problem?".
"The problem is your large mouth."

"Now wait a minute."
"You couldn't wait for your brownie points to be made, didn't you?" You made the decision that this story should be published and didn't care who might get hurt.

"Back off, Ron. "What are you talking about?"

"You know damn well about what I am talking about. That story was leaked to the

Washington Times article about our pilot in Nicaragua

"Now, wait a second. "I didn't do anything."

"The largest drug investigation we've ever had. We came so close to capturing the Medellin Cartel's highest-ranking men, but now we are dead."

"Well, it must have been a breakup somewhere."

North: "Yeah, there were some problems, North. It was all because of your precious Contras.

Ron, I don't think you want Communism to take over Central America more than I do.

Cafferty dropped the phone.

Unglesby, Barry's lawyer suspected that Barry had not provided enough information to him. Unglesby told Barry that he would only be able to defend him to his best ability if Barry updated him on all his activities. Barry pushed Unglesby's phone towards him and told him to dial a number.

The phone rang at the other end. "Vice President Bush's Office. "May I help you?" A female asked.

Unglesby stated, "This is Barry Seal.".
"Please wait while we transfer the call."

The line was then transferred to a man who claimed he was an admiral. "Barry, where have you been?"

"I'm Barry Seal." "I'm not Barry Seal." The admiral stood up and left.

Barry's lawyer told Barry as he entered a courthouse that this was just the hearing. It will soon be over."

Barry strutted in a light blue suit and said "Great." "I can't wait to go back to my cement block suite."

Joura stated, "The Witness Protection Program saves your life Barry.".
"Hey, listen! I'm a goddam prisoner inside a windowless cell. Joura, that's quite funny. "I testify against the bad guys, and I'm first to go to prison."

Joura stated that "The Witness Protection Program (not jail)".
Barry replied, "Then what in the hell do they call being locked up every day?".
Barry. Barry's lawyer placed his hand on Barry. "There is something more that happened today that we need to tell you about. Tomorrow, the State of Louisiana will present you to a grand jury to accuse you of cocaine trafficking.

Barry opened the doors to the men's toilet. He yelled at the agents who were accompanying him. He yelled, "What the hell are they talking about?" "You said they didn't have any case."

The lawyer stated, "I said that we could beat their case.".

"I put my money on the line here, Florida, to reduce my time. I end up doing twenty-years in Louisiana!"

The lawyer stated, "I can make an agreement with Louisiana.".
"What kind of deal?"
"You only plead guilty to one charge. There is no trial. There is only a sentencing hearing.

Barry took his sunglasses from his face and snatched them off. "Why should I plead guilty to Louisiana?"

"Because that's how it works! You can't get more time in Louisiana if you don't get what you got in Florida.

"How long am I spending in Florida?"

"You have a very solid defense."

"No, no, no! "How much time?"

"If we are lucky," the lawyer said. "Five years."

"What!"
Joura stated, "I have DEA agents lined-up around the block to testify on your behalf Barry,".
"The fuck!" Barry said.
The lawyer stated that it would take at least one year for you to testify at the Miami trial. Jacobsen stated, "I believe I can get that counted for time served.".
The lawyer stated, "And then Louisiana cannot touch you.".

Barry, you're out. Joura declared, "You're out of this game.".

"And rich," Jacobsen said.

"I want to get out of this fucking 10x10 room right now."

"What do YOU want?" "A house?"

"I want my home and my family."

Joura stated, "It's five hundred thousands dead and a billion alive." Barry, that's the bounty."

Joura asked, "Was i the best operative that you've ever had?".

Barry put his finger down and said, "Then you'll get me back on the street.".

Joura stated, "Barry it's not secure.".

"I don't want fucking lawyers to decide my life!" If I'm gonna go down, I wanna go down fighting."

His lawyer said, "Barry," shaking his head.

Barry asked his lawyer, "Is witness protection voluntary?".

"Yes."

"All right. Barry pointed at Joura and said: "You put me back undercover today.".

"It's unsafe," Joura hissed.

"Don't send me to Colombia. Ochoa has nothing to do. There are other places in this country. Other organizations. They will be set up. They'll be taken down. Or, I'll just walk." Barry marched to the exit and turned around. Joura asked, "Is it a deal?".

Barry replied, "All right!" "Now, I want everyone out of here. I've gotta piss. C'mon. Let's go." He was done and turned to Emile, who was standing at the door.

Barry stated, "They don't understand Camp.".

Emile, leaning against a wall, said "You don't want to escape.".

"That's right."

You think you have to get your scare fix. "You have to scare the crap out of yourself every now and again."

Barry laughed. "That's right."
"Well, you have to learn to live with that."

"Oh, yeah. How?"
Emile stated, "Stay down in Baton Rouge." "Go to church on Sunday and games on Saturday. It will become something you enjoy.

Camp, that's not me. It's not me. It's not over until I say it's done." Barry tried to open the door.

Emile closed the door. "Emile, my daddy used to tell me, 'Emile boy, you have to change your ways.' It turned out that the old man was right. It's time, Barry. We all have to change. Even you."

Barry looked at Emile and said, "Hey Camp, we gave them rides didn't we?"

"An eight-point barrel roll."
They hugged.

Chapter 21

Mena

Locals noticed unusual activity at Rich Mountain Aviation by 1985, particularly the larger planes. The hot money was flowing in faster than ever so the pilots Barry, Terry, and Emile used less prominent Senecas. Barry was carrying cash in duffel bags, which included transmitters to help people on the ground find the money.

Barry took out a pad and a pencil to a January meeting held in a hangar together with Terry, Emile, and Aki. "This is almost foolproof because the Agency has come up with a way. I will discuss how the Agency safely jettison cargo and moves it from green [cash] flights. Emile will discuss piggyback-flight procedures. Most smugglers don't know what they are doing and can't be trusted. To bring down the entire operation, all you need is an internal leak and a tip-off about the drop zone location. Terry stated that there was no way for the drop zone location to be compromised using our operation.

"'Cause it's not my fault that I don't know where the fuck is until I jettison its load and note the location on the LORAN [Long Range Navigation Equipment]. Piggybacking is when the plane sees the load go and denotes the same coordinates for a backup. The plane never relays coordinates over radio.

"How do you find the money?"

"We have a homing beacon that is located along with the cargo. There are many things that we can do once we are certain the jettison occurred unobserved. We can go back to get it since we have the coordinates within a few meters of the kick-out location. Option two: We verbally relay coordinates to a pickup crew using a scrambled frequency. They then fly a helicopter to the drop zone. Option three: We use the LORAN to guide us to a spot, and then we jettison it close to friendly forces that happen to have a receiver capable of tracking the frequency of our transmitters. This is combined with the fact that Uncle Sam has given us two targets to watch - one of which doesn't have any items at the time - makes it a foolproof system.

"You said transmitters." Terry asked.

You're a pilot. A pilot must have at least two copies of every item in order to ensure that one works. Three million dollars in cash is not something you would want to lose, right?

Emile began to draw the radio fix in Western Arkansas on Barry's pad. "I'll draw a map of a typical missions. Although it won't be perfect, the idea is there." He created two planes in piggyback, with one on top and the other slightly behind the other. Terry's plane joins the piggyback formation to become the bottom plane. It is slightly behind the middle plane. They would appear as one radar blip to air-traffic controllers. The money would be carried by the plane in the middle, Barry's plane. The plane at the top, Emile's, would take Barry's to Mena and continue on Barry's original flight plans. Together, Terry's plane and Barry's would continue on to Little Rock. Terry would notify air traffic control near Little Rock that there were two planes. Barry's plane would then dive towards the trees below radar detection, dropping cash at a area west of Little Rock. Terry would land in Little Rock. Barry would continue south, but he was still not visible on radar. Air traffic control would believe that only one plane had flown. Terry's plane would be considered the plane that landed at Little Rock if an additional plane was detected. It was extremely unlikely that three planes could be identified.

Emile, you forgot one thing. Terry, when you meet us for rendezvous, make sure you look closely at Camp and me before you go down to join us. The US Customs citations are blacked out and can be hard to see, so make sure you have your night-vision glasses on and take a close look. Terry stated, "If you see anything, come to our frequency and sing it out.".

Emile stated, "You can abort and just continue on to Little Rock." "Barry will see that I am being followed so he and I have several options. He would likely just break up, leaving him with two targets to chase. You don't have to worry about this. This is our problem.

Terry asked, "Aki? Is this all legal?" "Sounds as if we are going to great lengths in order to avoid detection from other feds. Who do we consider our enemy here?"

"Terry! We are CIA!" We are not law enforcement. We are not Justice Department. We are not Treasury Department. We are the CIA! We answer to the president, who in turn answers to the director. The very highest level is what you are dealing with. These agencies are not part of the loop. They are not authorized to make major foreign-policy decision. This is how the CIA must work around the world. We do not break the law. We are not above the law."

Terry stated, "I think this will require some pretty good flying coordination?" Terry said, "I would like us all to practice some close formation work before we attempt it, especially at night." Three identical Senecas could crash within a mile of one another, which would be a major blow to our plan.

Barry stated, "We'll accomplish better than that." "Tomorrow, weather permitting," Barry said.

Terry stated that Barry was the most likely to discover the location of the drop zone in Little Rock. Who's protecting the drop zone that you have set up in Little Rock?

Aki declared, "I am." "The Agency is. Because people who own land in the drop are under our control, it is safe. Don't worry about it. "Your job is to shadow Barry." Aki asked them to immediately start test flights. "There is a lot of pressure to increase Agency deposits in Arkansas."

Terry replied, "Barry, maybe you're just being nosy," Terry suggested, "but can you not just keep making deposits at Lasater's like you have been doing all along?"

Barry stated, "That was only the tithing money." "We are talking about more than that now. This seems to have worked so well, that Aki's folks decided to make a major financial investment here.

"Barry! It is not appropriate to speak freely about investments made by the Agency. They are confidential.

Barry exclaimed, "Aw, fuck Aki." He's going to figure it all out, now that he's a part of it. Terry did not fall off any turnip truck yesterday. He is a man I trust more than the Little Rock fucks I'm running around with. They are just a bunch goddam politicians with their fingers sticking out.

Terry was at 10,500 feet when Emile and Barry's Senecas flew in piggyback formation.

Barry replied, "You got a vision on us yet?".
"Roger! I have a visual on your face. You're at my 12 o'clock low, but you're so tight that all I can see is one plane from here.

Barry stated, "That's how it's supposed be," "Get down there with us. Try to convert your altitude into air speed and tuck under me.

Terry dived down to 4,500 feet. He approached Barry's plane from below Emile's and began to climb into position. He wasn't confident enough in the maneuver to be as close to Emile as Barry.

Barry stated, "Now, I'm going to have to jibber jabber a lot because you're in mine six [outof sight behind and below]. We'll reduce radio communication when we actually do this. For now, I will talk you through it. Emile is on centre frequency, squawking. Emile will ask for his ident just before the fix. When he does, I will bank in a standard-rate turning to get vector 573 to Hot Springs. You have to turn at the same angle as me and all other things, otherwise you will get in my wake turbulence, which can be quite hairy. When Emile says "Roger,ident", ident is the word we use to execute the turn on. Any questions?"

To avoid air-traffic controller, Terry and Barry's transponders were switched off. Emile then simulated radio conversations with Memphis air-traffic controllers. Barry banked to his right as soon as he spoke ident.

Terry's plane was rattled by turbulence. Terry focused hard, attempting to stay in Barry's plane. Terry wondered how difficult it would have been to do the manoeuvre at night.

Terry, remember what they taught in flight school. My wake flows outwards and downwards. You'll enjoy a smoother ride if you stay within my six.

Emile took pictures from his plane of Terry and Barry's piggyback. "From this point, it looks like you are either trying to fuck one another or refueling in mid-air."

Terry felt anxious that Terry would have to go down together.

"Terry, at Hot Springs VOR turn your transponder to 1,200 to start talking to Little Rock Approach. This will take us approximately 45 miles from Adams

Field. If they give you a code for squawk, I will dive in front of them as soon as you say "Roger, ident" to reach the deck before your radar blooms on my scope.

Terry radioed air traffic control. "Little Rock approach. This is Seneca. Level three-thousand five hundred Tango. Tracking the zero-seven-1 degree radial at Hot Springs VOR. Squawking twelve hundreds, inbound Adams."

"Roger Seneca seven-five Tango and squawk two-7-four-three and an ident."

"Roger Little Rock, Seneca seven five Tango will be at two-seven-fourthree. Squawking ident."

Barry dived so fast that his underbelly seemed to be crashing onto Terry's cockpit. Terry's plane jolted. A clipboard fell from its mount. Terry tried to control the clipboard but was unsuccessful. Barry laughed as Terry tried to grab the clipboard.

Terry, it's too late Terry. It can get really rough back there after a split. Ask Emile. Ask Emile.

Emile laughed. Barry glanced at the trees. They all turned around and flew back towards Mena. They were all ready for the real thing after another practice run.

It was dark and cold, but Terry flew clear. He tried to see Emile and Barry's planes. When he saw Emile's red and green navigation lights, his stress subsided. Terry stated, "Dodger 1 & 2, this is Dodger 3." "I have a visual on your target. "Request identification." Emile flashed flashing strobe lights to allow Terry to locate his target. As he descended, Terry increased his speed and was able to position himself underneath Barry's plane while scanning for US Customs aircraft. He was relieved to be alone up there and waited for the code word "ident" to arrive. His eyes swam towards Barry's tail hook, in an effort maintain a certain distance from Barry's plane.

Emile said, "Roger. Ident." "One nautical mile."

Terry felt more confident this time as he and Barry turned towards Hot Springs while Emile fled to Mena. To his right, the lights from Hope, Arkansas, were shining.

Barry asked, "Do you still have me Dodger 3?".

Terry stated, "Roger Dodger 2," "On my mark. Begin 500 feet per minute [feet/minute] descent to three thousand five hundred. Five, four, three, two, one, mark."

Both planes descended to 3,500ft in perfect sync. Emile called air-traffic control to request permission to land at Mena as they approached Hot Springs.

Terry switched on his transponder, and navigation lights. He called air traffic control to make sure that Barry's plane would land at Adams Field. Terry had set his plane so that he was right behind Barry. This minimized the turbulence when Barry dived. Terry's plane stabilized after a huge jolt.

Barry flew his plane parallel to an Interstate Highway with its lights off. He made a sharp left turn, passing a stable of horses and motorbikes that were winding through a field. Their headlights met the cargo that had been left at Triple-S Ranch, where Dan Lasater was an employee.

Terry estimated that Bill Clinton and his cronies were receiving $9 million per week from the skies. This was courtesy of CIA.

Dan Lasater used customer accounts to fund his money-laundering scheme. Dennis Patrick's account had been used to launder $109 million. Dennis was in a relationship with a Lasater employee who suggested that he open a trading account at Lasater & Company. Dennis was promised a share of the profits for the use his social security number. He received $20,000.

After he was called by Patsy Thomasson, who later became Clinton's Director of Administration at the White House, asking him to hand over the account due to litigation, the trouble began. Dennis refused. Dennis refused. The suspect was eventually arrested and convicted. The cash was a down payment for the hit. His house was then set on fire. The police were unable protect Dennis, a court clerk. He assumed a new identity and fled to Florida with his family. He eventually discovered the $109,000,000 in trades. Dennis stated years later that his account had more government securities trades than Chase Manhattan in the same year. "There is no reason to kill someone for $100 million knowledge or $100 million."

Chapter 22

Emile Camp

Barry and Emile had planned to fly from Mena in a Learjet on February 20, 1985. However, when they arrived at Baton Rouge Airport, they discovered that Barry's plane had been stolen.

Barry was contacted by Emile's wife from Disney World in Florida. She had gone to Disney World with her youngest child after a dispute with Emile. Barry should send Emile to Mena for a few more days so that she can find peace at her home after she returns. Barry gave Emile the task of taking flight records to Mena to be reviewed by an inspector. Barry flew Emile in Barry's Seneca, and Barry flew a commercial flight from Miami to Miami.

Terry moved into his new home later that day. After resolving manufacturing problems for the CIA, he was eager to enjoy a glass of Scotch while taking in the view of the river and the golf course.

Aki rang. "Emile's plane has gone missing. It's overdue on a flight from Baton Rouge, Mena. Because there is active search activity, I am telling this. It will most likely be featured on the news tonight, I'm sure. "I don't want you to draw attention to yourself."

"How overdue is he?"
"Only a few hours, Barry and I fear for the worst."

Barry joined the search from a helicopter. He knew from his gut that Emile had died. Barry found the wreckage on February 23. He was shocked. He was devastated. The plane contained the original logs from Fat Lady, which were not found at the crash site. Barry suspects foul play.

According to the official report, Emile died after Seneca hit the ground.

North Face of Fourche Mountain is located eight-and-a half miles north of Mena Airport. According to the National Transportation Safety Board crash inspector, Emile ran out of fuel. Barry and Terry were puzzled by this. Emile was flying a two-hour flight between Baton Rouge and Mena. He had three hours fuel left in his flight plan. Emile was able to operate and maintain the plane for two year. It was equipped with state-of the-art equipment. Barry stated that he was familiar with how to land. Barry also said that it should have been as simple as finding your dick at night.

Emile took off at 11:12 AM. Emile radioed at 12.55 pm to inform Mena that he would be landing in fifteen minutes. This would have made the flight time approximately two hours. His fuel was supposedly out of date and he went missing at 2:22 pm. Barry and Terry estimated that Emile would have needed an hour of fuel. However, there was no fire at the crash site 200ft below the mountain's peak. Pilot error was the cause of the crash. Barry and Terry found this unbelievable. They were puzzled as to why the Seneca was going off course, why Emile had not radioed for assistance and why he had climbed when he was off-course. Barry examined the wreckage and discovered that the engine controls had been modified to indicate that Emile was trying restart his right engine. With no fuel, if that were the facts, then where was the fuel?

Polk County Sheriff AL Hadaway said that another pilot, Emile, could find the airport at night without any lights and land there. It's something I've seen him do.

Rudy Furr was the Mena airport manager. He said to reporters that he had heard of murder. The bomb was aboard the Camp. He had 500 pounds cocaine and $3 million cash.

Arkansas State Police Investigator Russell Welch wrote a report which included Fred Hampton's quote. Fred Hampton is the owner/front man of

Rich Mountain Aviation. Fred claimed that the Seneca was sabotaged in order to stop Emile from giving evidence about Barry's covert work in Nicaragua for CIA and DEA. Fred claimed that Emile had documents in the Seneca concerning Barry's use in Nicaragua of the Fat Lady.

Barry was scared to death that he could have been on that plane.

Barry and Terry were grieving the loss of their friend but worried about the reports and rumours. Would they have been next if Emile had been set-up? Terry ruminated on possible scenarios, even though he stayed up late at night. What if Emile had been on a hot-money flight with Barry piggybacking, and then deviated from protocol for some unknown reason? That didn't make any sense. He was trying to steal a US Customs plane. How could the person who tampered Emile's plane get into such a tight-knit group? How would he survive if his plane was tampered? None. Terry examined his Seneca and found nothing. However, that didn't lessen his anxiety.

To ensure that Terry and Barry's planes were not sabotaged, the CIA hired a Puerto Rican.

Barry and Terry had dinner after Emile's death weighed them down. After dinner, Terry got into Barry's truck. Barry drove on the airport road until he reached the end of the field. Barry saw a four-door sedan coming towards them at an intersection. Barry jumped on the highway and flashed his headlights at the sedan before parking at a service station.

Barry stated, "Yep. It's time for the hogs to be slopped." Terry reached under his seat to find a paper bag. Terry took out a brown bag that had been wrapped in masking tape and sealed it with masking tape. Barry laughed as the sedan approached. Barry laughed as Barry drew near. Everyone should have one. They are very useful. He's one my inside guys, and it's now that I have to pay my monthly instalment for intelligence. Please, give me the sack."

The driver appeared apprehensive.
Barry said, "You've earned it this time." Barry handed the bag to the agent.

The agent asked, "Who's that with?".

"It's the Little Rock guy that flies around in Aki. Barry laughed. "Ain't that a hoot? Shit, that's what you told me back in November." The agent ended the conversation and left.

Terry, money is great! It can be used to buy pretty much anything," Barry said as he revved up the truck before driving off.

Chapter 23

Undercover

Barry was involved in various sting operations all over the globe in 1985. Despite eight years of investigation, authorities were unable to crack the Las Vegas case. Barry arrived in Nevada and within a month, all the conspirators were arrested. The largest ever seizure of cocaine in Nevada was made at $22 million. Barry's testimony led to the conviction of all co-defendants.

Norman Saunders was arrested in February as the Chief Minister of Turks and Caicos Islands and effectively the Prime Minister. Barry paid $20,000 to Saunders for the right to permit trafficking in his British colony south-of the Bahamas. This was captured by a hidden camera.

Barry stated, "I don't want to make you feel like I'm trying to force you into anything." "You can do what you feel in the heart."

Saunders was arrested along with two other officials of the government after a second meeting in Miami. This was a historic case for the DEA as it marked the first time that a foreign head-of-state was arrested on US soil for drug charges.

Barry surrendered on June 28, 1985 to the US marshals. He was sentenced for smuggling Quaaludes. His life was in peril so he started his sentence under the federal Witness Protection Program. He was kept underground for fifty days in a cubicle without windows that contained a toilet, TV, and a bed. He was not allowed to have visitors and ate alone in his cubicle. He was allowed to exercise for an hour each day at a permanent shelter. His wife and children flew 1,500 miles to visit him. However, they were denied entry because they weren't listed on his approved visitors list. Barry almost burst when he learned that they were denied entry.

Barry was removed from witness protection to appear in court on a regular basis. He was taken to Miami and Las Vegas in the summer 1985.

The prosecutor warned Barry that if you hold back any information, even the smallest, then those defense attorneys will come out and execute you. I want to know everything. If you have ever slept with a pygmy hippos in a Louisiana bayou, I would love to hear about it. Barry stated that there should be no pygmy hippos out there.

A videotape showing the corruption was shown in the trial of Chief Minister of Turks and Caicos Islands. The courtroom was packed with lawyers eager for Barry to be seen in action.

Barry stated on videotape that he was conspiring to kill Norman Saunders. You need to be cautious. It is important to know the identity of those you are dealing with.

Jay Hogan, a respected Miami lawyer, said that Barry is a "really good guy".

The jury was also impressed. Saunders was the first foreign head-of-government to be convicted in the USA of drug charges.

Next came Lito and three of his co-defendants. They were described as part of "one the largest cocaine organizations in the world." Barry's testimony was so shocking that Lito, along with two of his co-defendants, changed their pleas from guilty to guilty. The jury found the other codefendant guilty. Media attention was minimal to the convictions.

Even though they were convicted, Lito and his codefendants expected their associates to fly into the prison in a helicopter to kill the guards using machine guns and handgrenades. Max's testimony led to DEA agents finding the helicopter, a sleek, teardrop-shaped Hughes 500 Ranger. It had been purchased with $500,000 cash. The cartel offered $300,000. The authorities began inspecting the helicopter at Tamiami Airport in October 1985. The escape attempt was anticipated before November 1, when Lito and his codefendants were due to be sentenced. After that, they would be transferred to another facility.

The DEA alerted the prison, a complex of forty-two acres that houses 700 inmates. Lito and his codefendants were placed in medium security. They had jobs that allowed them to move about the jail.

Details of the escape plan were revealed in November. The helicopter would take off at 7 a.m. on an unknown date. This was just as the prisoners were getting ready to leave for their work assignments. They would fly at 160 mph from the helicopter to a farmhouse. They planned to blow up the helicopter and drive to an Everglades airstrip to fly to Colombia via the Bahamas. Agents observed the helicopter practice touch-and-go take-offs and landings. Agents wanted to let the helicopter enter the prison for arrests, but some said it was too dangerous. The DEA confiscated the helicopter before any escape attempt was made.

An agent stated that "our fear was that there might be a second helicopter" "We could have continued the investigation and let it continue longer, but it was running out of time."

Lito was sentenced on November 1, 1985 to 40 years, and his codefendants were given sentences of 12 to 40 year. They were moved to Atlanta's maximum security prison.

Chapter 24

Mena

Terry was offered a job in Florida by CIA in April 1985. He also had the opportunity to start a machine-tools company in Mexico. Barry talked to Terry in a restaurant about the Florida job and how it was a poor operation with outdated equipment and pilots who lived in poverty in Honduras. Barry saw greater opportunities for people with business skills and creative ideas, as the CIA lacked many.

Barry shared his thoughts with Barry over a plate full of oysters. "You won't apply to the job I have. You have to be assertive and take control of your time. Although they hate it, these guys love an aggressive level of insubordination. Understand? Understand? They wouldn't talk to you if they didn't know that you have the talent they are looking for. If I were you, I would pursue it. They see me as a pilot. I only transport the things they need and keep my mouth closed. Your expertise is what they really need. You'd be wise to jump at the chance if they talk about an offshore operation controlled or managed by Southern Air Transport. It was accused of drug trafficking and ended up in a mess. Keep me informed about what they have in store for you. If there is a way to get in on that, I would be very curious.

Terry was shocked to think Barry might be working offshore. Barry seemed so independent. He didn't know the extent of Barry's problems with government. "Why would you want to be involved in an offshore opportunity?" It would not be hard for you to become involved in another full-time operation.

"It's just like my dad said, 'You don't catch fish without a baited line in the water.' I am always looking for something. "Besides, they'll close us down in Nella after the new graduates graduate, given the problems Aki caused." The next graduation was set for August 1985.

Terry began to suspect that Terry was not just bribing Arkansas powerbrokers, but also with $40 million still falling from the sky each month. Seth Ward, a local businessman who had learned too much about the operation and tried to blackmail them, was also a concern. Terry discovered that Barry's money drop zone, Triple-S Ranch was actually owned and controlled by Seth Ward, his son-in-law.

"Finis Shellnut, the gofer who lives there is Finis Shellnut."

Barry stated, "I thought Dan Lasater was at that place all the time!" Finis, a Finis acquaintance. He is a bond-salesman for Dan. Isn't it interesting? What is Finis to know about weapons parts? Finis has nothing to be concerned with this. When I'm at Dan's, I don't talk to anyone except about money. Finis doesn't know who is flying the planes. Barry and Terry were worried that people would be more aware of the bigger picture as money and weapons operations became separated. "Well, that might explain some of the recent shortfalls I've been accused in relation to my nightly deposits. The books aren't compatible. It's all supposed to be accounted for when I take the cash down south. Recently, I was accused of having my hands in the cash register. Finis might be making a few bucks for the Ward family. Let me know if Dan is interested. You're implying that Ward has another connection?

Terry replied, "Yeah." Terry said, "He's got an underground pipeline that leads to the governor's office." Barry moved closer towards Terry.

"Ward's oldest child, Suzy Hubbell, is married to Webb Hubbell, Little Rock's ex mayor. Webb Hubbell is not only a close friend of Bill Clinton, but he's also a major player at the Rose Law Firm in Little Rock. Guess which office is next to Webb?

"With all the incestuous shit going, I hate taking a guess."

"How about Hillary Clinton, governor's wife."

"Bingo! Your fucking leak is now. Someone in the state government had the responsibility of informing the Ward family about Webb Hubbell's parts business. I would bet that someone is Bill Clinton, if he is as close to Hubbell as you are. These kinds of problems are normal in this industry. It's nepotism. This is how it works at a banana republic." Barry thought about the situation and said, "So Ward basically threatened us? Is it okay to let Ward in? Let's call him bluff. This could be very interesting. This whole thing is becoming very unprofessional. Let's get this straightened out! The Fat Man from Agency told him to go fuck his self.

Terry was worried that Seth Ward would tell the media about their operation. He envisioned the FBI raiding the Mena weapons-manufacturing plant. Barry, I don't see the benefit to that approach.

"Hey, you said that you wanted to work abroad for the Agency. You said you wanted to start a front business. You can expose the Agency and force it to close down if you really want to escape quickly. They would have needed your Mexican operation sooner. It could be run by you and me. That was all I was thinking. Barry traced a line from Triple-S Ranch to Dan Lasater's bond company, through Ward's family and into Rose Law Firm, ending up at the backdoor of the governor's house. Barry looked up at Terry and said, "This is turning to one big Chinese fire drill." You are ready to ride and hook it.

Terry was disturbed by Barry's attitude. Terry leaned towards Mexico sooner than expected and calculated that the Mena operation could fail. Terry was pondering if Barry was recklessly entering the Witness Protection Program as Barry was about to do so.

Terry was training the pilots in May 1985 with Emile's replacement Bill Cooper. He was a sharp, sixty-year-old man who was bald, and was very plump. They were flying in a Cessna on mountainous terrain, with rain pounding against the aircraft. A confused Nicaraguan tried to focus on the controls and ground controller in the dark cockpit.

Terry heard Bill whisper to Terry: "Shut down your left engine." Let's find out what this fucker is made of.

Terry pulled a red knob with a shrewdness. Terry pulled a red knob. The Cessna lean to the left. Terry shouted "Rudder!" when the pilot didn't respond appropriately. Rudder! Rudder! Now. Attitude. Bank angle. Airspeed. Airspeed. As the plane rolled, the pilot couldn't figure out what to do. "I'm going to die with you. Did you attend mass today? I didn't. I am not ready to go. If I can't help you through the recovery process, we'll all go down together. Believe in your tools! Push hard right rudder! Slowly, the pilot regained control. The Cessna rose out of a valley.

Terry was doing more night training in June 1985 when he received a distress signal from his command post. Barry, who had blown an engine, was landing at Texarkana. He needed someone to help him with his cargo. Terry saw Barry in a Rockwell Commander four-seater aircraft, with its engine cover on ground and an oil stain on its wings.

Barry stated, "I already checked out her," Barry said, "She was dead upon arrival. I have to get out of this place." I have a duffel bag in my hand. Drop me at

Mena then took it by hightail to Russellville to deliver the parcel." Barry gave Terry boxes. These babies should not be dropped. These are valuable electronics that the Agency lends to you. These are too valuable to be left behind. These keys are not for everyone. These are the keys to the secret door, or you might call them the key.

Barry and Mena parted after they reached Mena. Within two weeks, he was to join the Witness Protection Program.

Skeeter Ward was shocked to see Terry deliver the bag. Terry told him that Barry Seal was playing games with everyone.

Nella was the graduation site for Nicaraguan trainee pilots on August 25, 1985. Oliver North was contemplating promoting Terry, who was willing to move his entire family to Mexico. Terry asked Aki about Barry in September. He was told by Barry that Barry was working on a secret project.

In November 1985, Barry showed up at Mena. His face was aging and he had gained weight. He had made a deposit with Dan Lasater and arranged to meet Terry at SOB's.

Terry asked, "Where have you been?" "I thought the Bermuda Triangle must have swallowed you up. Or was it something that I said?

Barry apologized and said that Barry's absence was due to undercover work. Let's not discuss old business. Let's talk about new business. You are going to be impacted by some of my inside information. The good news? The Agency is interested in your Mexican venture. Cathey North [Oliver North] is really excited. "The bad news is that I have been so far out of the loop, you will need to get me back on track so that I can help you with this project."

Terry stated that he had taken his wife and their three children to Mexico. He had a plan for a weapons supply network after analyzing the situation.

Barry said that Arkansas is getting really pissed off at the Agency. Talk about growing out of their britches. They're stealing money from the Company. Terry, it's like robbing a mob. This is something you don't want to fucking do. Bill Clinton and his gang probably worked on much more than the ten percent cut. It has been decided to end the entire fucking deal.

"Operation Centaur Rose?"

"Yeah. It worked great here, and it was a success. The Agency has bigger plans for Mexico. Your proposal does not include larger plans. Terry, they want to make whole fucking guns using your machine tools. You really helped them to see the manufacturing side of things. I brought some blueprints for the first weapon they would like to build down there.

Two phases would be required for the Mexican operation. First, a Mexican front company would need to be established. Second, machine-tool equipment would be imported. Barry showed Terry a diagram of a weapon that could fire plastic explosive cartridges. It was being sold to the poor by the CIA.

"And another thing: Governor Bill Clinton will learn who is in charge the hard way. After they're done with him, he'll be lucky enough to become dog-catcher. It's up to you and them to accept their offer, go to Mexico, and then be in a position where I can receive you once I blow the lid off the entire Arkansas operation.

"How are you going to do that?"

Barry finished the oyster. "Let's not worry about that. Barry spoke of a secret meeting he had arranged with his CIA agent. Barry had to ensure that the meeting was secure because he was undercover. Remember how to piggyback?" "Remember how to piggyback?" "I'll refer my handler to as my brother. For security reasons, I am trying to arrange for this meeting to be held outside of the country. We won't be away for long. If I'm away from the country for longer than a few days, they'll be missing me. Be ready for me to call you and don't say stupid things over the phone. It is not secure.

"Can you give us an idea of where we are going?"

Barry winked. Barry winked.

Barry called Terry on December 13, 1985. Santa Claus, I'm glad that I got you. It's time to go to my brother's house." Barry exaggerated and continued to code a message that directed Terry to where to meet Barry's plane.

They flew to Texas, where they filed a false flight plan to Mexico under Emile Camp's honor and name. They wanted to stop in El Salvador for fuel and then take off for Panama.

Barry carried two GNS500 navigational radios, each worth more than $1 million. Barry typed in the flight plan coordinates and said that he would just connect the ground-and satellite communications equipment to this box, then it would be time for them to vanish."

Barry was setting up everything to stop a Department of Defense satellite, which is designed to detect incoming missiles, from detecting his Learjet. Barry had arranged for US Army intelligence personnel from the US to emit energy bursts in order to jam US radar. Terry was impressed that Barry used satellites to plan the flight, rather than getting instructions from ground pilots. It was clear that Barry had access to the most advanced communications and weapons technology at the highest levels of US government.

"I will switch the transponders to standby. Barry turned on his radio. "Sea Spray. This is Lear one-three Sierra Nov. You are now only thirty seconds away from the window. What is the best way to read?

"Loud, clear. "We've been waiting for you."

Terry was told by Barry that Barry would tell Terry to switch the transponders to standby when the clock reads thirty. Then, let's hit the brakes and dive the bitch to the deck. Your emergency decompression checklist should be used." The transponder interrogation lamp went off. The Learjet descended and shook with its speed brakes extended. Barry called Mexican air traffic control to request that they cancel the flight plan. We're going to somewhere else." Now, the Learjet was off radar and self-navigating towards El Salvador using a flight plan beam from outer space. This was used to conceal top-secret military flights, such as Air Force One that transports the US President.

The Learjet landed in El Salvador and was immediately surrounded by soldiers who provided lunch and Coca-Cola for Barry and Terry. The plane was refueled without any money exchanged or receipts being created. Barry instructed Terry to apply the brakes as the plane was about to take off. Barry got up and removed a Mylar mask from the Learjet. This changed its serial number.

Barry, flying to Panama, said: "Now, keep in mind that you got something these fuckers actually want. It's your reputation in the machinetool industry. That's what you have to offer. You have the credentials to build a strong front that nobody will notice. Don't be too modest and don't discuss money during this trip. This is an operational discussion. Remember, Leroy is just a fucking beans counter." Leroy was Barry's long-standing CIA contact. "Sometimes, he acts as if it's his money, not Uncle Sam's. "I'll handle the money discussions later."

Barry, what do you want from this?

"I wanna new life. This program will require significant air-transportation capabilities. I have always wanted to be a part of Air America. Perhaps this is my chance.

They landed in Panama at Howard Air Force Base. They were taken to the terminal by a pickup truck.

Leroy, a slim, wrinkled man in sunglasses, said "You guys are always on time." "I love punctuality. This meeting has been moved to Chagres. A few people attending the meeting don't want their photos taken here.

Barry flew them in a Cessna 172 to a dirt runway on the banks the Panama Canal. This was formerly part the US Armed Forces Aeroclub, which had hangars and outbuildings. The meeting took place in a building that overlooked ships.

A man claimed to be Max Gomez, an alias Felix Rodriguez, and was waiting patiently inside. He is a friend of George HW Bush. He led Barry, Leroy and Terry into a corner away from Terry.

Barry returned to Terry after a short chat with Felix. "This is an extremely sensitive topic that we must discuss. Another person is present outside, representing another government and may want to get involved in this operation. The other person, however, would like to be a part of this meeting but cannot be identified for security reasons. Terry asked, "Do you have any problems with that?".
He just wants to be fully informed at the end of this meeting and to then submit a report to his boss. He wants to make sure he understands the horse's words. If you don't, I have no problem with that."

Terry smiled. Terry shrugged. I suppose

"I can't trust this guy yet.

Barry nodded and said "Spook shit." Let them have their fucking fun."

Felix brought in a businessman with a clear eye and sat at one end of a long conference room table.

"Terry," Leroy stated, "I'm sorry for the security precautions taken not to divulge the identity our guest." To allay your doubts, I will show you my identification.

Terry felt calmer when he saw the CIA ID for Leroy Tracta at the table. Terry and Barry sat next each other with Terry opposite Terry and Felix opposite Barry. The stranger sat at the other end of the table and read his pen over a yellow notebook. Felix reached for his briefcase and pulled out a file that contained Terry's business plan.

Felix replied, "Mr Reed." It seems that you have been very busy. It is time to move beyond feasibility and get into the real world of building this front company. This is why we requested this meeting. Thank you, Mr Seal, for being so accommodating. It was best to have a face-toface meeting with Mr Tracta and ask you detailed questions. He wanted to meet with you in person.

Leroy smiled at the man with the glasses eye who was introducing him as a potential foreign investor and was preparing a report for his family. Leroy gave everyone a copy Terry's business plan, stamped with TOP SEECRET. A map of Mexico was included, as well as a diagram showing trade routes from Asia, Europe, and the US that could be used to enter Mexico directly or through other countries. From Mexico, export lines ran to Latin American countries.

Terry described the plan and the interest of companies from Japan, Germany, and Hungary in setting up a Mexican machine-tool operation. He was concerned about Mexican licensing requirements for foreign-owned companies and the laws that apply to them. This was exactly the type of company Mexico needed to expand its export market using modern machine tools.

The stranger spoke in a nondescript accent, "This is something that's not-existent in Mexico." "And this is the main attraction of Mr Reed's plan, according to what I have heard. This is what I intend to emphasize in my report. I will also expand on the joint-venture idea." The stranger was impressed. Felix enjoyed the Hungarian connection.

Terry stated that Mexico's poor road infrastructure makes air transport essential for fragile electronics needed for computerized machine tools. Air shipments would disguise the weapons trading.

Barry stated that with all the air-cargo activity, Barry suggested that we need a specialized carrier that can move sensitive cargo worldwide and operate without restriction. I propose to form a small, elite air-cargo organization based out Mexico. It would be similar to a smaller version of Southern Air Transport. I'll put it all together for you. And, given the black operations capabilities from Operation Seaspray we'll be in a position to travel undetected across this region. This type of operation is well suited to the US army's antidetection capabilities along the corridor between Panama and the Bahamas.

Leroy asked, "How much is this going to cost me?" "With you that's a question that I'm always afraid of asking."

"Leroy, haven't you always gotten your money's worth? You know that I am a professional and professionals are expensive. Terry has been instructed by me to not discuss any money figures. This is something he's still learning. After Terry and I have had the chance to sharpen our pencils, you can come to Terry later and we'll talk about money.

Leroy exclaimed, "Oh, shit!" "Just what I want. Everyone laughed.

Barry replied, "How did I know that I said that?" Leroy, you got my phones again bugged!

They laughed harder.

Terry was referring to Oliver North when Felix stated, "This is Mr Cathey's project." He is the boss. As the project progresses, you will need to file all reports with him. If it's possible, I will become the operations manager for this project.

Barry and Terry felt euphoric after three hours. They flew back to Howard Air Force Base where they were assigned rooms in the Bachelor Officer Quarters. They couldn't sleep because it was so dark outside.

Terry saw Barry's lights and knocked at his door. Barry was lying on his back, staring up at the ceiling fan like he was contemplating the day. Barry, tell me more about Max Gomez [Felix Rodriguez] man. You said that he was a loose-cannon back in the States and that we had to play ball. He'll be the one in charge here, from what I can see. It's not clear if he is driven by greed or ideals. Is that something you find bothersome?

Barry stated that Terry had ideals similar in youth to his. My role was to play an early part in a group of men who wanted to liberate their country, just like your Nicaraguan freedom fighters. Anybody whose ideals drive them is a bit crazy. Gomez is one of those people. My Agency service has shifted around a group ragtag Cubans and now Panamanians. They are just there to help you. They are always at the edge of right and wrong, and sometimes they will pull you along with them. Keep your head straight and remember why it was you were involved. You can end up in serious trouble if you make their war your own. From an Agency perspective, I can only tell you that they are the only game in town. At least not on this side. You have to associate with men like Gomez if you want to play this game. They have made fighting Communism their full-time, selfish profession. It's not clear what motivates them, whether it is greed, ideals, or hatred. However, I do agree that fucking Communism can be dangerous. Although I might be a free-spirited entrepreneur, I am also a patriot.

Terry oversaw the Learjet's refuelling after a large breakfast at the Officers' Mess. Leroy asked for a private meeting. Terry heard Barry apologize to Leroy as they left. This is business, and I have to do what I have to do."

The CIA would no longer have to operate outside of America because it could solve the problems in Mena. These included the snooping by local law enforcement and confusion among federal agencies about Barry's position and who he was working with. The FBI was believed to have been able to take control of the investigation because Barry was involved in drug trafficking. The FBI hoped that by leading the investigation into Barry's drug trafficking, it would be able to keep the attention of state and local authorities. Anyone later trying to access FBI records pertaining Mena would find a criminal probe. However, Terry Reed said that the FBI was containing the investigation or "a shadowing a dark operation." The FBI used other resources, including the Justice Department, to stop arrests and prosecutions. Barry's drug trafficking led to surveillance of Mena which helped conceal the activity at Nella twelve miles away. Barry wasn't just transporting drugs for Medellin Cartel. This was just a cover for decades-old CIA facilitation of drug entry into the US.

Barry felt a natural high on the return flight. Terry was stunned when he shouted "Yee-haw!" repeatedly. "I'm going to fucking make it!" Terry, we're going to do it! These assholes are eating our hands. Yee-haw! Barry reached for the control column. The plane did a series sideways rolls with each one a complete 360deg rotation.

Terry fought the urge for a urination.

Barry replied, "OK, enough with that shit!" "You have the plane. "I'll hook up radios." Barry crouched beneath the electrical panel to make radio connections.

Terry asked Barry why he was so happy at the controls.

Barry returned and punched the dashboard so hard that it nearly fell off. Terry, there is nothing more powerful in the world than good old fucking Blackmail. Don't ever let anyone tell you otherwise. Jesus

Christ, I had some great shit with some big people."

"Will your party allow me in? Barry, calm down! "Tell me about it!"

"Terry: It's important that you play ball with these guys right now and get down to Mexico as soon as possible. I'm not able to travel to Mexico right now. There's a small matter that I need to attend to. But, you can get on down there. You can get in touch with me to have me join you. This will be amazing, Goddamn. It'll be great fun to work together and spend all their money.

"What's the blackmail you're talking of?"

"Have you ever heard the expression, "It's not about what you know, but who you know."? That was a lie. Vice President Bush had not caught his children in dope. "Cause I can assure you that what you know can be even more important than who and what you know."

"You have to calm down, and tell me about what you are talking about, if I want to know. What do you think about the vice president's children and dope?

"I don't want to tell you too much, 'cause honestly you don't need to know. Terry, as you may have guessed, I've worked with many federal agencies over the past few years. One can't help but come across sensitive information in the course of this business. Some of the Medellin Cartel's most important players, who I know personally, came across valuable information that could be used by both the Republicans as well as the Democrats. This is real national-security stuff. Barry chuckled. "Well, I can only imagine how valuable such information would be. This could help you get out of any type of jam. Have you ever played Monopoly? Barry laughed. "Yee-haw!"

"Barry, are your telling me George HW Bush's children are in the drug industry?"

"Yup, that is what I am telling you. One guy from Florida who flipped for DEA has the goods on the Bush boys. This information was provided by a Colombian source. I received it earlier, but I kept it in my possession, ready to use as a trump card should I need it. It's time to use it. I have names, dates, and places. I even got some tape recordings. Fuck, I even had surveillance videos of the Bush boys caught red-handed. This stuff is my insurance policy. It makes me and the mole who's feeding me the stuff invincible. This is very sensitive information inside the US Customs and DEA, and they are well under control. As usual, it's all damage control. It's interesting to see what the Republicans do to the Democrats to make it look worse for those who might use the information against Bush.

"So, you have direct knowledge of Republicans trying to neutralise certain Democrats before they can nuke Bush using this?"

"Hell, yeah. It was my pleasure to be a part. Remember the meeting at SOB's where I said to you that you should have a good time with these guys, get down to Mexico, and be ready to receive me. Remember that I said in that meeting that I had a plan for the Mena deal to be blown off the roof and closed down due to negative publicity. But, I did not tell you that the project was in place and that Republicans were already trying neutralise important Arkansas people: the Clinton family." Barry radioed for ground control. "Yeah. That day you explained to my the connection between Ward family, Rose Law Firm, and Governor's mansion. I was about to spit. What you didn't realize was that I was actually on a secret mission to dirty up some governor-related people. This was something I was working on through Dan Lasater. Although he is a nice guy and all that, he has a drug problem and the guts to steal from the Agency. According to what I heard, Dan has been investing in questionable out-of state investments. He actually has a lot of cash stashed in New Mexico. That was what I was being told. This new connection is what you have to offer. Dollar signs began to dance in my head when you revealed that Finis Shellnut was the ranch owner. There was an instant way to get white stuff around Bill Clinton. Don't be mad, that duffel bag you had me take to Skeeter Ward was not really money."

Terry said, with his eyes fixed on the flight director, "I'm afraid I don't know what it was.".

Let's not call it cocaine. Let's call it neutralizing powder. At least that's how the Bush family viewed it. This is not a family fighting another. It's just like the mob.

"Goddam, Barry. This is a lot of shit! You are claiming that you were responsible for the cocaine being distributed to Arkansas. Just like the ones I read about in the newspaper. "There's a big scandal going down there." Both fell silent. "Did your involvement with Roger Clinton and the investigation of Lasater's company?"

"Terry. I told you when we met that I was in transportation and that I transport the government's goods. The Republicans, in this instance the Bush family, wanted to transport some items through Mena and into Arkansas. This would have the effect of putting some prominent Democrats under their noses. Yes, I admit that I was involved in this. Yee-haw! It's not about who you know; it's about what you know.

Terry was shocked and didn't know what to do. He watched the plane fly above the clouds and contemplated, disoriented by Barry's revelations, and more annoyed that Barry had unwittingly transported drugs. Terry thought about Roger Clinton, who was serving time in a Texas federal jail for drug possession. Terry had heard from other players that Roger Clinton was being investigated and that it would lead to them. The possibility of the local bond market being exposed for laundering proceeds from cocaine was real. If Arkansas' business confidence were to be undermined, it would spell doom for the economy. Dan Lasater and other Clinton cronies were targeted. Barry was correct, Bill Clinton was George Bush Sr.'s real target. Terry did not want to get involved in smearing the reputations so powerful people. Barry could be so happy to blackmail everyone! Barry was clearly biting off too much when he threatened to expose Bush's drug-business dealings. Terry was curious why the CIA would investigate its money-laundering operations. This didn't make sense. Perhaps Barry was trying to destroy the operation so that he could flee to Mexico. Barry was he playing with everyone, as Sketer Ward warned Terry? What else could he have lied about if he had tricked Terry into transporting the drugs?

Terry was shocked and then became angry. "Barry, I gotta tell you. I'm pretty pissed. This whole idea of putting cocaine up people's noses is not my thing. John Cathey brought us together and I think he made a great choice in bringing us together. However, I have to admit that I am having second thoughts about some of this. You have to promise me two things if we are going to be friends. The first is a lie. But I don't think it goes against intelligence. I need you to start telling me everything so that I can make my own decisions. We are treading in dangerous territory. Our relationship is becoming more than a need to know. Second, don't ever put cocaine near me again. If this is what you must do for the Agency then go ahead. It's not something I want to hear about."

"Terry is my friend and I really need you right now. I am sorry for any offense caused to you or for any compromise of your values. These days, it's difficult to find a person who has values. They are rare." The conversation was interrupted by a radio call. Barry apologized for the Skeeter cocaine deal after landing in Little Rock. I swear I won't do it again. Captain, we have many good times ahead. You have everything I know about me. It's time to go solo.

Terry asked, worried that Barry was using solo to end their relationship.

"I don't know for certain. Barry stated that he had to attend a Baton Rouge legal orgy. This refers to an IRS deposition in which Barry would have to answer questions regarding money laundered through Arkansas banks. "Be careful with these men and I'll be seeing you down south soon."

Terry got out of his plane and turned towards Barry in the cockpit. Barry smiled and gave Barry a thumbs up sign. Barry smiled as he stepped onto the runway.

Chapter 25

Sentencing

Barry appeared in Miami Court on October 24, 1985 for a Rule 35 hearing. He hoped that his work as an informant would reduce his sentence. This was his reward for taking the risk of his life. Barry was praised by the DEA for his success as an undercover operative and for his brilliant witnessing. He had infiltrated the Medellin Cartel's highest levels and exposed the sophisticated technology traffickers, including Defense Department navigation equipment that could be used in nuclear war.

Joura stated that "The DEA considers Ochoa the largest investigation the DEA has been involved since its inception." Over my career, I have had the opportunity to work with many informants. I have never seen someone with as much potential or as much output as Mr Seal. He has been my friend for more than a year now, and we have kept in touch almost every day. He has been extensively debriefed. He has never been caught in a lie. He was a cooperative person once he made the decision to cooperate. He has realized the impact cocaine has on American society. I doubt he fully understood it before he was arrested for bringing drugs into the country. As someone who provided transportation, I don't believe he realized the consequences of his actions. He has realized this through his work with the DEA and is now determined to rectify some of the mistakes he made in the past.

Barry's lawyer stated to Joura that if Mr Seal had done the same things he did, Barry would have been a cooperating defendant. "And if he were a DEA agent instead of a cooperating indictant, can you tell us how much he would have gotten?"

"I think he would have been recommended for the Attorney General's Award. This is, to my knowledge, the highest award that a person can receive in the DEA."

The judge removed his glasses when it came time to sentence. "When I first sentenced Mr Seal, I believed that the evidence showed a defendant who was smart, cunning, and frankly, moral. I would have given Mr Seal ten years more, as he seemed to me to be a man who, if I could use a word that Americans avoid these days, was evil.

"I believe it's well-known to all people within this district that promises of cooperation don't cut any ice. The only time I release anyone from jail completely, rather than just a reduction in sentence, is when they cooperate to the point where their lives are in danger. When they do this, I believe they are worthy of being rewarded. Therefore, I will reduce his sentence to the time he has been served. Enjoy your life, Mr Seal. It's your right. "You're a freeman." The gavel fell.

Barry reached out to hug his wife and lawyer. Barry was not concerned about the Baton Rouge sentencing. The plea-bargain stated that he would not have to serve more time in Louisiana than he did for his Florida conviction. He would go to the hearing as a matter of course. He would be gone in no time.

A press conference was held by Stanford Bardwell, the Baton Rouge prosecutor in December 1995. He said that Barry had agreed on two charges: money laundering and cocaine conspiracy. In an attempt to save face after Uncle Sam Wants You, Stanford said that Barry had pleaded guilty to two charges: cocaine conspiracy and money laundering. He also claimed that Barry was beaten by a fifteen-month investigation.

John Camp, the investigative reporter behind this documentary, intervened with some probing questions:

"Is there any plea-bargain agreement that Mr Seal can receive that guarantees he doesn't get time that is excessive to the Florida sentence he was given?"

Bardwell stated that he was not ready to comment on the matter at this point. Barry, he believed, would need to serve at most a portion the ten-year sentence for Quaaludes smuggling. "It is my opinion that the sentence won't be reduced."

Camp asked, "How can you possibly make that judgment if you haven't spoken with the judge?".
"Well, based on previous experience. "I just feel that he isn't in a position...
He has no reason to change it."

Barry pleaded guilty in Baton Rouge to the two counts of Bardwell's indictment. Judge Polozola, a close friend and confidante of Bardwell, questioned Barry about the statements he made in Uncle Sam Wants You. He also asked whether Barry could identify any wrongdoing that he had been accused of by federal officials in Middle District. Barry stayed quiet.

Barry thought it irrelevant because the outcome was already decided when the DEA did not appear in court on December 20, 1985.

His lawyer, sitting on the front row and leaning towards Barry, said that he had a problem. I received some amazing news from the CIA. I asked for a letter attesting to your honesty and cooperation when dealing with them."

"Yeah. Barry replied, "Regent said he'd send it right over.".
The lawyer stated, "There is no Regent.".
"What!"
"Regent is a false name. According to the CIA, they have never heard of anyone with this name. They gave you a false name."

"Bastards." Barry looked around the room and frowned.

"Don't worry, Barry. This judge can only grant you probation. Florida is the only exception. This is the deal.

Judge Polozola asked Mr Seal: "Do you understand that we're here to sendencing today?".
"Yes, sir."
The judge looked at him with a scowl. The judge scowled. To me, drug dealers such as Mr Seal are the most deplorable and lowest offenders I know. They have no concern for the public... People like you, Mr Seal should be in a federal penitentiary. You should be working hard. Drug dealers would not be satisfied working in the hottest sun or coldest days.

Barry's lawyer stated, "Now, please, Your Honour." "Mr Seal is in an unusual position. Only one American man can testify against Jorge Ochoa who is known to be the largest drug dealer in the country.

The judge replied, "Let's tell you what," "I don't care about who Mr Seal believes he is. He's nothing to me."

The lawyer stated, "Your Honour".
"In this case, you received probation in another court. This court has not extended your penalty." It's not what I want, but it's all I have right now.

The lawyer stated, "Your Honour".
Polozola said that Barry would be sentenced to five years imprisonment if he violated any conditions of his probation. "You will not leave Louisiana without permission from the court, even if you work for a government agency. It doesn't matter if it's in the Drug Enforcement Administration. It doesn't matter if it is in the Drug Enforcement Administration. It doesn't matter if it is from the State Department. It doesn't matter if it is US Attorney. It doesn't matter who it is. You can't go anywhere - anywhere! Without my written consent.

Unglesby asked, with a touch of sarcasm: "Do you want to me to refer all those agency?" "Because he talks to all these agencies, to you?"

"I don't care. "I don't care about who they are. It will be reviewed by the probation department. The US Attorney is present. He is the lawyer for the government. There is only one government.

Unglesby stated, "I have found this, in the case, not entirely true.".
The judge stated, "It has been brought to my attention that certain people are around you who carry guns." "If guns are in your homes, you're going have a serious problem regarding revocation," the judge said. This was in reference to Barry's probation being revoked.

Barry stated that he didn't own a gun and doesn't plan to. However, I do plan to have bodyguards.

"Well, your bodyguards will have to be without guns."

Barry replied, "Well, why would they do that if they have legal permits?"

Barry was fined $35,000. "As a condition of probation, Barry must reside at the Salvation Army Community Treatment Center 7361 Airline Highway Baton Rouge, Louisiana for six months."

Barry and his lawyer turned their heads toward each other, and began to talk in urgent whispers. None of the parties had ever suggested a halfway house during negotiations. The Colombians would not take long to kill the man they had stripped of his guns and force him to live at a specific location.

Barry's lawyer stated, "Well, we want you to talk about it, judge.".
"There's nothing to talk about."

The lawyer banged on the table. "This is a double-crossing by the government!" The judge pointed at himself and said, "This court, I'm the government!".
"This isn't a double-crossing by the government."

The judge stated, "Read the plea agreement for count two.".

"I have read it. It is very well-known to me. It was a tedious task. OK. It says no incarceration."

The judge grimaced, "This isn't incarceration.".

"Six months in Salvation Army is incarceration!"

The judge dismissed the claim, saying that he was free to work as much or little as he likes. He goes to work at 6 p.m., but can't leave until 8 a.m. the next day.

The lawyer said, "This is wrong!" "This is a death sentence. He has $1 million on his head. He's dead without any protection."

The judge stated, "Let's tell you something." "I would love to see this plea agreement broken immediately!"

"Is that why?" shouted the lawyer, approaching the judge.

"Mr Seal still has one week to go before he can start his Salvation Army stay.

"That's my sentence," the judge blasted his gavel repeatedly.

Barry's expression was blank. His wife reacted with shock.

"Do something! Debbie shouted at the lawyer, "They'll kill him!" They'll kill him!" Debbie yelled at the lawyer. Do something!"

Stanford Bardwell was smiling.
Barry sat down, shaking his head and gazing down depressedly.

The prosecutor smiled and left the courtroom.

Barry's lawyer, on his way out of the hall, asked one of the assistants to the prosecutor, "Does he know the extent of Barry's cooperation with Miami DEA?"

The assistant replied, "That's Florida or Las Vegas." "Barry has not done anything in Baton Rouge for us and we aren't that concerned until he does."

Barry left the court and was approached by the media. "What are your plans?"

to do now? Go into hiding?"

Barry stated, "Oh, no, I don't hide.".
"Mr Seal are you not afraid for your safety?"

"If it comes it will come."

"What about federal Witness Protection Program?"

"That's just another name to jail, you know. I don't want to go to jail. It doesn't matter what you call it.

"Are you afraid the cartel will find your Baton Rouge home?"

"I can see a Colombian coming in from a mile away in Baton Rouge."

Barry, like everyone else, didn't notice that there was an American private detective in their midst. He was in the courtroom with the Medellin Cartel and was paying his taxes.

Barry called Vice President George HW Bush after the sentencing hearing. Bush told him that if he didn't help, he would expose illegal weapons and drug trafficking. Bush's reaction is not known.

Barry woke up one morning to a knock at his door. He got up from his bed and looked out the window. The whole family was woken by more knocking. The room was occupied by his two teenage sons, and his little girl. Barry went downstairs to open the door.

One lady, seated with several people dressed in business suits, identified herself as an IRS agent. "Mr Seal. This is a declaration for back taxes owed the government. We will collect your assets to partially pay that debt.

Barry replied, "Show me your warrant.".
They looked nonplussed.
Barry stated, "You are not coming in without warrant.".
"We'll be back with warrants then."

Barry called Vice President George HW Bush. Bush's response to Barry is not known.

The IRS issued a warrant. Barry tried to bang the door against their faces but a man wearing a boiler suit and a large man opened it. The removal men entered the house and began to take the furniture.

The lady replied, "Mr Seal. You're on probation." "Resisting an Officer of the Law would be a violation that probation and result in your immediate imprisonment."

Barry looked at the paperwork. He looked at the paperwork. "It states that I owe $29,000,000 in back taxes.".
"It was based upon the earnings you reported to court for drug transport."

Barry stated, "But you don't take Debbie's stuff, lady." "You take my planes, and my boats."

"We already have."
Barry went upstairs and grabbed some papers. He then locked himself in the bathroom and began to burn them. He was finished and joined his family at top of the stairs. Debbie grabbed their daughter and hugged her before

turning around. Barry watched as the men removed the furniture from the house.

Doublecrossed was visited by Jacobsen, a DEA agent.

Jacobsen stated, "Barry. I'm sorry about that hearing.".
Barry sat on the steps and said: "Where were your men?".
"I'm sorry. It was going to be routine, they said. There was nothing to go wrong.

They said we couldn't make it."

Barry nodded. "They weren't ever on the streets, Jake?" "Too filthy."

Barry began to cry. Barry began to cry.

"I don't know, Barry."
"What did I not do for you?"

"You did it all."
Barry smiled regretfully.

"I'm sorry. "I can't help but to apologize."

"No. It don't matter."
"My hometown. They wanted me to come home and they got me."

"What about the Colombians?"
Barry stated, "I don't believe the Colombians would try to kill me." It's business.

Chapter 26

Assassination

Barry would have been a long-serving member of the Salvation Army halfwayhouse.

Many thought that Barry would give up and go to the Witness Protection Program. Barry surprised everyone with his determination to remain put for six months.

In May 1985, Cumbamba was given the hit to murder Barry after Max had been arrested. The Colombians were unable to get Barry into the Witness Protection Program. Jorge Ochoa was threatened with extradition from Spain to Miami because of his shifting legal fortunes on January 21, 1986. Barry began staying at the halfway house starting at 6 pm on January 24, according to reports by the private investigator who attended Barry's sentencing hearing.

After 15 days at the halfway house, a Colombian hit squad flew to Mexico with the intention of illegally crossing the border into America. Cumbamba arrived at Kenner Airport Hilton on February 16. He rented room 312 under the alias Miguel Velez. The hit team arrived on the following day. Mary Cook purchased a 1982 Buick grey for $6,500 using 100-dollar bills. Two Colombians stayed at Jay Motel Lounge Restaurant for $15.91 per night. They could see the Salvation Army parking garage from room 228, which is a few hundred meters away.

Barry called a friend, a missionary pilot, on the morning of February 19. "Joe! They're closing in."

"Barry, keep your eyes focused on Jesus!"

The Colombians were also given baseball caps and raincoats that day. Cumbamba drove Luis Carlos Quintero Cruz from his home to the halfway house's parking lot. Cumbamba reversed his Buick and parked it in a spot on the lot, three spaces above three large Salvation Army boxes for clothing donations. Quintero Cruz and Cumbamba got out of their Buick to drop off something in the donation boxes.

Cumbamba sat back in the car smoking, patiently waiting for Barry.

Barry used to wake up at 7 AM and leave at 7 AM for his halfway house routine. As an extra precaution, he returned to the halfway house at 6pm. He was usually accompanied by a friend. He ate lunch at his home with his family. He received bad news in the mail he received at home. His home was under seizure warrant. The FAA had already revoked his pilot's license because he was a felon.

Barry was preoccupied with resolving his tax problems after the IRS had seized his assets including his helicopter, two boats and three planes.

Barry stated to a journalist on February 19, 1985 that the IRS had made his life very difficult. I have been working with lawyers twenty-four hours per day. It's become a very complicated thing to talk with attorneys while I'm at the Salvation Army.

Barry called Bill Lambeth on his car phone when he returned to the Salvation Army to inquire about purchasing a propeller to go to a plane. Barry, sounding anxious and stressed, promised to call Bill at 6:15 PM from the halfway house.

Barry was overwhelmed by all the thoughts and feelings he was experiencing, so he arrived at the halfway house. He passed the Cadillac with the Colombians, and he reversed it into the space next to the drop boxes. On the other side of drop boxes, the Colombians were riding in a grey Buick.

Quintero Cruz had just dropped a bundle in one of the drop boxes. He then hid it behind them and waited for Barry to open his door. Quintero Cruz pulled the bundle out of the box as Barry tried to open his door. He removed the outer layer of a raincoat to get to a MAC-10. It didn't make an explosive sound that would bounce off buildings but a crackling sound because it was silencing.

Quintero Cruz jumped toward Barry until the MAC-10 was less that two feet from Barry. The gun fired twelve shots in two seconds. It made a loud sound similar to firecrackers. Three shots hit Barry on the left side, and two entered behind his ears. He was also hit with more. He was left with his head down and his hands crossed over his ears.

Barry was approached by a witness. A witness ran to Barry, seeing a hole in his head that seemed to have been all the way through. He said, "Barry! Can you hear me?".

Although a Colombian pulled the trigger, a hitman is just an instrument in the hands the criminal. It appears that the hitman was working for Pablo Escobar and the Medellin Cartel. Barry was working in a world that often used smokescreens to make his appearances. Before we can draw any conclusions about the conspirator, it is necessary to look at the lives of our suspects, Pablo Escobar, and George HW Bush. Finally, it is important to consider information from outside of the US government.

You can skip the section on Pablo Escobar: Beyond Narcos if you've already read the War on Drugs Trilogy's first installment, Pablo Escobar.

Part 2
The Murder Suspects

Murder Suspect 1
Pablo Escobar

Chapter 27

Early Years

Pablo Escobar was born in a cattle ranch during The Violence's second year. This civil war saw millions flee their homes and hundreds of thousands of people die. People were popularized by cutting them up with machetes, which led to new types of slaughter methods that had ornate names. The Flower Vase Cut started with the cutting of the head, arms, and legs. The limbs that were freed were then stuffed down the neck to create a vase with body parts. The victim was stabbed in his neck. His tongue was pulled out of the gap and his chest was hung. He was wearing a Colombian Necktie. Nearly every family in Colombia was affected by the turmoil. It made Pablo's generation more accustomed to violence and the expectation of a brutal and short life.

Pablo's parents were Abel de Jesus Dari Escobar (a hardworking peasant farmer who traded horses and cows) and Hermilda Galviria (an elementaryschool teacher). Hermilda took care of her family while her husband was away at work. She cooked, cleaned, and looked after them. Pablo was the third child of seven.

Pablo, a tiny boy, wandered off from his home one day. Hermilda discovered him playing with a snake under a tree.

Pablo told the snake, "See, I'm just not hurting you.".
Hermilda gazed affectionately at Pablo, knowing that he was a sweet boy who loves animals.

Pablo and Roberto had to get up at a very early hour because the nearest school was far from their home. They walked for an hour in their worn-out shoes, as they had no transportation.

Pablo refused to wear shoes that had holes, and instead chose to walk barefoot to school. He was sent home by his teacher. Pablo was so upset that his teacher sent him home. She didn't have any money so she shopped for shoes. She noticed that each shoe was different in size at home. She was devastated and confessed her grief to a priest who suggested she return the shoes and obtain credit for them.

She purchased the shoes and returned home exhausted and anxious. She complained about the lack of money, as she had a large family.

Pablo replied, "Don't worry mom." "Wait till I grow up. "I'll give everything to you."

The violence between the Conservative and Liberal parties escalated. The family was advised to leave or risk having their bodies reassembled into art. They chose to stay despite not having a safe place to go and adored the animals and the stunning countryside with wildflowers.

Pablo was seven years old when the guerrillas invaded his village, near Rionegro on the Black River. He heard the machetes pricking at his front door, and was terrified. He held on to his mother who was praying and crying. They would all be killed, his father stated, but they could save the children. They covered the children with blankets and mattresses.

The front door was so strong, the guerrillas gave up on trying to break into it. They instead set it ablaze. Pablo's parents feared for their lives, wincing and coughing in the smoke-filled house. The soldiers arrived, and the guerrillas fled.

The street was lit by a burning building, and the survivors were taken to a schoolhouse. Pablo will never forget the burned bodies and the dead hanging from the lampposts. The horrors of The Violence were ingrained in Pablo as a fearful child. He would later kidnap, murder, and bomb to keep his empire going.

Pablo was the closest to Roberto, his two-year-old brother, as he grew up with six siblings. Roberto was an intelligent man who loved mathematics, electronics and cycling. Pablo loved watching Roberto build things like radios. But rather than joining in, he would sit around and think for most of the day.

Pablo and Roberto were taken from their ranch to live with their grandmother in Medellin. This city is known as the City of the Eternal Spring because of its steady climate of 22.2degC (72degF) or around 22.2degC. Downtown was made up of skyscrapers made of steel and glass, separated by roads that were lined with trees. As the surrounding area of houses became more shabby, there were many slums, garbage dumps, and shantytowns. These places were home to displaced people, as well as thieves, pickpockets, and street children. Medellin's hardworking residents worked hard to make it a success.

Pablo's grandmother, who was a savvy businesswoman, bottled sauces to sell to supermarkets. Roberto and Pablo had to attend church every morning under her loving, but firm guidance.

The mountains and beautiful weather were their favorite things about Colombia. However, the second-largest city with its over a million inhabitants intimidated the brothers who are used to ranch life and its speed cars. Their parents were thrilled to have them join them. However, their father didn't like living in the city so he moved back to the country to help on other farms. The brothers eventually fell in love Medellin.

At home, the atmosphere was strongly religious. The couple had a figurehead.

Jesus with real blood. Young Pablo was so upset that his mother had told him Christ's story and he ate a piece of meat from his corn cake. He then took the figurehead with him. "Poor man! Who made you bleed?" His mother was convinced that he was religious and kind. Pablo would sleep with an image or two of Jesus near his bed every night for the rest of their lives.

Pablo was enchanted by Hermilda's stories about Roberto Gaviria his grandfather who had smuggled whiskey. Roberto the bootlegger was a master of long-range planning. He also had a creative imagination and outsmarted all authorities. Pablo wanted to be like his grandfather.

The children grew up in Envigado, a suburb of Medellin. They built wooden carts and raced down the hills. They created soccer balls out of old clothes, wrapped in plastic bags and set up goalposts. Pablo loved it. One popular trick was to put chewing gum on the doorbell so it would ring continuously.

Some of Pablo's criminal and leadership traits began to emerge on the streets of Medellin. He was the youngest member of his group but he would take the initiative. He encouraged his group to throw stones at the police car after they took their soccer ball. The police arrested several members of the group and threatened them with imprisonment for the rest of their lives. Only Pablo spoke up for the commander. He assured them that they had not done anything wrong. They got tired of seeing the ball taken so they agreed to pay for the retrieval. Pablo and some of the children in the group went on to start their own business.

Pablo, in his teens, was elected president of the school's Council for Student Wellness. This group demanded food and transportation for students who were poor. Pablo learned about US meddling in South America to its advantage. This often led to more suffering for the poorest people. He hated the fact that the poor were the most vulnerable to violence and injustice.

He absorbed anti-imperialist phrases during this period, which became his mantras throughout the rest of life. Rumours circulated that Jorge Eliecer Gaitan was assassinated by the CIA. Gaitan was a leftist presidential candidate who defended workers' rights, and promised equitable land reform. Pablo's family was threatened by The Violence after Gaitan's assassination.

Pablo began to hate the structure of society. Only a small percentage of Colombians owned most of the land and wealth. More than half lived in poverty. He was determined to stop that from happening and claimed that he would commit suicide if he didn't make a million pesos before he turned thirty.

Roberto, Pablo's brother, said that Pablo was interested in poetry, history, and world politics. He read law books at the public library. He practiced public speaking in front of student audiences during lunchtime and on the soccer field. Roberto recalls Roberto passionately speaking about his ambition to become the president of Colombia. He also wanted to take ten percent from the earnings of the wealthiest people to help the poor build schools and roads. He wanted to create jobs by encouraging Asian companies to build plants in Colombia.

Pablo was a troubled child at school. He was distrustful of authority figures and felt more comfortable with street gangs. He tried small scams to make some extra money. He believed school was a waste and dropped out after two years. He learned how to avoid the dangers and refined his skills on the streets.

Hermilda persuaded him to continue his education so that he could graduate with the three required grades. He loved his mother and returned to school. He ended up having constant arguments with his teachers, whom he considered foolish and absurd. He was eventually expelled.

His mother had a stern look on his face and he replied, "Mother! I keep telling you, I want to become big, and I will." I'm poor, but I'll never die poor. I promise."

Pablo, then sixteen years old, was showing an incredible amount of confidence when he walked the streets. He often looked at his reflection through windows, always carrying a comb in one's pocket. Later, he mimicked the mannerisms of Al Capone as well as The Godfather (Marlon Brando). He smoked marijuana to intensify his deep thinking. He grew quieter. He paused before answering a question and generally became quieter when asked. Many wondered if he was trying to imitate The Godfather. However, it was just a natural trait that was worsened by being stoned.

He saw his banditry in a way of resisting an oppressive society and channeled his energy into criminal activities, which included selling fake lottery tickets and assaulting people. Armed with a rifle, the man entered banks and instructed staff to empty their safes. He smiled and chatted with the bank tellers as he waited for the cash. Some mistook Pablo's bravado for drugs, as he was unable to see that he had lost his fear. His cleverness and farsightedness, which included evading police officers, led to him having more faith in himself.

His combination of intelligence and street-smarts allowed him to surpass his peers. Some of them sought his guidance and joined his gang. His company was safe for those who were anxious or frustrated. He was calm and cheerful even in difficult situations, earning their respect.

One person said that he was like a God and a man with a powerful aura. It was the most significant day in my life when I first met him.

Mark Bowden, the author of Killing Pablo, described Pablo as a skilled car thief at twenty-five. His gang forced drivers out of their cars and had the cars taken to chop shops. He dictated orders, managed the logistics, and collected the cash.

His gang began stealing new cars. These cars were difficult to resell if reported stolen. He offered to bribe the police in order to get around this. His relationship with the police was so strong after a year that the chiefs of police followed his orders. All complaints about his reselling of stolen cars were ignored.

The money from the sale of car parts was used as bribe to get car certificates issued to officials so that stolen cars could be sold without being cut. He was receiving complaints from the same officials who issued him the titles for his new car.

He created a protection scheme where people paid him to stop their cars being stolen.

He was always generous with his friends and gave stolen cars to them with clean papers. The factory told those who received new cars to come pick them up. Pablo's friends informed the factory workers that the fake paperwork was forged. They were then prompted to hand the keys over by the workers.

Gustavo, Pablo's cousin, and he built race cars out of stolen parts. They also entered rallies. Pablo, who was suspected of stealing a red Renault, was arrested in 1974. However, he bribed his escape from a conviction.

Pablo ordered the execution of those who attempted to stop his accumulation of power, such as those who denounced him or refused to follow his rules or accept his bribes. He found that murder was cheap and effective public relations. Putting people in the spotlight on their deaths or those of their families helped them to behave better. To increase his earnings and reputation, he killed without any regret.

Pablo money was owed to some people. Some were abducted. The victim was executed if the debt was not paid by his family or friends. His reputation was enhanced and his business grew in a world full of cutthroats and opportunists. He also kidnapped and held people for ransom.

Diego Echavarria Misas, a powerful industrialist, lived in a reconstructed medieval castle. He was highly respected by the upper social circles and aspired to be a philanthropist. However, despite the many hospitals and schools he opened in his name, his efforts to hide his evilness did not deceive the poor.

His textile mill workers worked in terrible conditions and earned a pittance. He fired hundreds of them without any severance pay and in abusive ways. He expanded his territory, just like many wealthy landowners. He forced the expulsion of peasant villages. Some peasants tried to defend their homes and were either imprisoned, or even murdered. Rest were forced to settle down in the slums.

Pablo was tired of hearing about Echavarria. His kidnapping was soon reported. His family paid the ransom quickly, but it remained a mystery as to his fate. His body was discovered in a hole close to Pablo's birthplace six weeks later. He was beaten, tortured and strangled. His death was celebrated by the poor.

Many believed Pablo had brought them justice. However, there was no evidence linking him with the crime. He was not charged. People stopped to shake his hands or bow to him in reverence on the streets. He was called "Doctor Escobar" or "The Doctor".

Roberto claimed that Pablo's enemies made false accusations about his brother's brutality in the beginning.

Pablo began to use his organizational skills to counterband, which was a thriving industry in Colombia, a country steeped with corruption. Medellin was a major hub for smugglers. People who were caught often bribed their way to freedom.

They would be confiscated by the police if they refused to pay a bribe. It was a cost of doing business, and it is a common practice in Colombia.

It was difficult to distinguish between police officers and criminals with so many police officers on the payroll of the crime bosses. Not only did the police release their criminal associates from prison, but they also committed crimes on behalf of the gangs including kidnapping and contract killings. Sometimes, shootouts occurred between police officers on the payrolls rival gangs.

The court system was basically the same. A judge who made $200 per month could be charged up to $30,000 to dismiss an instance. Judges who refused to comply were threatened or beat. Staff at courts could be bribed to give up files. This was cheaper than hiring a judge. The judge could be killed if this didn't work. Pablo would learn how to manipulate the court system, which was considered the most vulnerable target in law enforcement.

Pablo was the subordinate of a powerful contraband kingpin, who specialized in shipping cigarettes, electronics and clothing in shipping containers to Japan, England, and America. Panama was used to ship the goods to Colombia.

Pablo met the kingpin at a soccer match and asked him to act as his bodyguard in order to reduce worker theft. Pablo told him that protecting the merchandise was the only way to make money.

Pablo bought the wine and seafood from the low-paid workers. Pablo offered to pay half of his salary for them to work with him forever. He promised to return in two weeks if they stopped stealing. They agreed to return the stolen goods that they had left and were paid back by the workers.

Pablo, who was a specialist in cigarettes drove across Colombia in a jeep in front of half a dozen contraband trucks. He also paid the police the required bribes along the way. The kingpin was pleased with Pablo's performance and offered him ten per cent of the business. Pablo wanted fifty. Pablo was called crazy by the kingpin. Pablo claimed it was fair, as the kingpin sometimes lost more than half the goods. Pablo would have to give Pablo fifty percent. However, the kingpin would still be able to make more money since there would not be any theft. The kingpin accepted to 40 percent.

Pablo was a skilled smuggler through the contraband trade. He didn't have to pay any taxes or fees. He earned up to $200,000. Supervising two convoys per month. His profits were hidden in his walls, so he kept them. He created electronic doors that only he could access. Roberto was hired as an accountant to handle the payroll, make investments, and deposit money in bank accounts with fake names. The money was used to invest in farms, construction companies, and real estate over the years. Pablo bought him a gun because his brother handled so much money.

He gave half his salary to workers, earning their respect and the nickname El Patron or Boss. He purchased a house for his mother, a taxicab to Gustavo, and an Italian bike for his brother. He donated truckloads worth of food to the garbage dump scavengers. He brought around twenty family members to Disney World, Florida. There, he rode all the rides with his son.

Pablo was moving a policeman to another area on his payroll, so he took over the operation. They waited for a convoy to arrive and then ambushed them. The police would make a lot of money by stealing so many goods. Pablo stopped for lunch and instructed the convoy to go on without him. Thirty-seven trucks were seized. Pablo, a driver, said that he would tell other drivers to not speak to the police. He was escorted by the police to his bus ride back to Medellin. The drivers were released by lawyers, but the law firms could not retrieve the merchandise.

Pablo found a better business opportunity, even though his contraband relationship with the kingpin was ended.

Chapter 28

Cocaine

The Cockroach introduced Pablo to Gustavo, a supplier of cocaine paste in Peru. They were selling it at $60 per kilo. This was at a time when cocaine paste was being sold for as high as $60,000 in America.

Pablo used Renault 4s to smuggle the paste from the Andean Mountains across three countries, Peru, Ecuador, and Colombia. Each country had its own Renault 4 with the appropriate country's license plate. Gustavo, his cousin with sharp dark eyes and square faces, was sometimes raced by him to see who could return to Medellin first. All proceeds were kept by the winner. The paste was found in a hidden compartment above the passenger's side wheel that the checkpoint police never looked into.

The paste was found in a residential area and ended up in a covered window house where it was converted into cocaine. The second floor was where the cooks lived. The first floor was converted into a kitchen. Pablo converted old refrigerators into ovens to cook the cocaine. He gave away ten samples to get feedback on his first batch. Most people preferred it to marijuana and asked for more. Others claimed it gave them energy. Some people claimed it gave them energy. Others said that it calmed their nerves. Pablo didn't like it. He preferred to smoke pot.

Cheap paste was easily available because the coca plant is widely grown in the jungles of Peru. The price of cocaine in America skyrocketed due to drug laws. The US authorities focused on heroin and marijuana coming from Mexico, rather than cocaine. Pablo calculated that he could make more selling one load of cocaine in America than from a convoy hauling normal contraband.

Pablo found out that he had underestimated the demand for cocaine while testing the export business. Pablo could sell cocaine to any country, but especially to America, which is the biggest consumer of the drug.

Pablo's drug smugglers flew with drugs and returned home with large sums of cash. The Renault 4s were replaced by trucks. There were more workers.

Pablo's driver was Vulture. Vulture began to show off his wealth by purchasing a car, a motorbike, and clothes as he made more money from his trips. One of his relatives at the DAS (the Colombian equivalent to FBI) noticed this. Vulture informed his relative that he was transporting potatoes.

Pablo was stopped by the DAS and asked for a bribe. They were both arrested when Pablo and Gustavo turned up. Pablo's mugshot appeared on the newspaper's front page the next day. His mother cried for hours.

Pablo spent eight days in prison and paid for his transfer to a facility that offers outdoor recreation, including soccer. After two months of bribery, he was allowed to transfer Pablo to a facility with outdoor recreation. His lawyer warned him that he could be sentenced to a lengthy term. Pablo said to a guard one night that he needed to stretch his legs in order to relieve stress. He was allowed to leave the soccer field after he had spoken with a guard.

Pablo's mother was called by the prison director, asking her to call her son. Otherwise, he would end up in jail. Pablo called his mother and she insists that he return. Pablo and his mother arrived at the prison with some xrays of a sick person. Pablo claimed he was ill and showed his mother to his military escorts. They were happy about his absence. Pablo eventually bribed the judge. Gustavo and Pablo escaped. The driver was sentenced to five years in prison. Pablo provided a home, a car, and money for the driver's family.

Pablo continued his cocaine business after his release. However, the police were aware of it. Gustavo and Pablo were stopped by two DAS agents, who had previously arrested them. He and his cousin were taken to a remote location by a trash dump, where they tied their hands and forced them to their knees. The agents demanded one million pesos for their lives in return for roughing them up. Gustavo was able to obtain the money while Pablo offered him more cash to identify the person who had arranged to kidnap Gustavo. It was the Cockroach, which he was shocked to discover.

Pablo planned revenge against his captors and was freed. It was inexcusable to be forced to his knees by gunmen. Two DAS agents, inspired by their success were ready to kidnap Pablo's worker. They saw Pablo as a potential drug-trafficker and considered him an easy target. Pablo's men abducted the agents and took them into a house. Pablo forced them to kneel. Pablo placed a gun to their heads, and they were shot multiple times. Their bodies were discovered by the news.

Pablo met Maria Victoria Henao Vellejo in 1974. She was a beautiful local girl. Maria's mother wasn't too enthusiastic due to her being fourteen years old and Pablo being twenty-five. He persevered, even showing up at her house with a guitar player to serenade her. They were married in 1976 when she was pregnant. Juan Pablo was born three months later. Maria's mother took two years to get to know Pablo. But she finally did and accepted that he loved her daughter.

Pablo created his own gang, Los Pablos. They had a reputation for being dangerous on the streets in Medellin. His organization absorbed rivals. Pablo helped to broker a deal that saw them enter a partnership with him after a conflict broke out between two drug traffickers in Medellin.

Pablo found it easier to ship cocaine to America than smuggling large quantities of marijuana. Pilots would dispose of the used tyres at Miami with up to 40 kilos. They were then taken to a dump and followed by Pablo's worker who would retrieve them. The cocaine was distributed by a network made up of Latinos living in Miami.

Pablo stopped smuggling drugs. He hired others to do it. To frustrate drug agencies' efforts and avoid giving any evidence verbally that could be used against him, he used code words like emeralds or diamonds on the phone.
He changed his smuggling methods constantly to stay ahead of the DEA. He stopped using plane tyres, and had Colombians and Americans board planes

carrying cocaine in their suitcases or dressed in special clothes. The suitcases, which weighed up to five kilograms each, had double walls and could hold as much as five kilos. They received $1,000 and their flights tickets. Some wore shoes with hollowed out bottoms. Shoes with cocaine inside were made. Pablo also recruited passengers and crew members. Pilots and copilots were also included in the crew, which made it easy to get through airports without being searched. In the frames, people in wheelchairs could smuggle as much as $1 million of cocaine. Some of the smugglers disguised themselves as nuns. Some posed as blind men with canes filled with cocaine. Many people ingested cocaine from condoms. They would die if the condom was opened. Newspapers reported such tragedies.

The authorities were obsessed with eliminating the drug, which had been stigmatised in America for decades, and marijuana was allowed to slip into the US without being noticed. The federal government classified marijuana as a Schedule 1, more dangerous than cocaine and as deadly as heroin. It remains there to this day.

Pablo stopped sending people suitcases. They were loaded onto a plane and taken to the other side. Officials at airports were offered hundreds of thousands of dollars in bribes to turn their backs. A man on a low salary was arrested after he had $27 million in his bank account.

Pablo took bigger bribes to keep his empire growing. Pablo gave huge amounts of cocaine to the police officers on his payroll in order to allow them promotions and raises. The media captured the busts and reported them to the news. These seizures were a delight for the government as they allowed them to obtain more money from America to help fight the War on Drugs. Pablo received the confiscated cocaine, which was then reported to have been destroyed and returned to Pablo. It was then exported to the USA. This scam continues to be perpetrated by corrupt governments around the globe.

Pablo moved his kitchens to the jungle because of the strong smells from cocaine.

El Poblado is one of Medellin's most wealthy neighborhoods. It has lots of white stucco homes, with heavy marble, glass, and armed guards. Locals dined in fancy restaurants that offered views of the city and shop at high-end boutiques. Although his brother encouraged him to focus on real estate investments, Pablo was still addicted to power, money, and lifestyle.

Pablo attracted investors by offering high returns. A $50,000 investment would pay off with $75,000 within two weeks. Investors would receive half their money back if the drug ring was busted. People sold their homes and saved to get investment capital.

Pablo created a form insurance that allowed businessmen to invest a few thousand dollars in order to own a portion of a shipment of cocaine. The profits would be distributed after the shipment was shipped to America. Pablo assured their original investment, even if the shipment were seized. He took ten per cent of the American value for this insurance premium. He even offered loans to businessmen to invest.

Pablo made millions, but the sum was still small.

Chapter 29

Death to Kidnappers

Pablo was not the only trafficker in his network. Jorge, Juan David, and Fabio Ochoa were also involved. They are alleged to have been more involved in the plot to kill Barry than Pablo. Doublecrossed, which featured Pablo as a sidekick, reveals this. Most of Barry's orders were given by Jorge Ochoa (the leader of the family's cocaine business). Barry stated that he was a member of "the Jorge Ochoa cocaine cartel" in 1985. The Ochoas started trafficking their own cocaine in the mid-1970s.

Jorge was calm, firm on family values, and did not use drugs except for the occasional glass of wine. He enjoyed riding vintage Harley Davidsons, and also attended horse shows. His ability to avoid the law was a great asset. The Ochoas lived on La Loma, a hilltop home south of Medellin where their friendly ponies ate from visitors' hands. They also had Hacienda Veracruz where they kept horses and had their own Zoo.

An alliance formed between Pablo Escobar, the Ochoa family and two other traffickers, which was later called the Medellin Cartel by the US authorities. Their bond was cemented by the kidnapping of Martha Ochoa, the youngest sister of the Ochoa brothers, by a guerrilla group known as the M-19.

The M-19 took Martha Ochoa, a student at the University of Antioquia, Medellin on November 12, 1981 and demanded millions of US dollars from the Ochoas. Jorge Ochoa, seconded Pablo, hosted a meeting where he proposed the formation a military, Muerta a secuestradores (MAS), which translated to Death to Kidnappers.

Rodriguez Gacha, Carlos Lehder and Carlos Gacha were also present. Gacha, a short-stubby man, rose in the emerald industry which was known for its violent reputation. Gacha was a pioneer in trafficking through Mexico and the US, killing anyone that stood in his way. Lehder, a German-Colombian descendant, was Barry's comrade in crime. He forced Barry to fly a heavily cocaine-loaded plane at gunpoint.

The meeting was attended by two hundred twenty-three businessmen from all over Colombia. They approved Death to Kidnappers. These included pilots, traffickers, and smugglers. Each gave two million pesos, ten hitmen and each donated two million. Following the MAS meeting, which saw the drafting and distribution of a communique by the participants, they went to a picnic on a ranch near Medellin where they found that they shared many commonalities. They had never before gathered together to create public policy.

The MAS communique was loaded onto a plane that flew to Cali on Sunday afternoon just before a match between Medellin & Cali. Leaflets fell from the skies onto the pitch after the referee gave the start whistle. They spoke of a general assembly that would not tolerate kidnappings by rebels trying to finance revolutions through the sacrifices made by people like themselves... The primary objective will be to execute all kidnappers immediately and publicly starting from the date indicated in this communique.

The government offered twenty million pesos in exchange for information that would lead to the capture of the kidnapper. It also guaranteed immediate retribution. The guilty would either be hanged from trees in public parks, or shot and marked by the sign of our group - MAS. Kidnappers in prison would be executed. If this is impossible, then "our retribution falls on their comrades and closest family members."

Pablo said to a journalist that if there wasn't an immediate and strong response, then the M-19 would continue to screw our families... We paid eighty million pesos to law enforcement for the information they had at the moment, and they began to fall the next day. They were taken by my soldiers to our secret homes, our secret ranches and then people from law enforcement went to them and hung them up.

Many of the M-19, as well as anyone else suspected of involvement in Martha's kidnapping, were killed in the tradition of The Violence, Pablo's childhood, which included the Colombian Necktie, the Flower Vase Cut, and many others. In six weeks, more than 100 M-19 were dealt with. This was a shame for the Colombian army, who hadn't captured that many people since 1974 when the M-19 began.

A terrified woman was found chained to a gate made of steel on December 30, 1981. She was wearing a sign around her neck stating that she was Martha Ochoa's wife. Because the MAS Constitution forbids harming innocent children, her kidnapped daughter was returned to her family.

The MAS released a statement on February 6, 1982 stating that their patience was wearing thin. Martha Ochoa was uninjured on February 17.

Informants were treated the same way as kidnappers by the MAS. Brian Freemantle, in The Fix, says that the informant who informed the DEA of the first MAS meeting did not fare well. Before they killed him, his hands were tied behind the back with barbed wire and his tongue was cut.

The victory against the M-19 was a demonstration of what unity can do. Different groups began to realize the advantages of not competing with each other. They could all make more money if they combined their resources to ship cocaine to America. Independent operators began to work together in the production, distribution, and marketing of cocaine while still running their own businesses.

Trafficking methods were simplified in future meetings. They offered government officials plata o plomo, which is silver or lead. This meant that they could accept a generous amount of bribes or be executed. Officials knew that their network could access anyone in Colombia and they would be subject to the death penalty. The M-19 was under control, and officials accepted bribes. Medellin's cocaine business thrived. Traffickers from all over Colombia attended a meeting called by cartel leaders. The American market was split between the Medellin Cartels and Cali Cartels. Cali had New York. Medellin had Miami. Los Angeles was divided between them.

As business expands, so did the need for new ways to outwit the authorities. In remote areas of the jungle, massive cocaine labs were constructed. They became towns with their own housing and schools. To disguise jungle runways, houses on wheels were used. Cocaine was transported in fridges and TVs with hollow interiors. Electric industrial transformers that weighed more than 8,000 lbs were gutted and filled up with up to 4,000 kilograms. Mixing 23,000 kilo of cocaine with dried fish was the result. American and European chemists mixed cocaine to make plastic, metals, or liquid. Other chemists removed the cocaine at the destination. Cocaine was often mixed with fruits, wine, cocoa, and flowers. All kinds of drinks were made from liquid cocaine. It was used to soak lumber and clothing like jeans. Cocaine was made black by mixing it with black paint. It was chemically mixed into PVC, religious statues, and fibreglass shells for boats. Drug-sniffing dogs tested all of these methods.

Pablo purchased planes to transport cocaine, cash, including DC-3s - fixed wing propeller-driven airliners. He decided to invest his money in submarines. He decided to invest in submarines because he was afraid of being noticed. His brother built two subs with the help English and Russian engineers. Manufacturing was carried out in a quiet shipyard. They weighed in at around

1,000 kilos. They were unable to reach the shore so divers loaded the cocaine onto boats.

Pablo made $500,000 per day in 1982. This grew to $1 million by the mid-80s. Millions of dollars were hidden underground. However, ten percent of it was destroyed each year by rats and water damage. People were paid to live in apartments and houses with upwards of $5 million in Styrofoam-protected walls. Millions of dollars were stored in wooden boxes wrapped in Styrofoam and placed below swimming pools in storage cabinets. In ten different offices, accountants kept track of the money. Some of it was invested in famous paintings, antique cars, and property around the world. He never forgot the poor and continued to build schools, houses, hospitals, and give away truckloads upon truckloads of food. He also paid college tuition and built soccer fields.

Inadvertently, Panama received refrigerators with $7 million worth of cash that were intended for Colombia. The money vanished. Pablo calmly replied that sometimes he won and sometimes he lost. A plane carrying $15 million was lost in the jungle, and it exploded, igniting the money. Workers who had lost cash or drugs were given additional drugs to make up the difference. They were executed if they made a mistake again.

Pablo had plenty of murderers in Medellin. His reputation for extreme violence allowed him to expand his business. Gustavo de Grieff (an ex-Colombia Attorney General) claims that Pablo authorized the use of a hot knife to remove the eyeballs of victims while they were still living. A heated spike or nail was also used to puncture the skull of victims. This was fatal. One victim was tied to the tree with barbed wire and given a telephone to tell his family about his situation. He was then tortured to death as they listened.

Chapter 30

Lara Bonilla

Pablo ran for the presidency in an attempt to fulfill his childhood dream. He vowed to help the poor and sought to get exemption from laws that would allow him to be extradited.

Pablo knew a lot about politics, having so many of them on his payroll. Cartel members competed for the most powerful, much like they did with luxury cars, homes, and zoos. With brown envelopes stuffed with cash, cartel lawyers approached politicians. If they refused the bribe, they would be called asking if they would prefer to die. It was easy to answer yes, considering how many of their coworkers were taking money and the Colombian cocaine business bringing in so much wealth. Many felt that cocaine was America's problem, as it was consumed most often in America. Colombia would not produce cocaine if they didn't need it. Many Colombians saw the US dimly due to its history in Central and South America. This included supporting right-wing death squads, assassinating democratically-elected left-wing leaders, and a bloodlust after foreign resources. Some believed cocaine was the atomic bomb of the less-developed world against the US and that imperialism would be destroyed by its own excesses.

Pablo, who had built a power base in Medellin's barrios, was elected to Congress as an alternate in March 1982. This made him exempt from any prosecution under Colombian law.

Pablo wore chino pants, polo shirts, and a Rolex gold Rolex when he gave speeches as a politician. Pablo spoke softly and politely at the openings for soccer pitches, roller-skatingrinks, hospitals, and schools that he had invested in. He also started a radio program, Civics on the Mar, and Medellin Without Slums. Barrio Pablo Escobar was a project that included five hundred two-bedroom houses constructed over a garbage dump. It also provided truckloads of food. It was located in north Medellin. This area was a popular spot for Pablo, who was a recruiter for young enforcers and hit men. Pablo made the rounds while accompanied by two Catholic priests, who were board members at Medellin Without Slums. He was introduced at public events by the priests, and accompanied him through the slums. They also blessed the charity art auction that he hosted at Intercontinental Hotel, Paintbrush of Stars.

Pablo hired journalists and publicists to help him build his man-of the-poor image. Medellin Civico's column praised him: "Yes, I recall him... His hands, almost priest-like growing parabolas in the air of friendship and generosity. Yes, I do know him. His eyes are filled with tears because there isn't enough bread to feed all the nation's hungry. I've seen his despair when he looks at street children. They are angels without toys and without a future.

Pablo was dubbed "A Paisa Robin Hood" by Semana in April 1983. Pablo said that he started his business renting bicycles when he was sixteen. Then, a few years later, a company bought and sold automobiles. Finally, Pablo got involved with real estate. Although he didn't have much money, a member of my community, Semana, promoted the construction and creation of a scholarship fund for students in need.

In March 1982, Pablo was elected president. His goals were to make peace with the guerrillas, improve housing and education. His agenda did not include drugs. Why should we upset any feathers when the majority of politicians accept donations from traffickers? Many previous presidents have taken drug money. Those who didn't took drug money didn't last long in office. The traffickers loved the fact that the president declared he was opposed to extradition of Colombian citizens. They feared the possibility of living life sentences in America.

The Reagan-Bush administration was not satisfied. Reagan declared in 1982 that "my very reason for being present this afternoon isn't to announce another short term government offensive but to call for a national crusade to combat drug abuse, a sustained relentless effort by every segment of our country to eradicate this scourge."

Reagan-Bush tried to link FARC guerrillas to marijuana trafficking by intensifying the War on Drugs. The Reagan-Bush administration also attempted to incite war by labeling the 5,000-strong proCommunist army as "narco-guerrillas", hoping to provoke conflict. The propaganda was not believed by the Colombians. The outside interference had disrupted peace negotiations with the rebels, and the new Colombian president was furious. They changed their strategy. Reagan-Bush ordered their emissaries to search for a Colombian politician who was compatible with their goals. Rodrigo Lara Bonilla was the one they settled on.

Lara, who had studied law at the Externado University of Colombia at the age of 23, was elected mayor of his hometown. Lara, a member the New Liberalism Party he had helped to create, was elected as the mayor of his hometown in August 1983. He became the minister for justice. His anti-corruption campaign upset his bribe-dependent contemporaries. He attracted the attention of the DEA in Colombia who encouraged him to pursue the traffickers with help and support.

Pablo and his bodyguards arrived at Congress on August 16, 1983. It was packed full of reporters, photographers, and spectators. The hallways were filled with people ruminating about the confrontation between Lara and traffickers. Pablo, dressed in a cream suit and a tie, was stopped at the doors for not having a tie. Pablo was given a tie with a floral design by someone and allowed to enter. As he sat at the back, people closely observed him. The house president asked for the release of his bodyguards. Pablo nodded and they were off.

Jairo Ortega was Pablo's ally and began to address the allegations that Pablo had taken money from traffickers. He asked Lara if he knew Evaristo Porras Ardila.

Lara shook his head and said "No.".

Ortega stated that Evaristo Porras, a Leticia native and a drug trafficker from Amazonia, had been imprisoned in Peru. Porras wrote a cheque to Lara for one million pesos in April as a campaign contribution. He held up the cheque and showed it to ministers who were present for the debate. The cheque was distributed in copies. In a telephone call, he said that Lara had thanked Porras about the cheque. Ortega used a tape recorder to have an unintelligible conversation.

"Let Congress analyze the minister's conduct towards the person who offered him one million pesos. According to Peruvian police, Mr Porras has been identified as an international drug dealer. I will not attempt to stop the brilliant political career of the minister. I want him to let us know what morality he expects from the rest of us. Relax, Minister. Let the country know that you are the same moral person as Jairo Ortega, and all of us.

Carlos Lehder's gallery was filled with cheers, which other people tried to suppress. Pablo sat quietly in a leather swivel chair and watched, occasionally picking at his teeth or making an uncomfortably smile.

Lara, 35 years old, stood ready to answer in a business suit with tie. His thick dark hair was swept away and his charming face was shaved. He was not a person who is used to scrutinising the source of donations.

Lara stated that his life was an open book and that he was always blameless. This made him immune to the claims of his enemies. He said he would resign if suspicion was placed upon him, "knowing that my actions will not be followed up by complacent ministers affected from the blackmail, the extortion perpetrated against Colombian's political class." It's another to run a campaign entirely with these funds," Lara said.

"[We] have a congressman, Pablo, who was born in a very poor region, and then, after he has made astute business deals with bicycles and other items, creates Death to Kidnappers and nine planes. He also owns three hangars at Medellin's airport and creates charitable organizations with which he tries bribe vulnerable people. There are also investigations underway in the US regarding the criminal conduct of Mr Ortega's alternate. I can't tell you about them here in the House.

Some of the respondents supported Pablo. They claimed that they were all guilty of receiving tainted donations. Pablo was attacked so Lara could gain political capital.

A congressman stated that "only when Representative Escobar joined us movement that all kinds were thrown at him about the sources of his wealth." "I, as an elected official, do not have the power to investigate the origins of assets... Representative Escobar does not need to rely on anyone to defend his personal conduct which, to my knowledge, has not been subject to any lawful or government action."

Pablo didn't reply, his anger boiling over. He re-joined his bodyguards and walked out of the chamber into a crowd of reporters whom he attempted to dodge.

Lara was notified the next day that he had one day to prove his claims or he would be sued. Lara began gathering evidence and made statements critiquing drug-trafficking. He said that he had a day to prove his claims with evidence. My accusers couldn't forgive my clear denunciation Pablo Escobar, who has made a fortune through smart business deals. This is an economic power concentrated within a few hands and criminal minds. They can't get what they want by blackmail. They get it by murder.

Porras was interviewed by media and acknowledged that he donated a million pesos (a million) to Lara. He also admitted to being indicted for trafficking. This he attributed to youthful indiscretion. Porras, who worked in the coca leaf business for Pablo claimed that his wealth was derived from three winnings of the lottery. Lara, confronted by Porras' testimony admitted to receiving the cheque. He said it was for a family loan. Pablo requested that a judge investigate the cheque. The investigation was unsuccessful.

Lara was helped by El Espectador newspaper. It ran a story on Pablo's 1976 cocaine arrest, with mugshots of Pablo as well as Gustavo. Pablo ordered his men buy every copy of El Espectador, which increased sales and encouraged the newspaper's publication of daily stories about him. The article described how Pablo had played the system, having his case transferred to different courts and judges and how his criminal records disappeared. This led to an investigation into his murder and the deaths of the officers who arrested him. Pablo was granted a new arrest warrant, but the judge was killed in his car.

Lara obtained a recording from an ABC News documentary, DEA-assisted, about Colombia's largest traffickers. They included Pablo - who they claimed was worth $2Billion - and played it in Congress. Pablo demanded proof while giving Lara a death stare.

Pablo stated that his money was earned from construction, rebutting Lara's allegations. Although denying that he was trafficker, Pablo extolled the many benefits trafficking brought Colombia like creating jobs and capital for numerous projects that have contributed to economic growth. Pablo argued that the claims of trafficking were false and showed him a visa he had recently received from the US Embassy. The visa was cancelled by the embassy within days. Pablo criticized Lara for being an instrument of US foreign policies.

Lara remained firm. He revealed how traffickers had funded Colombia's major soccer teams. He attempted to cancel the licenses for 300 of their small planes. He tried to seize Pablo's zoo animals, and he named thirty politicians that he believed were involved in drug deals.

After the Supreme Court's decision in favor of America, a warrant was issued for Carlos Lehder's arrest on September 2, 1983. Lehder, who had already vanished, claimed that he knew it was coming "because my friends from the Ministry of Justice alerted us regarding Lara Bonilla's intentions." He also told reporters that the only way to extradite him was to his dead body.

Pablo was asked by Senator to give up his immunity as a parliamentary member and answer the charges against himself on September 10. Pablo refused to answer the charges against him on September 11.

Pablo was arrested for conspiring to murder DAS agents. This happened within two weeks. Two of them were executed in 1977. 1981 saw hit men riding motorbikes assassinating the officer in charge.

The Supreme Court ruled that two marijuana traffickers should be extradited in October. Lara signed it off, but the president rejected it. He referred the matter to the Colombian courts. Lehder's extradition request was not signed.

Lara demanded that Congress lift Pablo's immunity against extradition. Lara was praised by the newspapers while they reported Pablo's 1974 indictment for car theft. The largest newspaper asked: "How will democracy continue in Colombia if it's managed and manipulated by criminals?"

Pablo was fined 450,000 pesos on November 17, 1983 for illegally importing eighty-five animals including elephants and camels.

Pablo's evidence was so overwhelming, that he couldn't save his political career. He was expelled from the Colombian Liberal Party. In January 1984, he quit Congress and released the following statement: "The attitude taken by politicians is very different from the opinions and aspirations of the people."

His presidential plan had gone so wrong that the media was covering his cocaine business, and the police trying to get in on it. He fought back in court and got his extradition warrant withdrawn February 13, 1984.

Lara made a statement that upset traffickers after Pablo was killed by a politician who wanted Pablo to be extradited. I will not again refuse to extradite one of these dogs. The narcos will only fear US judges as long as Colombian judges fear drug dealers.

Pablo's men were watching Lara. His conversations were replayed back to him when he answered the phone. He declined large amounts of money offers. His death threats increased.

He retaliated by busting all the cocaine labs in the country. The DEA helped Colombian authorities locate a huge jungle lab known as the Land of Tranquillity. It was owned mainly by Gacha, the cartel leader. It had produced cocaine worth $12 million over two years. There were nearly 200 residents. It was 250 miles away from the nearest road, so authorities were aware of it.

Barry was apparently required by the cartel for his services because of the raid. Barry told the DEA that Jorge Ochoa had set up facilities in Nicaragua in response to the destruction of the raid. However, Dominic Streatfeild, author of Cocaine: An unauthorised Biography, quotes Jorge Ochoa saying that they knew that the raid was coming and that they had removed all the valuable stuff. The authorities then claimed that they had seized tons of cocaine, but that only chemicals were seized. Jorge denied ever transferring cocaine through Nicaragua. Barry had taken Barry's photos and he admitted that Pablo may have been involved in something in Nicaragua.

Roberto stated in Escobar that Pablo made a deal to construct a laboratory on an island off Nicaragua's coast. However, the lab never was built. It was used to refuel planes. This would mean that Barry was lying to George HW Bush and the DEA.

Pablo sent a statement to the US ambassador in which he denied any involvement in the Land of Tranquility. His conscience is clear." Lara was accused of being the representative of your government in Colombia's cabinet.

The Medellin Cartel decided it was time to let Lara go after the raid on Land of Tranquillity. Pablo controlled Los Quesitos who received the $500,000 contract. Three of the gang's field commanders took a green Renault loaded with guns and grenades from Medellin, Bogota, and equipped with bullet-proof vests. They settled into a four-star hotel and discussed the hit over food. The Snore was a Medellin hitman who had many kills under his belt and was available to help if the others failed. Ivan, a 30-year-old drifter, would act as the shooter. Ivan was a serial killer, robbery victim and had been assaulted. The driver was Byron, a teenage boy who wanted to be admired by the big boys. These teenagers, who were poor and had nothing to lose, were easy to recruit to perform hits. They could make thousands of dollars for each murder if they were unemployed or had only $1 per week. The team waited for several days before calling Medellin, then went out to eat.

Lara was encouraged by the US emissaries to extradite Pablo. They arrived with a bulletproof vest. "You should be more cautious. "You should be more cautious." Lara declined the vest but they took it with them.

Lara was aware of the danger to not only him, but his wife and three young children. Lara stated, "I am a dangerous minister to those who act beyond the law." "I hope they don't take us by surprise," Lara said. Lara then called the US Embassy and enthusiastically revealed that he was being transferred to Czechoslovakia to serve as ambassador.

The US Ambassador stated that "you'll be safe here." "All terrorists are within the government."

Lara stated that he needed somewhere to hide with his family and friends as the transfer would take 30 days. He felt the Colombian government could not protect him anymore. For as long as he needed, the US Embassy offered to place him in a safe house in Texas owned by a wealthy businessman.

Lara thanked his journalist friend for publishing an article on his work, April 30, 1984. "I am going be killed today. But that article can be mine will for the Justice Department." Lara played his friend fifty death threats he received that morning and then said to Lara, "If you don't answer the phone, it will mean that I am dead."

Ivan and Byron went to Santa Maria Auxiliadora near Medellin in the afternoon to say a prayer. Byron wore a picture of the Virgin Mary in his underwear to bring good luck. They boarded a Yamaha motorbike at 7 pm and set off for Bogota, armed only with grenades, a MAC10, and a motorcycle.

Lara sat in a back seat with his bulletproof vest beside him.

Ivan and Byron stopped by an address they had been given earlier in the day. They were told that Medellin was talking about them, which was coded for "Find Lara, kill him." As they searched for a Mercedes-Benz limo in white, the roads were still blocked. They spotted Lara around sunset. They weaved around cars and eventually came to a halt.

Ivan removed the MAC-10 from his jacket and took aim at the figure in back of the limo. The MAC-10 emptied its magazine and smashed the rear window. Lara was struck seven times in the neck, head, chest, and chest. Lara's escort limousine pursued the attackers. The Yamaha's gasoline tank was set on fire when a bullet struck it. The motorbike collided with a curb. Ivan was blown to pieces by machine gun fire. He was hit in the arm by the Yamaha and died. Byron was hit in the arm and was taken into custody.

The president and his cabinet discussed what to do until 3 AM. In Colombia, no cabinet minister has ever been assassinated. Maybe cocaine wasn't an American problem. The reputation of Colombia was being damaged by drug trafficking. It would seem that the president was losing control of the country with the departure of the justice minister. Lara's murder swayed them in favor of extradition. The president declared war on drug traffickers in an emergency radio broadcast and stated that they were "the greatest problem Colombia has ever faced in its history".

Lara's closed coffin was visited by thousands in the Rotunda of the Capitol Building. Military guards then took it to the National Cathedral. Outside, mourners of all ages were singing and crying for Lara. Emotions were high in the cathedral. The president seemed tense amid the top brass of the military and government.

Lara was flown by plane to his hometown, where he was buried. The president stated that "We have reached an important point in our country's history." What does the term citizen actually mean? Stop! Stop! Colombia will give criminals wanted by other countries to Colombia so they can be punished as an exemple." His eulogy was met with a standing ovation.

The president signed an order to extradite Carlos Lehder on May 8, 1984. Traffickers would be tried before military courts. They would also be denied bail. With limited parole options, prison sentences would increase.

Gun permits for suspected traffickers will be revoked.

Many were immediately arrested and taken into custody, including Fabio Sr., the father of the Ochoa brothers. Helicopters were seen landing at Hacienda Nápoles. Armed with rifles and search dogs troops stormed into the building, prompting raucous cawing by Pablo's exotic birds. The troops took weapons and evidence and threw them out. They also handcuffed the low-ranking workers who were gathered by a swimming pool. They left the animals at the zoo to starve after the raid. After receiving complaints from the public, the government reopened their zoo.

The traffickers responded by declaring war on Colombia. There was chaos: bombings. Kidnappings. Mass murders. Death squads. Lara's murder was investigated by a judge who was murdered.

The chaos created by the sale of arms to all sides, US weapon manufacturers made a profit. They accepted drug money as one form of payment through the CIA. While George HW Bush was putting Pablo on the War on Drugs' enemy list, secretly the CIA was facilitating drug smuggling in order to finance a war against Nicaragua. This was despite the fact that cocaine was flooding America. This covert activity required constant smokescreens and Pablo was the ideal choice. His crimes made him the American media's favorite cocaine scourge. However, journalists seldom mentioned that his cocaine empire was built on a black market that was created by US drug laws. George HW Bush was in a win-lose situation. Although he knew from America's previous experiences with alcohol prohibition that Pablo would not alter drug flow, fighting traffickers justified US military expenditures. It also allowed the US to expand its influence in Colombia, where oil and other resources were coveted by US banksers and corporations perched like vultures.

Chapter 31

Panama

Pablo hid in the jungle for a time until Lehder, Gacha, and the Ochoa brothers fled to Panama. They stayed in a large house near a golf course under the protection Manuel Noriega. Manuel Noriega was a military dictator who had been a CIA informant whose hospitality cost them millions. Pablo had authorized the deal with a $2 million down payment, just a few months prior to Noriega's rise to power.

Pineapple Face, named after his pockmarks and nicknamed Noriega, had been elected to power in Panama. The bomb was planted by the CIA in the plane of Noriega's predecessor. His leftist stance - he believed in democracy, the rights of the poor - had led him to reject Communism. Noriega was a master at playing all sides and had lucrative relationships with both the CIA (and the Colombian traffickers) who were supporting the Nicaraguan rebels in their fight against Communism. The cartel contributed to Nicaraguan causes in expectation of CIA protection. America's security was provided by Noriega for the Panama Canal. The American bases housed over 10,000 military personnel. His contributions to America's antiCommunism crusade include money laundering and hosting guns for-drugs flights for Nicaraguan rebels.

Pablo had made a deal in 1982 with Noriega. Panama was used to transship cocaine from America to America. Noriega received six-figure loads. Noriega also received fees from the billions of dollars that drug cartels and intelligence agencies like the CIA poured through Panama. Jeb Bush is alleged to have tapped into this money by establishing bank relationships between the CIA, the Medellin Cartels and the Cali Cartels. Jeb allegedly disguised drug money from oil industry revenues through front companies like Texas Commerce Bank while he was in Venezuela as a CIA director father.

The cartel leaders were protected by Noriega's bodyguards. They enjoyed swimming, playing golf, and working out at the gym. They eventually rented their homes. Barry and Jorge Ochoa met around this time in Panama.

Pablo wanted Panama to be a temporary hub. Noriega didn't like the idea. The agreement was to make Panama a transport point and not an operations center. Pablo received word from a Panamanian Colonel about Noriega's overtures to DEA. Noriega had authorized the construction of a Panama cocaine lab. However, his military confiscated 16,000 barrels of ether intended for the new lab, and arrested 23 Colombian workers. An angry group of cartel leaders demanded explanations, but were informed that Noriega was in Europe.

A meeting was organized for Noriega and the Colombians through President Fidel Castro. The cartel had attended a preliminary conference in Panama with the Panamanian government before Noriega arrived. The meeting ended with Noriega releasing the Colombian prisoners, and returning $3 million in cash as well as lab equipment to the cartel.

The cartel became homesick and distrustful towards Noriega. They tried to reach an arrangement with the Colombian government. They asked for consideration of the possibility of their reintegration into Colombian society in near future. Their memorandum gave a history of Colombian drug trafficking and stated that their organizations "control between 70 and 88% of Colombia's drug trade." This equated to an annual income of about $2 billion. Pablo offered to transfer billions of dollars from foreign accounts into Colombian banks and to end the cocaine empire. However, the deal was rejected.

The cartel lost 1.2 million tonnes of cocaine in the form of perfume cartons and frozen drugs to US Customs agents in Miami on June 15, 1984. The cargo plane transporting the cocaine was owned by a Panamanian charter company. 6159 drums of ether were confiscated by Panamanian authorities the following week.

Pablo advised fellow Colombians that they leave Panama. Private planes and helicopters arrived. The Colombians fled to Medellin (Brazil), Spain, and Brazil. Roberto claims that Pablo and his brother traveled to Nicaragua. Pablo brought 1,100 kilos cocaine with him in an attempt to convert it into cash.

Even though extraditions had started to America, things had settled down in Colombia after Lara's passing. Due to lack of evidence, corruption and other reasons, most of the people who were arrested following Lara's murder were released.

Pablo spoke from abroad and said that he knows that Pablo is involved in construction, industry, and ranching. The fact that Pablo attacks extradition doesn't make him extraditable.

Traffickers never stopped putting pressure on authorities. They had obtained the private telephone number of the president, which had scared the president, and were issuing threats.

A man approached a judge outside a courthouse and asked for a temporary dismissal. He was indicted by the cartel for Lara's murder. "Ask for anything you want and they'll place it wherever you want it in Colombia or elsewhere... You can then relax. "Neither your life nor your family's will be at risk," the judge said. Five men from a Mazda shot him as he climbed into a taxi.

US Embassy staff were transported by armoured vehicles. The children were transported to school by armed jeeps equipped with machine guns. Staff kept an eye out for motorbike assassins on the roads. Some people kept their windows closed to hear the motorbike approaching. They heard gunshots every night in their secure living areas. A car carrying an empty object aimed at the Embassy rolled down a hill and hit a curb. It exploded sending flames three hundred yards into the air. The staff of the Embassy was reduced to a minimum.

Locals who were working with the Americans were brutally murdered. One victim had pins inserted underneath his fingernails before he was shot in the head. A sign around his neck read: "Killed For Being a DEA informant." The DEA closed the Medellin office after Pablo learned that a guerrilla hit crew had been hired to kidnap key members.

Pablo believed it safe to return home in the second half of 1984. Pablo convened a meeting with seventy people of importance, from traffickers to priests. He arrived with 200 bodyguards. The topic of extradition was raised. Pablo suggested that Medellin have a single group of bodyguards, divided into zones. Gacha was the most powerful of the Medellin Cartel's four founders, while Lehder was losing power. Lehder was given the responsibility of overseeing jungle operations and maintaining relations with the guerrillas that guard the labs.

The arrival of a Mercedes at the farmhouse came just after midnight the night before the meeting. A well-dressed woman appeared. The woman knocked at the door, claiming to have flowers for Dr Hernandez. Roberto informed her that she was not at the right address. Roberto warned his brother that he had never seen anyone from the flower-delivery industry arrive in a Mercedes-Benz. Pablo dismissed the incident as trivial. Roberto ordered the bodyguards, to shoot in the air if anyone appeared.

Shots were fired at 2 AM. Pablo and his brother fled the back of the farmhouse with their guns. Roberto was hit in the leg by a shot and brick fragments struck him in his face. This caused a lot of bleeding. One of their bodyguards was returning in a car when they came upon them. Gustavo and Gustavo escaped from the car.

Cali's trafficker, who had a history with Medellin, attended the meeting at the farmhouse. He then snitched Pablo out in the hope of a government guarantee against extradition.

Pablo had paid $50,000 per month to the colonel who was in charge of the raid. Pablo wrote to him, "Now you're against me and I know what you think about that."

Jorge Ochoa was in trouble in Spain after he emigrated with Cali Cartel's boss. He settled in an 8,000-square-foot home with a swimming pool and tennis courts. Four Mercedes-Benz were also available. The Special Prosecutor of Spain for the Prevention and Repression of Drug Trafficking was told by an informant that Ochoa was living in Madrid under a false name, Moises Moreno Miranda. The two Colombian bosses were arrested along with their wives on November 15, 1984. In an effort to capitalize on the money, the Americans made offers to the Spanish to get the Colombians extradited. It was the beginning of a long legal battle.

Even forming an army called the Death to Kidnappers wasn't enough to deter criminals in volatile Colombia. Pablo's father was abducted by policemen in 1985. Six men riding in a jeep pulled him over while he was on his way to Pablo's farm. They tied up the workers and drove him away. They wanted $50,000,000.

Pablo's mother was furious when she learned the truth. She spent hours crying, yelling, and praying after her son's death. Pablo said that even if their father was beaten, the ransom money they received wouldn't cover their burials.

Pablo remained calm and devised a plan to capture his kidnappers. His father required medicine for open-heart surgery. Security cameras were installed in many of the Medellin's two-hundred drugstores. He put cameras in the ones that didn't have them. He offered a reward if anyone bought the heart medication his father required. Two kidnappers were found. Pablo instructed people to tune in to a particular radio station, as the kidnappers were using payphones. The station broadcast a song dedicated Luz Marina whenever Pablo was called by the kidnappers. The transmitters were heard by the listeners and they ran to the nearest payphone.

Pablo's brother managed to negotiate a ransom of $1 million in just 18 days. The ransom was paid in duffel bags that had electronic tracking devices. The kidnappers then took the money to a farm. The house was attacked from all directions and was surrounded. Pablo sentenced three of the kidnappers to death. His father was unharmed.

Pablo was wrong to think that Colombia wasn't as safe as Pablo believed. He was accompanied by bodyguards and moved around extensively with extra precautions.

Chapter 32

The Extraditables

Pablo met Ivan Marino Ospina after the MAS began to eliminate the guerrillas that kidnapped Martha Ochoa. Ospina presented Pablo with the sword of Simon Bolivar, the Venezuelan military leader who helped Colombia achieve independence from Spain in 1810. Jaime Bateman was the founder of M-19. He had taken the sword, a symbol for unfulfilled liberation, from a museum in 1974. He announced that he would not return it until the government made peace with the M-19. Pablo initially hung it on a wall. He eventually gave it to his nephew to hide.

The relations between the guerrilla groups of the cartel and them were in flux. However, after the handing of the sword, Pablo and Ivan had maintained a friendship. The M-19 is known for their spectacular attacks on the government. Pablo was inspired to target the government's extradition files, which are located in Bogota's Palace of Justice. Pablo might be able to take control of the country if he can inflict terror on the Colombian judiciary. He would go after the Supreme Court.

Six of the 105 Colombians on the US list were expelled by September 1985 and nine were already in prison. Pablo founded a group called "The

Extraditables" with the motto: "Better to a grave in Colombia than in a prison cell in the US." The cartel leaders made an agreement that they would kill themselves rather than die in a American prison. They preferred to kill themselves behind the ears, circumventing the skull to allow a bullet to enter the brain.

Pablo's intimidation techniques against judges have been refined since his initial arrests. A bright, young and well-dressed lawyer would visit a judge in a narcotics matter. He would carry a briefcase. He would place a brown envelope on the desk of the judge.

A lawyer might say, "You have a choice. The lawyer would say, "You have a choice. You can have silver, bullet in the head, or lead. Some money is a payoff." It's your choice." If the judge evaded, the lawyer would reach into his briefcase to find a photo album that contained photos of the judge's closest family and friends. The pictures included their children leaving their home at dawn, going to school, playing on the playground, and talking with friends... Most judges were convinced by the threat of losing their entire family.

Pablo was just about to perfect his tactics once again. The Extraditables wrote to the Supreme Court justices requesting that they declare illegal the extradition treaty. These letters were not intended to provide any evidence to police officers. Block letters were used. These letters were signed either by the Extraditables, or Manuel. Pablo didn't write the letters on behalf of Extraditables, but he wanted people know that he had authored them. He wrote the letter in his own handwriting and signed it with his name. Many people wondered if Pablo was the Extraditables. Others thought he was just a front.

The Extraditables obtained justices' private numbers and threatened them. The justices were terrified after receiving a ruling on extradition. The justices received more letters stating that the Extraditables knew everything about their lives.

We declare war on you. We declare war on your family members. We know where they are, and we will take your family with us. We don't have compassion - we can do anything, absolutely anything.

On November 6, 1985, the Palace of Justice hosted a full-blown pomp and circumstance in the Protocol Salon of The National Palace. National anthems were being played. In the courtyard, armed grenadiers marched. Although the gunfire was initially difficult to hear through the noise, people began to wonder what was happening when they heard the marching boots.

At 11:40, hundreds of guerrillas armed with machine guns, rifles and grenades stormed the Palace. They attacked security guards, joined their compatriots in civilian clothing and stormed the Palace. They had nearly 300 hostages by the time they reached their destination, which included most of the justices. Others hostages included secretaries, lawyers, shoe shiners, and shopkeepers. They erected machine guns on top of the furniture, and blocked stairs with guerrillas. They demanded that the highest court in the country bring the president to trial for breaking his promise to create peace.

Some hostages were saved by the police, but they were repulsed with gunfire. The army arrived with tanks, helicopters, grenade launchers and hundreds of soldiers with hard helmets. They positioned themselves against different walls to provide cover. They launched rockets at the huge building's masonry façade, causing holes in its walls. The sidewalk was littered with debris. The entrance door was smashed by rockets and tank fire. Helicopters flew up to the roof and troops were greeted by sniper fire from the skylights. Machine-gun fire was fired at those who were able to gain entry. The guerrillas remained in control of the building for a day.

Around 7 p.m. the next day, smoke began to penetrate the building. The fire spread to the wooden building walls, where it was ignited by burning files. Some of the hostages on the top floor started to gag and cough, and they were eventually taken down by the guerrillas. They were placed on top of 60 hostages, who were all crammed into a small bathroom. Some were bleeding. Some had stopped breathing. The air was stale from sweat and bodily fluids.

The troops gathered to enter the building in the afternoon. The president authorized a military attack instead of complying to the guerrillas demand for negotiations. The front door was rammed by a tank and troops stormed in. They ordered the living to be raised and sorted through the bodies. The army decimated all hostages who were forced out of the doors. Some of the hostages were thrown out by the army, and some were left bleeding and/or dead from the impact of grenades. Guerrillas tossed bodies down the stairs, including one justice who appeared dead but was still breathing. His artificial leg was also torn by a bullet. The injured justice crawled up the stairs and to the cellar after the guerrillas had left the area. He gathered energy and raised his arms. "Don't shoot!"

Around one hundred people died in the bloodbath. This included eleven justices, half of the Supreme Court. All guerrillas, eleven police officers and soldiers died. Some survivors vanished immediately after the attack, and the government is suspected of their murder.

The role of the cartel was not obvious at first. Roberto Escobar said that the Extraditables funded the operation to destroy the records, not mass murder. The traffickers offered to double the fees to the guerrillas if negotiations with the government had been successful.

The government's failure to negotiate was criticized by survivors, including the justice who was thrown down with the bodies. The survivors were not able to attend the funeral of the president in the church for the deceased justices.

Some people left Pablo after that, while others worked for the government, which included many judges.

The violence escalated into 1986 when journalists, judges, and prosecutors were killed by motorbike-riding hit men.

Chapter 33

War

The Medellin Cartel was beginning to show weakness, and the Cali Cartel began to take aim at it in the late 1980s. Both had different organisational structures. Cali, on the other hand, was managed by a four-man executive committee. The Medellin was an alliance of independent operators. The board included engineers, accountants, lawyers, and the rest of the workforce. Some of the executives had law degrees and considered themselves to be sophisticated. They were known as the gentlemen in trafficking, while Medellin members were called thugs. According to the New York DEA's head, they would kill you if necessary, but prefer to have a lawyer.

Pablo wanted the cartels to work together against the government, but the Cali Cartel refused to oblige. Instead, the Cali Cartel made a deal with authorities that its business operations would be allowed to continue in return for information about the Medellin Cartel. The Cali Cartel revealed to the Medellin Cartel's enemies the location of Pablo's hiding and safe houses. These enemies included paramilitaries and special units from Colombian police that were assigned to Pablo's search. Although they claimed to be after Pablo to end his illegal cocaine trade, these authorities were actually working with Cali Cartel who were also in Pablo's business and were growing thanks to their assistance.

Pablo fled Monaco with his family after he had eaten dinner. It was a reinforced steel building. He fled to a farm 10 miles away. A bomb went off in Monaco at 5:30 AM, alarming people two miles away. The building was completely destroyed. Roberto arrived and Pablo claimed that he knew the perpetrator. Pablo said that he knew who was responsible for the explosion half an hour later.

Pablo was aware that Gilberto had been in Spain as a bombmaker for Basque guerrillas. Pablo tracked down the bomb-maker, offered him training for his workers, and promised him great prices on cocaine for sale in Spain. Pablo then asked the bomb-maker if he had ever worked in Colombia. He said that he had met someone in prison who had brought him to Colombia to train them to make a bomb against the government. Pablo, surrounded by armed guards, said that the bomb had been used against him. The bombmaker was now completely white. Pablo encouraged him to not worry and to get Pablo's workers trained in bomb manufacturing.

Gilberto called Pablo to protest that Pablo had not done anything. Pablo advised him to stop lying, and to prepare to be hit.

Pablo's mother was attacked by a car bomb at 4 AM. She was cut by glass and taken to the hospital. The fourth-floor was also where his six-month-old sister, who was also pregnant, had been sleeping. She gave birth in hospital to a baby who had to be kept alive for several weeks in an incubator. A fifth-floor sister was also treated for shrapnel injuries.

Cali Cartel offered Pablo $5 million to get his killers. Pablo hired the killers by himself, exposing Cali's money-grabbing ways. Pablo ordered the destruction of drugstores Cali had laundered their cash through.

In 1989, bombs were popping almost every day, and many international mercenaries joined the hunt to find Pablo.

Chapter 34

The Cathedral

Pablo used a strategy to kidnap elite hostages and negotiate with the government. Pablo wanted to surrender to La Catedral del Valle (a prison he built himself), which was located on a mountainous slope above the Honey Valley at 7,000 feet above the sea level. This would allow the guards and occupants to see any dangers from a bird's eye view. Fog in the evenings and dawn made it difficult to launch a surprise attack from the air. This provided an opportunity for the occupants of the prison to escape unnoticed if necessary. The forest was dense with wildlife, including sloths, armadillos and large iridescent butterflies, so they could easily lose their trackers.

Pablo had registered the building and 30,000 m2 of land in the name of a friend, an old ironmonger. Pablo requested that only local guards be present and that the police and army had no involvement in it. The Cathedral was named after the mayor of Envigado who approved the transfer.

It had cement floors, tile roofs, and green metal doors. The administration section was once a farmhouse. It contained three rooms: a kitchen and a courtyard. It contained a large dormitory, library and study, as well as six cells each with their own bathrooms. A large dayroom had four showers, six toilets, and a dressing area. It was being renovated by seventy men who worked around the clock. Because it was difficult to access, furniture had been brought in on mules: water heaters and military cots, yellow tubular armchairs, potted plant...

Pablo requested a permanent army of bodyguards to guard the prison, despite its security. "I won't surrender alone," he stated, while noting that he would not abandon his associates to the Elite Corps. He also said that keeping his network close allowed him to continue his operation. This was added insurance.

Pablo and Roberto dug up weapons near their designated cell. Roberto was told by Pablo that they would need the weapons one day.

Pablo arrived by helicopter. He was escorted out by fifty blue-clad guardsmen who pointed guns at him.

He replied like thunder: "Lower all your weapons, damn it!"

Before their commander gave the same order, the guns were taken down.

They marched to a house that contained the official delegation, Pablo's men who had surrendered, and his wife.

Pablo was shaken by the prison director. "Senor Escobar. "I'm Lewis Jorge Pataquiva."

Pablo reached for a trouser leg and revealed a Sig Sauer 9 mm pistol. It had a gold monogram on it. The handle was made of mother-of-pearl. He removed each bullet and threw it on the ground, as the crowd looked in awe. Pablo was trying to express his confidence in the warden, whose appointment had been a concern. Pablo informed his brother via a mobile phone that he had surrendered. He addressed the journalists and said that his surrender was an act for peace. "I gave up when I saw the National Constitutional Assembly working to strengthen Colombian democracy and human rights."

Pablo began to change his surroundings to fit him by spending some of the millions that he had smuggled into prison. Pablo kept his cash in milk containers, along with fresh fish and rice cans. These items were allowed inside as they were food rations. The excess money was hidden near the soccer field, as well as in underground tunnels that could be accessed through trapdoors within the cells. Helicopters were used to transport cash from the Cathedral to employees who needed it.

He also added a bar, lounge, and disco where he hosted weddings and other events. The Cathedral was the scene for famous people, models, politicians, and soccer players dancing and cavorting. He also installed a sauna in his gym and Jacuzzis in his bathrooms. He had a rotating bed in his bedroom and two additional beds for his family. Pablo was able to spend more time with his family, which was one of the greatest benefits of not being on the run. A gold-framed portrait depicting the Virgin Mary was placed above his bed.

Roberto's son drove a truck loaded with soda crates to conceal the contraband. He was able to smuggle large items like computers and large-screen TVs in. Women were also allowed in by the truck. Even though there were restrictions on visits to official days of the week, people kept sneaking in. Fake walls in vans could hold up to twenty people. This entry method was perfect for those who wanted to keep their visits secret, such as politicians and criminals.

Pablo's vast record collection was present, including albums signed in Las Vegas by Frank Sinatra and Elvis records bought during a Graceland visit. His books included Bibles and Nobel Prize winners. His novels were by Gabriel Garcia Marquez, and Stefan Zweig (a prominent Austrian writer of the 1920s). He had several movies on videotape, including The Godfather trilogy and films starring Chuck Norris. Pablo had valuable paintings on his wall, while most prisoners had posters. Pablo's closet was filled with neatly pressed jeans and shirts, as well as Nike sneakers. Some of them had spikes to protect him from fleeing. Pablo did not tie the laces on his sneakers. It was believed that if he did so, something dangerous would happen. Pablo could turn off all lights from the prison's interior with a remote control in case of danger.

Cabins were built further up the slope to provide privacy for female visitors as well as hiding places in the event of an attack on the prison. They were brightly painted and featured sound systems and fancy lamps. To allow for quick escape and to let the prisoners walk in the freshest air, paths were built into the forest.

Because the location was within easy sight of his family's home he set up a telescope to see his wife and kids while calling them. His daughter was given a playhouse and it was filled with toys.

Night lights were installed on the soccer field and wires placed above it to stop helicopter landings. Pablo was able to play centre forward despite having a bad knee. His associates made shrewd allowances by giving him the ball to score winning goals. Pablo's men won every game against professional teams. Pablo always had a backup in case he became tired. After he had regained energy from rest, he would rejoin the group. The guards provided refreshments for the players. His lawyers sometimes had to wait hours for him to be seen if he was playing football.

Pablo was concerned about being poisoned and so the Stomach Brothers introduced two chefs. He enjoyed beans and pork, eggs, and rice. For the prisoners, he had installed weights and bikes to help them get in shape. However, once they stopped being on the run and had unlimited food and alcohol access, they began to gain weight.

The Cathedral was renamed "Club Medellin" (or "Hotel Escobar") by Hustler magazine. An illustration of Pablo and his friends in prison throwing darts at President George HW Bush was published. Pablo obtained the illustration from Hustler magazine and hung it up on his wall.

Communication was a top priority. Pablo owned cell phones, radio transmitters and a fax machine. He also had beepers. Roberto denies that Pablo used carrier-pigeons, as claimed by other authors.

Pablo's cocaine business flourished because the government protected him rather than hunting him down.

Prison security agents from DAS discovered that the Cali Cartel had purchased four bombs in El Salvador and was trying to purchase a plane to drop them at the Cathedral. The guards began firing at planes that flew too close to the prison.

Pablo employed thirty lawyers to help him with legal issues. He was accused of being the intellectual author in the assassination of Galan, the presidential candidate. One of Pablo's accomplices was charged with being a participant in the attack on Avianca Flight 203. During an investigation of Pablo's property, authorities discovered paperwork that linked Pablo to Guillermo Cano, a journalist.

Pablo spent most of his time reading or calling the telephone when he wasn't with his lawyers. He attempted to learn Mandarin. He would sit in a rocking seat and watch Envigado's lights at night, thinking about his family.

Pablo received many letters asking for money, advice or help. Pablo would often send them money if their stories were confirmed. Pablo sent a teenager a picture of himself in a wedding gown and a letter in which he offered his virginity in return for paying her college tuition. After she confirmed her story, he paid her fees without accepting her offer. Pablo was also sought out by people who gathered at the prison gates with money and notes.

Pablo turned forty-two on December 1, 1991. He celebrated with a party at the Cathedral where his friends ate caviar, pink salmon, and listened to live music. A Russian fur hat was one of his gifts. He was photographed wearing it and declared that it would become his trademark.

Pablo went on trips to Medellin to see soccer matches at the stadium he had built. To allow his cars access, the police diverted traffic. He went to a mall to shop for Christmas. He celebrated the one-year anniversary his surrender by going to a nightclub with his family and friends.

No construction company was willing to take on the task of building a maximum security prison that would transfer Pablo from the American model. One man said, "We are not going to build the cage with the lion already in it." Finally, an Israeli security expert tried to construct it with apparently corrupt workers. Pablo's men began to write down the license plates of the workers and attacked many, leading to them all being forced to quit. The project was abandoned.

The attorney general's office published photographs taken at Hotel Escobar in early 1992. It included photos of waterbeds and Jacuzzis. The embarrased president requested an investigation. However, the justice minister determined that the furnishings were legal as each prisoner was allowed to have a bed and a bath tub, and TVs were allowed for good behavior.

The president declared, "I want all these things removed immediately!" "Tell the army that you want everything taken out immediately!" Escobar must know that we aren't kidding.

The job was not wanted by any government department. The minister of defense said, "No way." "I can't do it because it doesn't cost me the people." He refused to accept the assignment even though he had 120,000 troops.

The police could not do it because of the agreement with Pablo. DAS stated that they could not act as they were only permitted to enter the prison in the case of riots.

A lawyer was instructed to get a truck and workers and go to prison to collect the goods. The lawyer replied, "What have you ever done to me?" "Why did you assign me this assignment?"

The lawyer hoped that the truck would not be allowed into the prison so that he could return home. Pablo opened the prison gate and welcomed them inside.

Pablo replied, "Certainly Doctor. These things were not something I knew. Please take all the items out." Pablo and his men helped them transport the goods until they were gone.

He ran to his boss, armed with photographs of the prison in its naked state. All of the goods were being returned to the Cathedral while the president was looking at the photos.

Pablo claimed that his imprisonment was a personal act of sacrifice for all traffickers, for whom he had single-handedly gotten rid of extradition.

They were required to pay a tax to offset the benefits they received. Pablo, thanks to his vast communications network, was able to keep up with everything outside of prison. He was reprimanded severely for those who attempted to cheat him or were believed to have swindled his tax.

Pablo's close friends Fernando Galeano, and Kiko Moncada ran two of Pablo's most lucrative trafficking organizations. Pablo had set up a route through Mexico to allow them to smuggle cocaine into America. The Cathedral heard that they had been deceitful to Pablo. He viewed their deceit and plot to take over his organization. Pablo discovered where the money was hidden. His men took $20 million. Galeano, Moncada and Moncada denied Pablo's claims. Galeano and Moncada asked him for it back. He said he would like to talk about it at the prison.

Pablo gave Moncada and Galeano a lecture on everything he had done for them. Roberto claims that they were killed shortly after leaving the Cathedral. Popeye killed Moncada, and Otto shot Galeano. Their brothers were also murdered within days. Their devastated families begged Pablo for proper burials and Pablo gave them the address.

Pablo demanded all property belonging to their organizations. They told their employees that Pablo was their boss. Many of their key employees thought they would die when they were smuggled through a tunnel into the Cathedral to attend a meeting.

Pablo declared an emergency. Pablo said, "Your bosses have already died. I'll now take all their resources. He reminded them that he was their boss. He assured them that they would all be safe if they paid the tax.

The DEA created a version of events based upon an informant's statements:

Escobar claimed that, while he and his associates were in prison and needed money to fight the Cali Cartel's expensive war, Galeano, Moncada, and Galeano preferred to store their money until it turned moldy, rather than using it for their friends. Escobar convinced other cartel members, who really liked Moncada, that if they were not killed, then the Medellin Cartel could be at war with itself and all would die.

The news of the murders in Galeano, Moncada and others spread quickly. This made the president seem weak for not taking action. George HW Bush, and the Cali Cartel, were two of Pablo's greatest enemies. They were insisting on the government to get rid of Pablo by either moving him to another prison where he could be assassinated or extraditing to the USA, where he would never escape from prison.

Roberto said to Pablo that he was feeling something terrible. He asked Pablo to look into it. Pablo was informed by the government and military personnel that he had to leave the Cathedral. He was informed that George HW Bush threatened to invade Colombia, claiming that the government wasn't capable of exchanging Pablo.

The Cathedral was spotted by military trucks. Pablo was informed by officials that they were coming to talk to him.

Roberto and Pablo's weapons, which were buried before they arrived at the Cathedral, were found. Pablo also carried a Uzi across his shoulders, along with the pistol in his pants. They used the fog to cover them as they approached the perimeter. Roberto, who was surrounded by soldiers, used wire cutters to cut through the electrified fence. This created a gap large enough for someone to pass through.

Pablo tried to contact the president while he was preparing to flee.

Pablo said to his men, "Either you flee or all of us die." Roberto and he entered a secret room and seized a lot of cash. Roberto used his emergency remote to control the darkness in the prison, scaring everyone inside, including the hostages, to stop spy planes.

Pablo listened to different radio stations reporting on Pablo's story. One radio station claimed that he had been captured and was flying to America. Another claimed that the military had taken control of the Cathedral, and that many lives were lost.

He was worried about the news reaching his family. "Don't worry. Listen to the news. He is currently resolving the matter directly with the president." He hung up and called his mother to reassure him. Pablo sat down and tied his shoes. "Roberto! Let's get our radios on one frequency!"

Pablo instructed his men to walk through the holes Roberto had made in the fence. They were covered by rain, fog, and darkness. Most of the men were wearing army fatigues in an attempt to blend into the military units around the prison. Pablo went first. He stood up to observe the others emerge and all that was going on around him.

Roberto lost his way due to poor visibility. Roberto wandered around in fear, and he finally found the hole in the fence around 2 AM.

The group began to descend a slippery, wet surface that could cause injury or even death. The group was confronted with a rock face and the bravest one went first. They walked down another slope together, despite the pain from the thorny vegetation. The fog began to thin and visibility improved after two hours. They realized they had gone in circles and weren't far from the prison.

They exchanged shock and frustration. They had to move because they could be shot. Pablo said that they only had two hours to evacuate the area.

They reached El Salado when the sun was rising. People went to work, and the children went to school. Pablo and his men arrived in filthy, ripped clothes. They set out for Memo's farm, a friend and trusted source.

They knocked at the door. They knocked on the door. The groundskeeper answered but didn't recognize them. He finally realized what it was and allowed them to enter. They took off their soaked clothes and rolled them up to relieve tiredness. They finally got to rest after their clothes were washed.

A frantic banging sound came from the door about an hour later. They grabbed their guns and prepared for a gunfight. The door opened. The neighbours arrived with hot breakfast for the guests. Others stayed on the streets to keep an eye out for the army. Pablo and his men washed themselves and changed into fresh clothes.

Five of Pablo's men were captured in the raid. Seventy-eight guards were arrested on suspicion of cooperating in the raid with Pablo.

Pablo was having coffee at Memo's home and listening to radio reports while helicopters buzzed overhead. Roberto's son called radio stations and said that the family was hiding under the prison in a tunnel with weapons and food. A reporter asked him if Pablo would surrender to him and go back to the Cathedral if the original terms of the agreement were restored.

In an effort to find the tunnel, the government sent equipment to the prison so that troops could begin digging. The fields were exploding with explosives.

Pablo viewed the activity through a glass. Pablo looked through a window at the activity. He said that the only thing they would find was the money in the barrels, which he meant the $10 million that had been buried.

Radio reported that Pablo had ordered assassination all top government officials. Numerous hoaxe bomb threats and evacuation drills in schools were common.

The president called for calm on TV and promised to save the lives of the escapees if they surrendered. However, he never mentioned reinstating Pablo's original agreement.

Some US news outlets reported Pablo and his men stormed out from the prison in a hailing of gunfire, their guns blazing. These stories prompted support for George HW Bush's decision to send troops to Colombia to capture Pablo and imprison him in America.

The men left Memo's when it was dark and began to trek through the woods. As the troops searched for the tunnel, the Cathedral was still exploding. Pablo called his family from another farm and asked them to ignore the news. They ate, then set off to go again.

Five German Shepherds fired at them from the outside of a farm. The dogs were too loud to be shot because it would have alerted authorities. El Mugre bit one of the legs, drawing blood. Pablo gave the dogs snacks to distract them. Pablo stayed with the dogs, while others went on. He then followed everyone.

They arrived at a friendly farm around 3:30 AM. Roberto was taken by a driver to his mother so that he could tell the story. Although he didn't want the wait, his mother insisted that he and Pablo eat. Roberto refused to leave, and he sat at the window watching for police.

Roberto returned to his farm to find that some members of the group had left. Pablo believed it would be more difficult to find them if they broke up. In an effort to flush them out, more soldiers kept arriving at the Cathedral area. They stayed on the farm for two days, listening to radio and watching TV reports.

Pablo made a statement on July 24, 1992. He offered to surrender if the Cathedral would allow him to return to it. Pablo stated that the troops' arrival had taken him by surprise. "As regards the aggression against us, it is not yet our intention to take any violent actions. We are ready to continue the peace process and surrender to justice if we can guarantee that we will remain at the Envigado prison [the Cathedral] and also hand over control of the prison to the special forces of United Nations.

He said that he was in Colombia's jungles, which led to the government sending soldiers and helicopters there.

After being at the farm for twenty-days, 5,000 soldiers arrived to assist them. They ran into the forest, escaping into the jungle, as helicopters arrived. The army continued dropping bombs, but failed to find their location. They slept in hammocks for twelve days, occasionally being awakened by explosions around them.

Chapter 35

Los Pepes

George HW Bush used Pablo's escape to distract from domestic problems and boost his popularity. His chances of being reelected would be greatly increased if he caught the man he had called the largest cocaine trafficker in the country. Bogota's DEA sent a cable from Washington:

The BCO [the US Embassy in the local area] believes that Escobar may have finally crossed his self-perceived illegal boundaries and is now in a precarious situation. Escobar's bravado and gall could lead to his downfall. The GOC [government in Colombia] has never refused to comply with Escobar's demands. The current situation gives the GOC an opportunity to show its commitment to bring all narcotraffickers to justice. This includes Pablo Escobar, the most dangerous and notorious cocaine trafficker in history.

George HW Bush sent Centra Spike, DEA, FBI, ATF, CIA, Bureau of Alcohol, Tobacco and Firearms, and the army, navy, and air force to Pablo amid rumors that Pablo might assassinate and set off bombs in America. Centra Spike was the fastest to achieve results, flying planes above Medellin using technology that recognized Pablo's calls.

Pablo replied to America's involvement by sending a fax:

We, the Extraditables, declare that if Mr Pablo Escobar is ever hurt, we will hold President Gaviria accountable and again launch attacks against the entire country. We will attack the United States Embassy and plant the most dynamite in history. We declare that President Gaviria is responsible for all this mess. We will immediately launch attacks across the country if Pablo Escobar and any other suspects turn up dead. We are very grateful.

George HW Bush approved a $2million reward for information that led to Pablo. For any useful information, the US Embassy in Colombia offered relocation to America and $200,000 The reward program was advertised on television and featured pictures of Pablo as well as his henchmen.

The authorities were able to discover that Pablo was using at most eight cell-phones through the Centra Spike surveillance. He saw himself as a victim in violation of his agreement with government and desired to return to the Cathedral. Pablo's liberation allowed the Americans to retarget his location for assassination. The Delta Force arrived and trained the Colombians. Centra Spike returned to the case. His enemies multiplied.

The CIA collaborated with Los Pepes (People persecuted Pablo Escobar), a death squad that included ex-members of the Medellin Cartel as well as police officers frustrated by the laws that prevent them from using the same force against Pablo. Los Pepes had one mission: to retaliate against Pablo and his family, and his associates, for every terrorist act that injured innocent people. Los Pepes was provided intelligence by and funded by the Cali Cartel.

Los Pepes had inside information about Pablo's organization and kidnapped and tortured anyone they could find, including his family and workers, as well as lawyers and accountants. Many of his workers fled to the Cali Cartel which flourished. Although the Americans claimed they were in Colombia to stop the supply of cocaine, the Americans were actually passing intelligence to Los Pepes, the Cali Cartel and those who were increasing America's cocaine supply.

Los Pepes members, which included policemen, used terror and torture methods that were taught to them by the Search Bloc. Pablo was able to burn down one of his mother's homes and set fires to several other Pablo's homes. Outside Pablo's apartment, bombs went off. His aunt and mother were injured by a bomb that was dropped on a ranch house.

Pablo wrote a note in which he blamed Colonel Martinez for the recent head of the Search Bloc:
Your supervision allowed car bombers to attack buildings in El Poblado where my relatives reside. Your terrorist actions will not stop me fighting under any circumstance, I want you to know. Your threats and car bombs that you used against my family are now added to the many young people who were murdered in Medellin at your school Carlos Holguin headquarters for torture. I hope the Antioquian community is aware of your handling of the dynamite that you seize and the criminal acts of men wearing ski masks. Because you are part the government, I want to warn you that I will take vengeance against any relatives of government officials who do not punish you for your crimes. Remember that you also have a family.

Pablo's warning didn't stop Los Pepes from getting to work on their mission of annihilating all Medellin Cartel personnel. Los Pepes had the Medellin Cartel organisational charts from Centra Spike and the CIA. They knew who to target in order to cause maximum damage. They made Pablo's associates aware of their plans and offered reward for information.

A low-ranking cartel manager was found murdered in February 1993. The sign that was attached to his neck read: "For working with the narcoterrorist and baby-killer Pablo Escobar." Colombia. Los Pepes." Pablo's associates and employees were killed by them up to six times a day. One of these included a director of National Police of Colombia who was on Pablo's payroll. Multiple times, they shot the man responsible for financing operations in the head. Pablo's warehouse, which was stocked with antique cars valued at $4 million, was set on fire. Pablo's brother-in law, Pablo Search Bloc, was killed by the Search Bloc on February 28, 1993.

Pablo was enraged by Los Pepes and wanted his family to leave the country. The US authorities intervened in Pablo's favor to stop his family from fleeing.

Los Pepes murdered the brother of Pablo's real estate broker and destroyed properties owned by Pablo's bankers, lawyers and other property owners. The corpse of a lawyer found in the body was discovered on March 4, 1993 with a note from Los Pepes warning the rest of Pablo's legal team. Two of them were killed quickly, as well as Roberto Escobar's attorney, who they took after Escobar had left a prison that he had been visiting. One of Pablo's top attorneys and his 18-year-old son were tortured and murdered. The father and son were kidnapped by 15 men with machine guns. They were found in the trunk with their car. Their heads were shot, their hands tied together with Los Pepes notes. What did you think about the Pablo Escobar exchange for bombs in Bogota?

Pablo's top attorneys resigned. One thought he could outwit Los Pepes by working undercover. He was walking in Medellin with his brother, when Los Pepes shot him 25 times. One lawyer fled the country. Pablo responded by dropping bombs every so often, but he was losing the ability to resist violence that spiralled out of control. Los Pepes were the only ones who could stand up to them, even the authorities that made up a large portion of their membership.

Pablo wrote an April 29, 1993 letter to the attorney General:

Los Pepes has their headquarters and torture chambers at Fidel Castano's house on El Poblado Avenue, near the country club... They torture lawyers and trade unionists. They have not been searched or taken their assets. The government offers rewards to the Medellin cartel leaders and guerrilla leaders, but no rewards for paramilitary leaders nor those from the Cali cartel who are responsible for numerous car bombs that were set off in Medellin.

Pablo complained in the note that neither the murders or kidnappings of Los Pepes had been investigated nor were any arrests made. If the government would agree to certain guarantees, he offered to surrender.

Los Pepes were threatened by the Colombian government. Los Pepes responded by announcing that they had been disbanded. But the killings didn't stop. Los Pepes executed Roberto Escobar, the trainer and rider of Roberto Escobar's prize stallion, and castrated Roberto Escobar on July 14, 1993.

Chapter 36

Demise

Pablo, aware that his time was numbered, left a recording to his daughter pleading with her to be a good child and promised that he would save her from the evil one. Authorities relied on Pablo calling his family to track his calls back to him. Pablo called his son numerous times to express concern about Los Pepes. Centra Spike, the Search Bloc, and Pablo made numerous calls to his son. They traced the calls back to Los Olivos in Medellin, which is a neighborhood with a lot of two-storey houses. Los Olivos was monitored by the Search Bloc.

Pablo celebrated his forty-fourth year on December 1, 1993, at building number 45D94 on Street 79A. It was a two-storey home that he owned. Limon was his bodyguard. Luzmila, his cousin, was his cook. Limon drove Pablo around in a yellow taxi when Pablo needed to make phone calls. This gave

Pablo a false sense security. Pablo was more interested in receiving birthday congratulations than usual, so he stayed on the phone with his family longer than usual. He celebrated his birthday with champagne and restaurant food.

Pablo decided to hide in the jungle to evade his pursuers. Pablo wanted to say goodbye first to his mother, so he took the risk of going to her apartment at night. He informed her that this was his last visit to Medellin. He planned to create a new group and establish an independent country, becoming its president. His mother left him without crying.

Pablo woke up at noon on December 2, 1993 and ate spaghetti. His cousin was sent to purchase supplies for him in the jungle, including stationery and toiletries. He made calls while he was in a taxi. He made phone calls from the taxi, and he returned to his apartment by calling the taxi driver.

Pablo called his family pretending to be a journalist on the radio at 1pm. Maria Victoria, his wife, was crying. Los Pepes had killed many of their relatives and friends. The family was devastated.

Pablo asked, "So, what's your plan?".
She cried, "I don't understand," and continued to cry.

"What does your mother think?"

She said that it was like her mother had fainted. This was referring to the time the family tried unsuccessfully to flee to Germany a few days prior. "I didn't call her. "She said bye and then-"

"And you haven't spoken to her?"

"No. "No.

Pablo softly asked, "What are your plans?".
"I don't know. "I mean, I'm not sure.

"No!"

"So?"

"Don't give me this coldness!" Pablo said, "Holy Mary!".

"And you?"

"Ahhh."

"And you?"

Pablo replied, "What about me?".

Maria Victoria asked, "What are your plans?".

"What do you want?"

"What would I want?"

"If you have any questions, don't hesitate to call me.

"OK."

"You call me now, quickly," Pablo said. "There's nothing else I can say. What can I add? "I have stayed on the right track, right?"

"But how do you know? "Oh my God, I don't know!"

"We must keep going. It's amazing, think about it. Pablo said it, referring specifically to his offer to surrender to government.

Maria Victoria replied, "Yes," Maria Victoria said, "Yes," and added, "Think about your boy and all the other things, and don't rush to make decisions. OK?"

"Yes."

"Call your mom again to ask her if you want to go there, or what ..." they said. "Ciao."

"So long."

Pablo called his son at 3:00 pm. He said that a journalist wanted information about Pablo's conditions to surrender to him. The Search Bloc members began to walk street to street in the hope of finding Pablo's location.

Tell him: "My father cannot surrender unless he has security guarantees

The search bloc was driving up and down Pablo's street when the call went on for so long. The Search Bloc noticed a man with a beard standing behind a second-story window. He was holding his phone and watching the traffic. The man vanished into the house after a few seconds.

"This is the house!"
They radioed Colonel Martinez, who shouted "Stay exactly there!" Place yourself in front and behind the house. "Don't let him out!" Search Bloc units sped up to the house.

Many stories have been told about what happened next.

The front door was knocked down with a sledgehammer. Six Search Bloc members stormed in, firing at the garage space that was empty except for a taxi. One member of the Search Bloc team fell down the stairs as if shooting, causing panic among the rest.

According to authorities, Limon had escaped from a window onto a orange-tile roof. Search Bloc members placed behind the house spray gunfire at Limon as he fled. He was shot multiple times and jumped off the roof onto the lawn.

Pablo threw his sandals on the ground and jumped down onto the roof. He didn't want to be like Limon and he kept his feet against the wall. This blocked him from getting any clear shots, even though there were marksmen all around. Pablo ran along the wall in an attempt to escape down a back street.

Shots erupted. It was intense gunfire from all sides. Some Search Bloc members thought that Pablo's bodyguards were attacking them. They radioed for help.

Pablo fell.
The shooting stopped.
"It's Pablo! It's Pablo!"
Troops approached the bloody corpse and turned it over.

"Viva Colombia! Pablo Escobar has been killed!

"We won! We won!"

Roberto describes the police coming down the stairs and Pablo sending Limon to investigate. Limon was shot multiple times and died as Pablo reached the roof. He then looked around to see that he was being surrounded. To make sure the government could not claim that he had been killed or captured, Limon shot himself in the head.

Pablo was shot in the back, leg, and above his right ear. Roberto believes that the suicide shot was the one above his ear.

Troops put a Hitler moustache on Pablo's head and took pictures with him.

The news broke the hearts of the poor, while the wealthy celebrated. Over 5,000 people rushed to touch and touch the coffin at the funeral. Pablo's wife was evacuated. Ten thousand people joined the procession as it travelled along the streets. His grave was guarded by an armed guard for the first time in his life.

Pablo's passing did not affect the flow of cocaine into America.

Pablo would not have thought twice about ordering Barry Seal's assassination. He gave the death penalty to informants. Some of them were tortured with the most horrific methods, including having their tongues pulled out of their necks. Others had their eyeballs taken out with hot spoons. Some had their skulls pierced with sharp tools. Pablo had the motivation and the means to kill Barry. However, his hit men had failed repeatedly. They were able to succeed because of the outside assistance provided by the US government. It is necessary to look at the life of George HW Bush, a suspect in the murder of Barry.

Murder Suspect 2
George HW Bush

Chapter 37

War Hero

Anti-aircraft fire was flying above a blue sky and a few puffy cloud over Chichi Jima (one of the Bonin Islands) in the Pacific on September 2, 1944. The US bombers, which were a chunky grey color, were avoiding flak and dropping their loads. Some hit the island, causing an explosion, while others splashed into the dark-blue sea, causing water vapor to rise into the air. George HW Bush was strapped to his knee with a target map and was in command of an Avenger torpedo-bomber. The canopy that covered its top allowed for a view of the green island with dense vegetation and the aquamarine waters of the bay. Bush was trying to drop a bomb against a Japanese radio tower. He felt a jolt as though a giant fist had struck the plane's underbelly. Bush escaped the plane and left his two crew members behind. He gashed as the tail assembly struck his forehead.

Chester Mierzejewski (rear turret gunner) had a clear view of Bush's plane being hit by anti-aircraft firing from a bomber about 100 feet away. Chester was so close to Bush's cockpit that he could see his face. Bush was soon freed from the cockpit by a puff of smoke and parachuted out.

Chester stated that the bomber was never on flame and "no smoke rose from his cockpit when he opened it to bail out... I was hoping to see other parachutes." I never did. I was there when the plane went down. I saw the men still inside it. It was an awful feeling... Bush could have saved their lives if they were still alive. Although I don't believe they were, at least they had a chance of survival if he tried a water landing. It's normal procedure to try a water landing when there's no fire. Chester was then debriefed and questioned by an intelligence officer. However, his statement did not make it into the official record. "I told him everything I saw. It's not in my report.

Chester was also accompanied by Lawrence Mueller, a gunner who stated that no one had ever mentioned a fire in the debriefing area. "I would have written it in my logbook, if I had heard it."

Bush's propaganda machine used the bomber story to generate a variety of versions:

In 1987, the incident was described in Bush's campaign autobiography. With flames rippling towards the fuel tanks, Bush risked his life unloading four bombs on targets and flying out to sea. There was no mention of his crew until he parachuted onto the South Pacific, inflated his raft and began searching for them. Only after being rescued by a submarine had he learned that neither had survived. One had gone down in the plane. The other had jumped, but his parachute had failed to open.

In a 1980 authorised biography, Nicholas King claimed that Bush's parachute had failed to open properly and had become momentarily fouled on the tail of the plane after Bush had hit the water. There was no mention of his forehead injury.

In *George Bush: The Life of a Lone Star Yankee* (1997), the award-winning historian Herbert S Palmer wrote an account based on interviews with Bush and from reading Bush's personal papers and diaries: Bush had jumped prematurely and pulled the ripcord. His head struck the horizontal stabiliser at the plane's rear and his parachute ripped as it became snagged on the tail.

In another account, Bush claimed that he'd seen his rear gunner machinegunned to death, while the plane was on fire. In a taped interview, Bush stated that one of the crew had jumped and his parachute had streamed. The other man had been killed in the plane and was slumped over.

In a book commissioned by Bush to extol his wartime glory, *Flight of the Avenger* (1991), Joe Hyams described Bush jumping from a burning plane at approximately 3,000 feet, his parachute opening successfully and him landing on the water. This account was a damage-control response to a 1988 interview with Chester Mierzejewski published in the *New York Post*.

Upset by Bush's false claims of war heroics made during the 1988 presidential campaign, sixty-eight-year-old Chester sent a letter, informing the vice president that his recollections differed from Bush's official story. After not receiving a response, Chester broke his forty-four year silence in the *New York Post*, "That guy is not telling the truth."

When the paper double-checked Chester's account with former Lieutenant Legare Hole, the executive officer of Bush's squadron, they were told, "The turret gunner in Melvin's plane [Chester] would have had a good view. If the plane was on fire, there is a very good chance he would be able to see that. The pilot can't see everything that the gunner can and he'd miss an awful lot."

Regardless of the facts, Bush was awarded the Distinguished Flying Cross and his bravery was parlayed into political capital. A grainy film showing submarines rescuing him was aired numerous times during his 1964 Senate campaign in Texas. During the Gulf War of 1990-91, Bush achieved record heights of worship for his military prowess. As his business associates cashed in on bombing Iraq, Bush compared Saddam Hussein – whom the CIA had installed as the leader of Iraq in the 1960s – to Adolf Hitler.

Chapter 38

War Profiteering and Eugenics

For almost a century, the Bush family has engaged in profiting from war with as much zeal as Barry Seal possessed for flying. To understand why Barry would end up transporting arms shipments covertly for the interests represented by George HW Bush – and become a liability to Bush for knowing too much – it's necessary to examine the history of the Bush family's war profiteering.

America entered World War I in 1917. In 1918, Samuel Bush – Bush's grandfather – became the chief of the Ordinance Small Arms and Ammunition Section of the War Industries Board. His duties included providing government assistance to weapons companies. Later that year, he became the director of the board's Facilities Division. The War Industries Board funnelled taxpayers' money to weapons manufacturers and holders of raw materials and patents. As thirty eight million people died in the war, the recipients of the taxpayers' money made billions.

In *War is a Racket* (1935), Major General Smedley Butler detailed the abnormal profits generated during World War I. "Only a small 'inside' group knows what it [the war racket] is about. It is conducted for the benefit of the very few, at the expense of the very many. Out of war a few people make huge fortunes." He added that World War I created 21,000 new millionaires and billionaires and that the most profitable operators were the bankers. He cited the du Pont family who manufactured gun powder. Their average earnings for 1910 to 1914 were $6 million a year, whereas their average profit during the war years, 1914 to 1918, was $58 million a year, an increase of more than 950 per cent. Du Pont's revenues from the sale of powder and explosives soared from $25 million in 1914 to $319 million by 1918, totalling $1.245 billion over five years. The same leap in profits happened for the producers of ships, planes, engines, steel, copper, nickel, leather, sugar, coal, mosquito nets, undershirts and hobnailed service shoes.

The weapons manufacturers didn't just arm their own countries in a patriotic quest to defend their homelands. They armed every side in the war. Before the war had even started, their salespeople were manipulating world leaders into fighting each other, so they could maximise their sales.

Hearings in 1934 exposed culprits such as Remington Arms and the British Vickers company, who were attacked for being "Merchants of Death."

In 1916, eight years before the birth of his son, George HW Bush, Prescott Bush was invited to join Skull and Bones, a Yale senior-year secret society with bizarre death-worshipping rituals, founded by children of the Wall Street elite. Several Bonesmen who graduated in 1917, including Prescott, were hand-picked to join Brown Brothers Harriman, the largest private investment bank in the world, which cashed in on World War I. Instrumental in the selection of Prescott was Percy Rockefeller, a co-owner of Remington Arms. Prescott was groomed by master warmongers and profiteers. World War I was kind to Prescott's associates, but Prescott's ability to profit from slave labour and the slaughter of millions would really shine during World War II.

With the Skull and Bones order originating at the University of Berlin, many of its US members supported financing and arming Hitler. Just like the Nazis, they believed in eugenics: the interbreeding of elites to improve the genetic quality of the human population, and the sterilisation or extermination of people with inferior genes such as the mentally ill, alcoholics, gypsies, Jews and people of colour. If the horses they interbred could display superior characteristics, then surely the same applied to humans – or so they thought. Prescott supported and helped to finance the American Eugenics Movement, which lobbied for the successful passage in many states of sterilisation laws for anyone judged unfit.

Inspired by the American Eugenics Movement, Hitler wrote, "There is today, one state in which at least weak beginnings toward a better conception of immigration are noticeable. Of course, it is not our model German Republic, but the United States... I have studied with great interest the laws of several American states concerning prevention of reproduction by people whose progeny would, in all probability, be of no value or be injurious to the racial stock."

By the time the US had entered the war, Prescott was the managing partner of Brown Brothers Harriman, which had helped finance Hitler's rise and was still laundering Nazi money.

In *George Bush: The Unauthorized Biography*, Webster G. Tarpley and Anton Cheitkin revealed the extent of Prescott's Nazi collaboration. In 1922, USA railway magnate W Averell Harriman met the Thyssen family in Berlin with a view to founding a German-USA bank. The Thyssens owned banks that allowed them to transfer their money from Germany to the USA via the

Netherlands. Fritz Thyssen was fascinated by Hitler's public-speaking skills. He donated $25,000 to the German National Socialist Workers' Party, giving Hitler an early boost. In 1931, Thyssen joined the Nazi Party. His steel company was at the heart of the Nazi war machine.

In 1926, Harriman and the Thyssens set up the Union Banking Corporation (UBC) with Prescott at the helm. That same year, Prescott was promoted to vice president and partner at Brown Brothers Harriman. Both firms allowed the Thyssens to send money to the US from Germany via the Netherlands. UBC ended up securing Nazi money. When the Nazis needed to retrieve it, Brown Brothers Harriman sent it directly to Germany. As the executive of both companies, Prescott was a primary banker for the Nazis.

After Hitler invaded Poland, Prescott ended up with a controlling interest in the Consolidated Silesian Steel Corporation – later changed to Silesian American Corporation – which used the slave labour of Auschwitz. While mostly Jewish prisoners – starved and skeletal – were worked to death and finally exterminated, Silesian coal enabled the Nazis to rampage across Europe. According to Dutch intelligence, Prescott managed some of the Auschwitz labour to maximise his profits. At least 1.1 million people died at Auschwitz. Instructed to take showers, they were shaved and herded naked into chambers, sometimes to music being played by a live band. After getting sealed in, they were gassed with the pesticide Zyklon B. The proceeds from the sale of their jewellery, belongings and the gold extracted from their teeth helped to finance the Nazis.

On June 14, 1940, Auschwitz was opened, thanks in part to the joint enterprise of the German company IG Farben and the Standard Oil Company of New Jersey (later renamed Exxon). The initial purpose of Auschwitz was the production of artificial rubber and gasoline from coal. The principal manager of the IG Farben-Standard Oil cartel was William Stamps Farish, the grandfather of the man who would later become George HW Bush's money manager. In 1942, William Farish pleaded no contest to charges of criminal conspiracy with the Nazis, and was fined $5,000, which was nothing compared to the millions he'd made from Hitler. Standard Oil was also fined $5,000, and several of its subsidiaries. Patents Farish had provided the Nazis had been illegally withheld from the US military. With US soldiers dying, Farish was summoned to the Senate committee investigating the national defence program.

Before he testified, the chairman, Senator Harry Truman, told reporters, "I think this approaches treason."

Farish protested that he had not been disloyal, but after the hearings, it emerged that Farish had prevented the US Navy from acquiring patents he'd given to the Nazis, and also that he'd supplied gasoline and tetraethyl lead to Germany's air force and submarines. Communications showed he'd intentionally deceived the US government. While Prescott's Nazi banking facility was quietly seized and shut down, the attention on Farish intensified. A heart attack saw him off on November 29, 1942. After Farish was lambasted for fuelling Nazi aircraft, his son, a lieutenant in the US Air Force, was humiliated. Training in Texas, he died in an accident six months later. The family fortune earned from the Nazis went to the grandson Will Farish, who used some of it to help launch George HW Bush's political career.

In October 1942, the US authorities confiscated Nazi bank funds from the New York UBC, whose president, Prescott Bush, was charged with running Nazi front groups in the US. Two of the remaining five directors of UBC were Skull and Bonesmen; the other three were Nazis. UBC was essential for the financial operation of the German Steel Trust, which had produced huge amounts of war material for the Nazis, including more than a third of their explosives. The firm was condemned as a financial and commercial collaborator with the enemy and its assets were seized. This is documented in The National Archives and Library of Congress. As investigators followed the paper trail, more companies were seized, including Silesian American Corporation.

It became apparent that the Nazi invasion of Poland in 1939 had in part been made possible by war material produced by the business interests of Prescott and his associates. During war, profits are maximised by investing in opposing sides, and true to the pattern established in World War I, Prescott and his associates had provided the technology for oil to be pumped from wells in Baku, which had enabled the Soviets to attack Poland from the East.

Yet again, it emerged that Remington Arms had been providing guns to both sides. Mr Pryor, the executive committee chairman of Remington Arms, was also a founding director of UBC, working in tandem with Prescott's Nazi banking facility. Remington was probed by US Senate arms-traffic investigators, who stated that, "German political associations, like the Nazi and others, are nearly all armed with American... guns... Arms of all kinds coming from America are transhipped in the Sheldt to river barges before the vessels arrive in Antwerp. They then can be carried through Holland without police inspection or interference. The Hitlerists and Communists are presumed to get arms in this manner. The principal arms coming from America are Thompson submachine guns and revolvers. The number is great."

Thyssen – whose bullets had been used to kill Allied soldiers and whose factories had employed slave labour – was arrested and interrogated. The chief interrogator was a plant, who banked with the Thyssens. Thyssen's war profits were preserved and parlayed into a multi-billion-dollar empire. The Thyssens are one of the wealthiest families in the world.

In 1947, the manager of a Thyssen-owned Rotterdam bank threatened to blow the whistle on the UBC money-laundering scheme when he discovered that he was sitting on a pile of hidden Nazi assets. After being fired by the Thyssens, he fled to New York City where he naïvely intended to talk to Prescott Bush. Two weeks later, his body was found in New York.

In 1996, a Dutch journalist, Eddy Roever, went to London to interview a baron involved in the money-laundering scheme. The baron was a neighbour of Margaret Thatcher. Two days later, Roever's body was found. Retired US intelligence agent William Gowen commented on the deaths of the Rotterdam bank manager and Roever: it was only a coincidence that both healthy men had died of heart attacks immediately after trying to uncover the truth about the Thyssens.

If Barry Seal had been born a few decades earlier, his covert operations would have included transporting American arms to the Nazi private armies that overthrew the German Republic, all with the blessing of Prescott Bush. By the time George HW Bush obtained the presidency such activity was performed by the CIA.

By banking for Hitler, Prescott multiplied the wealth of the Bush dynasty. Despite violating laws that banned US companies from trading with enemies, he never suffered any punishment. He even managed to claw back $1.5 million of the seized money. He was the perfect role model for his son, George HW Bush, who felt destined to continue the family tradition.

Chapter 39

Early Bio

Fifteen years older than Barry Seal, George HW Bush was born on June 12, 1924 in Milton, Massachusetts. Although the stock-market crash of 1929 had depleted the fortune built by Prescott Bush on the back of World War I, the family, including five children, lived luxuriously in an eight-bedroom Victorian home with four servants, a chauffeur and a view of two acres of lawn. His mother, Dorothy, raised her children to win at all costs. Prescott was a binge drinker who beat his boys with a belt, a razor strap and a squash racket.

At Phillips Academy in Andover, a boys' prep school used as a stepping stone to Yale University, Bush excelled at sports, but was mediocre in the classroom. Prior to his graduation, the US entered World War II. Despite his parents' concerns, Bush insisted on joining the Navy's air program. The prerequisite of having completed two years of college for entry was no obstacle as Prescott had established the career of the Navy Secretary for Air. In an accomplishment that would have impressed Barry Seal, Bush became the Navy's youngest pilot.

In June 1944, flying a Grumman TBF Avenger he'd nicknamed Barbara on a combat mission against the Japanese, his plane lost oil pressure. He made an emergency landing on the sea, where he was rescued after floating for a few hours. That year, he flew fourteen missions near Guam. He nicknamed his next plane Barbara II – the one that was hit by flak which he parachuted from, abandoning his colleagues.

On January 6, 1945, Bush still had a battle scar on his forehead when he married Barbara Pierce at the first Presbyterian Church in Rye, New York. She wore her mother-in-law's long-sleeved white-satin dress and veil. Bush had donned his Navy midshipman's dress blues. After honeymooning on Sea Island, Georgia, Bush returned for special combat training in anticipation of the final Allied assault on Japan. Barbara prayed for the war to end and rejoiced when it did while her husband was still training. After celebrating in the streets, they thanked God at a nearby church.

After Yale and Skull and Bones, Bush tried to get a job with Procter & Gamble, but failed the interview. Utilising the Skull and Bones network, Prescott got his son a job at Dresser Industries, a large oil-equipment manufacturer and a subsidiary of Brown Brothers Harriman, where Prescott had served as a director for twenty-two years.

In January 1949, Bush flew to Texas, where he started work as an equipment clerk at a Dresser subsidiary, International Derrick and Equipment Company. While working for Dresser, he lived in various places in Texas and California with his family, which had expanded with the births of George W and Robin, the latter named after Barbara's mother, who had recently died in a car crash.

Bush co-started the Bush-Overbey Oil Development Company Inc in 1951, which specialised in swindling farmers out of their land for a pittance and reselling it to big buyers such as oil companies at inflated prices. Bush and Overbey chose land based on leaked geological information or after observing major oil companies drilling there.

In 1953, he co-founded the Zapata Petroleum Corporation, which drilled in the Permian Basin in Texas. Zapata struck so much oil that its shares rose from seven cents to $23 dollars, delighting its investors.

By now, there were three children thanks to the addition of Jeb, but one morning, Robin woke up pale and said, "I may go out and sit in the grass and watch the cars go by or maybe I'll just lie in bed." The doctor diagnosed her with leukaemia. Her white blood cell count was the highest the doctor had ever seen. "You should take her home, make life as easy as possible for her, and in three weeks' time, she'll be gone."

The next morning, the Bushes flew Robin to New York to see Bush's uncle, Dr John Walker, a former cancer specialist who was the president of Sloan-Kettering Memorial Hospital. He recommended treatment to extend her life in case a medical advancement occurred in the field of childhood leukaemia. Brave Robin lasted for seven months of painful bone-marrow transplants and blood transfusions. She died with her parents present. Her body was donated for research. The shock turned twenty-eight-year-old Barbara's hair grey. In the following years, Barbara gave birth to three more children.

In 1954, Bush was named president of the Zapata Offshore Company, a subsidiary that specialised in offshore drilling. Big oil companies hired its services. The CIA used it as a front for some of its activity and money laundering. This fledgling relationship with the CIA would lead to Bush getting to know and employing the services of Barry Seal.

Chapter 40

JFK Assassination

High-profile people in power require others to do their dirty work. George HW Bush had at his disposal a stable of CIA good ol' boys, including Barry Seal. Bush was working for the CIA at least as early as 1961, but many researchers believe that he was recruited in his Yale days when he was in Skull and Bones.

The Bush family's relationship with the CIA goes back to its first director, Allen Dulles, a lawyer who helped facilitate the laundering of Nazi money with Prescott Bush. Allen Dulles was the CIA director fired by JFK, whom LBJ put in charge of the Warren Commission investigating JFK's assassination. Allen's brother, John Foster Dulles, was Prescott Bush's lawyer during the Nazi days.

Throughout the Eisenhower presidency, 1953-61, Prescott was a confidential ally of the Dulles Brothers. They concocted schemes to overthrow foreign governments by any means possible in order to further their business interests, which included the United Fruit Company.

In 1954, they toppled the democratically elected president of Guatemala, who'd come to power by offering land reform – detailed in Chapter 3. Under the guise of fighting Communism, the CIA removed the president and installed a ruthless dictator.

The CIA tried to oust the leader of Cuba, Fidel Castro, in numerous ways – detailed in Chapter 3 – including using George HW Bush's company, Zapata, whose Scorpion platform fifty miles away from Cuba provided an ideal training post for anti-Castro Cubans. According to the book *Prelude to Terror* by Joseph Trento, Bush was given a list of names of Cuban oil workers that the CIA wanted placed in jobs. CIA money and payments were filtered through Zapata, according to John Sherwood, ex-chief of CIA antiCastro operations. "We had to pay off politicians in Mexico, Guatemala, Costa Rica and elsewhere... Bush's company was used as a conduit for these funds under the guise of oil-business contracts."

Bush was a major organiser and recruiter for the Bay of Pigs invasion, codenamed Operation ZAPATA. Colonel Fletcher Prouty – a former Pentagon high ranking official who was the basis for the Colonel X character in Oliver Stone's *JFK* – obtained two Navy ships for the operation that were repainted to non-Navy colours and renamed HOUSTON and BARBARA. Zapata's worldwide oil rigs enabled Bush to vanish for weeks at a time on CIA business. Anyone getting in the way of the Bush clique tended to end up dead. Prime targets were foreign leaders and even domestic ones such as JFK.

A few hours after JFK's assassination, George HW Bush called the Houston FBI field office, identified himself and claimed that his location was Tyler, Texas. He reported that James Milton Parrot, a young Republican, had talked about killing JFK. An FBI memo declassified in 1993 stated:

Mr George H W Bush, President of Zapata Offshore Drilling Company, Houston, Texas, residence 5525 Briar, Houston, telephonically furnished the following information to writer by long-distance telephone call from Tyler, Texas. Bush stated that he wanted to be kept confidential but wanted to furnish hearsay that he recalled hearing in recent weeks, the day and source unknown. He stated that one James Parrott has been talking of killing the president when he comes to Houston. Bush stated that Parrot is possibly a student at University of Houston and is active in political matters in this area. He stated that he felt Mrs Fawley, telephone number SU2-5239, or Arline Smith, telephone number JA9-9194 of the Harris County Republican Party Headquarters would be able to furnish additional information regarding the identity of Parrott. Bush stated that he was proceeding to Dallas, Texas, would remain in the Sheraton-Dallas-Hotel and returned his residence on 1123-63. His office telephone number is CA2-0395.

Following up on the lead, FBI agents went to the house of Parrott, an unemployed twenty-four-year-old Air Force veteran who'd been honourably discharged. His mother said he wasn't home and provided an alibi. "She advised that James Parrott had been home all day helping her care for her son Gary Wayne Parrott whom they brought home from the hospital yesterday... Mrs Parrott advised that shortly after 1 pm a Mr Reynolds came by their home to advise them of the death of President Kennedy, and talked to her son James Parrott about painting some signs at Republican Headquarters on Waugh Drive."

Upon further questioning, both Reynolds and Parrott claimed that Reynolds had visited between 1:30 and 1:45 pm. But decades later in 2007,

Reynolds told an interviewer that he had not gone to Parrott's house that day. He said he'd been asked to accompany Parrott to the local Secret Service office. The encounter was documented as follows:

There was a young man who came around headquarters... and somebody said that he had made a threat against Kennedy and this was, I believe, this came up after the assassination... The end result was, it was suggested I contact the Secret Service, the local Secret Service, and I accompanied this young man... And we went down, and this was kind of a strange kid, mild-mannered, quiet kind of, seemed to be living in another world, and I took him down one day, escorted him down there.

When the FBI showed up to question him, Parrott was painting "Bush for Senate?" signs. Parrott admitted picketing members of JFK's administration. He denied threatening the president. As a member of the right-wing John Birch Society, he'd opposed Bush during Bush's campaign for GOP chairman of Harris County. The FBI decided that Parrott hadn't been involved in a conspiracy to kill JFK. So why had Bush sent them on a wildgoose chase?

Bush's call to the FBI had placed him in Tyler, Texas, approximately 100 miles away from the JFK assassination crime scene in Dallas. One theory is that Bush had dropped Parrott's name to the FBI as payback. Another theory is that Bush was joining in the hunt for the killer to camouflage his own role in the conspiracy. To camouflage their activity, killers sometimes join in the search party for their own victims or other false suspects. Bush may have been attempting a more sophisticated form of that strategy.

Two decades later, during Bush's 1988 presidential campaign, Parrott emerged as a volunteer for Bush, lending weight to the theory that Parrott was acting as a fall guy, enabling Bush to establish his Tyler, Texas location.

So what were Bush's actual movements around the time of JFK's assassination? Bush had booked two nights at the Dallas Sheraton: November 21 and 22. He and his wife spent November 21 in Dallas and took a private plane to Tyler, where Bush was scheduled to speak at a Kiwanis Club luncheon.

Aubrey Irby, the vice president of the Kiwanis Club (and later president of Kiwanis International during Bush's vice presidency) told author Kitty Kelley her version of the events on November 22. In *The Family: The Real Story of the Bush Dynasty*, Kitty Kelley wrote that Bush had started to deliver a speech to a hundred men gathered at Tyler's Blackstone Hotel. The head bellhop tapped Aubrey on the shoulder and said that JFK had been shot. Aubrey told the club president, who leaned over and told Bush.

After halting his speech, Bush said, "In view of the President's death, I consider it inappropriate to continue with a political speech at this time. Thank you very much for your attention." Bush sat down. Aubrey considered Bush's behaviour magnanimous. Recounting the tale in 2007, Aubrey described Bush as having been matter-of-fact and supremely well composed.

In her 1994 memoir, Barbara Bush published a letter that she had purportedly written on the day of JFK's assassination:

Dearest Family, Wednesday I took Doris Ulmer out for lunch. They [Al and Doris Ulmer] were here from England and they had been so nice to George in Greece. That night we went to …

I am writing this at the Beauty Parlor, and the radio says that the President has been shot. Oh Texas – my Texas – my God – let's hope it's not true. I am sick at heart as we all are. Yes, the story is true and the Governor also. How hateful some people are.

Since the Beauty Parlor the President has died. We are once again on a plane. This time a commercial plane. Poppy [Bush] picked me up at the beauty parlor – we went right to the airport, flew to Ft. Worth and dropped Mr. Zeppo off (we were on his plane) and flew back to Dallas. We had to circle the field while the second presidential plane took off. Immediately Pop got tickets back to Houston and here we are flying home. We are sick at heart. The tales the radio reporters tell of Jackie Kennedy are the bravest I've ever heard. The rumors are flying about that horrid assassin. We are hoping that it is not some far right nut, but a "commie" nut. You understand that we know they are both nuts, but just hope that it is not a Texan and not an American at all.

I am amazed at the rapid-fire thinking and planning that has already been done. LBJ has been the president for some time now – two hours at least and it is only 4:30.

My dearest love to you all,

Bar

According to Russ Baker, who wrote *Family of Secrets: The Bush Dynasty, America's Invisible Government and the Hidden History of the Last Fifty Years*, the first and only Bush family acknowledgment of where Bush was on that day came in a classic form: from the wife in the most innocuous swathing. That it didn't surface until 1994 is also peculiar. To whom the letter was mailed is unknown or whether an original exists or how it was unearthed thirty years after JFK's assassination. She wrote "Dear family," but all of her children were ten years old or younger, and why would she mail them a letter if she were flying home and probably would have been home before the letter arrived? Was she sending it to her parents? Unlikely, because her mother was dead. Her father had remarried, but Barbara Bush wasn't known to be particular close to them. She hadn't attended her mother's funeral. Although the letter has details, it didn't document Bush's call to the FBI about the potential assassin James Parrott. The letter did achieve one thing: it recorded that they were in Tyler, Texas during the assassination.

According to Roger Stone in *Jeb! and the Bush Crime Family*, Bush was in Dallas on the evening of November 21, attending an oil contractors' association meeting.

In 1976, Bush, now the director of the CIA, received a letter asking for help, which casts even more suspicion on Bush and his knowledge of the JFK assassination:

Maybe you will be able to bring a solution into the hopeless situation I find myself in. My wife and I find ourselves surrounded by some vigilantes; our phone bugged; and we are being followed everywhere. Either FBI is involved in this or they do not want to accept my complaints. We are driven to insanity by this situation . . . tried to write, stupidly and unsuccessfully, about Lee H. Oswald and must have angered a lot of people . . . Could you do something to remove this net around us? This will be my last request for help and I will not annoy you anymore.
G. de Mohrenschildt.

The staff at the CIA asked Bush if he knew G. de Mohrenschildt. Bush responded in a memo to the staff:
I do know this man De Mohrenschildt. I first men [sic] him in the early 40'3 [sic]. He was an uncle to my Andover roommate. Later he surfaced in Dallas

(50's maybe) . . . Then he surfaced when Oswald shot to prominence. He knew Oswald before the assassination of Pres. Kennedy. I don't recall his role in all this.

By not recalling, Bush was downplaying the extent of his relationship with de Mohrenschildt, who came from Russian nobility. His family had made a fortune from oil. Working for the czar, his father had been the governor of Minsk. His uncle and father had run the Swedish Nobel Brothers Oil Company in Baku, Russian Azerbaijan on the southwestern coast of the Caspian Sea, where, during World War I, Prescott Bush and his associates had provided the technology for the oil that had enabled the Soviets to attack Poland from the East. Back then, Baku hosted half of the world's known oil reserves and major players such as the Rockefellers were trying to get in on the action.

Born in 1911, George de Mohrenschildt had moved to the US and worked for Humble Oil, a company co-founded by Prescott Bush. By 1952, he was living in Dallas and a member of the Dallas Petroleum Club. He regularly attended the Dallas Council on World Affairs, which Bush's friend Neil Mallon started in 1951. He helped expand American oil interests in Cuba and other locations of interest to the CIA. He had a knack of taking business trips to locations where a political event or upheaval significant to the CIA was imminent. In 1961, as exiled Cubans and their CIA support team prepared for the Bay of Pigs invasion in Guatemala, de Mohrenschildt and his wife passed through Guatemala City on a month-long walking tour of the Central American isthmus. Another time, they appeared in Mexico just as a Soviet leader arrived on oil business and they just happened to have a meeting. Another time, they were in Haiti shortly before an unsuccessful coup was launched against its president.

According to the author Edward Jay Epstein, in 1961, the Dallas CIA told de Mohrenschildt that Lee Harvey Oswald was living in Minsk, a Russian city. He was asked to get information about Oswald and in return the CIA would help him with an oil deal in Haiti. In the summer of 1962, when Oswald was back in Texas, de Mohrenschildt started to become close to Oswald and eventually became his mentor. He helped Oswald find jobs and apartments, took him to meetings and social gatherings, and assisted him and his Russian wife, Marina, and their baby in various other ways. He provided information to the CIA about Oswald and in March 1963, his Haitian oil deal went through.

In 1964, de Mohrenschildt and his wife testified to the Warren Commission, which spent more time with them than any other witness except for Oswald's widow. The Warren Commission helped portray de Mohrenschildt as an eccentric, while steering him away from naming his powerful friends and associates. One relationship he never disclosed to the Warren Commission was that with Bush. The Warren Commission concluded that de Mohrenschildt's relationships were all coincidences that had nothing to do with the assassination.

Bush replied to de Mohrenschildt:

Let me say first that I know it must have been difficult for you to seek my help in the situation outlined in your letter. I believe I can appreciate your state of mind in view of your daughter's tragic death a few years ago, and the current poor state of your wife's health. I was extremely sorry to hear of these circumstances. In your situation I can well imagine how the attentions you described in your letter affect both you and your wife. However, my staff has been unable to find any indication of interest in your activities on the part of Federal authorities in recent years. The flurry of interest that attended your testimony before the Warren Commission has long subsided. I can only speculate that you may have become "newsworthy" again in view of the renewed interest in the Kennedy assassination, and thus may be attracting the attention of people in the media. I hope this letter has been of some comfort to you, George, although I realize I am unable to answer your question completely.

On March 29, 1977 – months after Bush wrote his response – de Mohrenschildt visited his daughter at a family friend's house in Manalapan, Florida, between West Palm Beach and Boca Raton. While in Manalapan, he was interviewed by Edward Jay Epstein for a feature story in *Reader's Digest*. The House Select Committee on Assassinations (HSCA) investigator, Gaeton Fonzi, showed up at Manalapan while George was out doing the interview. Fonzi was an investigative reporter from Philadelphia hired by the HSCA. He left his business card with de Mohrenschildt's daughter.

When de Mohrenschildt arrived home for lunch, his daughter told him in Spanish that Fonzi had visited and to not tell the maid and gardener. She gave him the card and went shopping. Later that afternoon, de Mohrenschildt's corpse was found in his upstairs bedroom with a self-inflicted gunshot wound. No one heard the gun go off. There was no suicide note. The next day, he was supposed to have testified before the House Select Committee on Assassinations. After his death was ruled a suicide, he was cremated within a week. Among his personal belongings, in an address book, was an old listing for George H W Bush at 1412 W. Ohio; also Zapata Petroleum Midland.

Just like Barry Seal, he died in possession of Bush's contact details.

Another JFK assassination connection is John Crichton, a former intelligence operative, and later, an oil-company investor, who became friends with Bush in 1964. According to Fabian Escalante, a former chief of Cuban counterintelligence turned author, Vice President Nixon had paired Bush and Crichton to raise funds for Operation Forty, a Bay of Pigs CIA assassination squad. Crichton rubbed shoulders with the elites of Texas and had worked during his military days with many of the Dallas police. His directorships included Dorchester Gas Producing Company, whose other director D H Byrd owned the Texas School Book Depository Building that Oswald had just coincidentally started to work at two weeks before JFK drove by.

Crichton was involved with JFK's Texas travel arrangements. The driver of the pilot car in Kennedy's motorcade was Deputy Police Chief George Lumpkin, who'd worked under Crichton in the Dallas Army Intelligence unit. Crichton provided the interpreter for Oswald's wife, Marina. According to author Russ Baker in *Family of Secrets*, Marina's words were mistranslated to implicate Oswald. The Warren Commission never asked Crichton to testify. In 2007, Crichton died. The George Bush presidential library holds his papers, which are all sealed.

Not only was he evasive when asked about his relationships with people such as de Mohrenschildt, but when Bush was president he claimed that he had never asked for any CIA files on the JFK assassination. Under the Freedom of Information Act, it was revealed he had submitted numerous requests for such files – when he was CIA director – as if trying to gather a range of information.

On September 9, 1976, he asked whether Lyndon Johnson had been told by a former CIA director that Cubans were involved in the assassination. On September 15, 1976, Bush asked his deputy director to look into reports that linked Jack Ruby with the Mafia boss Santos Trafficante Jr. Bush wrote, "A recent Jack Anderson story referred to a CIA cable, the subject matter of which had some UK journalist observing Jack Ruby visiting Trafficante in jail (in Cuba). Is there such a cable? If so, I would like to see it."

Bush was close to the former CIA head, Allen Dulles, who had a grudge against JFK, as well as being tight with the Texas elites heavily invested in oil and weapons manufacturing, with close ties to intelligence operations that had used assassination teams in attempts to overthrow foreign governments. Bush was in Dallas on November 21, and maybe even on the morning of November 22, yet since then, he has claimed that he can't remember where he was on those dates. He created a record of being in Tyler, Texas by sending the FBI on a wild goose chase after James Parrott, and through his wife's letter that materialised decades later. Lastly, JFK's attitude towards the war and the CIA stood in the way of the pattern of profiteering dating back to Prescott and the Nazis that multiplied the wealth of the Bush dynasty and from which they continue to profit to this day.

It seems that Bush at the very least had insider knowledge of the JFK assassination or at the most was a co-conspirator. Anyone who'd go so far as to conspire to kill a president would easily order the assassination of Barry Seal.

Chapter 41

CIA Director

After CIA Director William Colby spoke too honestly with congressional investigations, a decision was made to get rid of him. Colby made the mistake of putting the American Constitution before the CIA. He believed the CIA had a moral and legal obligation to cooperate with Congress. Colby's natural replacement was someone esteemed for subterfuge: George HW Bush.

Bush wanted to become the Vice President – a title he considered his birthright – which a CIA directorship would have precluded. On December 18, 1975, President Ford told Bush that he'd been ruled out of the candidacy for Vice President, and that Ford had written a letter stating such to the committee chairman. Bush convinced Ford to alter the letter to make it appear as if Bush had withdrawn from the candidacy.

The amended letter stated, "He [Bush] and I have discussed this in detail. In fact, he urged that I make this decision. This says something about the man and about his desire to do this job [CIA director] for the nation..."

The next day, Bush was approved for the CIA directorship. He was sworn in on January 30, 1976.

Frank Church, whose committee was investigating CIA assassinations, commented on Bush's appointment, "There is no question in my mind but that concealment is the new order of the day."

Lucien Nedzi, a Democratic congressman in Michigan, wrote to President Ford, "The director of CIA must be unfettered by any doubts as to his politics. He must be free of the appearance, as well as the substance, that he is acting, or not acting, with partisan political considerations in mind... Accordingly, I respectfully urge that you reconsider your appointment of Mr Bush to this most sensitive of positions."

Richard Nixon wrote to Bush: "You will be tempted greatly to give away the store in assuring the members of the Senate Committee that everything the CIA does in the future will be an open book. I think you will be far better off to stand up and strongly defend the CIA and the need to maintain, particularly, its covert activities."

Bush replied: "I couldn't agree more. We must not see the Agency compromised further by reckless disclosures."

The Church Committee was investigating how the CIA had used the media to manipulate the public. Senators requested the names of journalists on the CIA payroll. On February 12, 1976, Bush stated that he would remove from the CIA payroll all "full-time or part-time news correspondents, accredited by any US News service, newspaper, periodicals, radio or TV network station."

In April, the Senate Select Committee on Intelligence Activities found there were at least twenty-five journalists and reporters still on the CIA payroll. When called to account over his earlier statement, Bush responded that he'd only referred to correspondents accredited by US News services. This excluded a large number of freelance reporters, editors, news executives and foreign news organisations still on the CIA payroll.

Two senators drove to the CIA headquarters in Virginia and demanded Bush release the names of the journalists still on the CIA payroll. Bush responded that the CIA was "not at liberty to reveal the names."

On February 18, 1976, the *New York Times* reported that, "Bush now had more power than any other director of Central Intelligence since its creation."

Bush approved Executive Order 11905, authorising the CIA to conduct foreign counterintelligence activities in the US. He obtained money from Saudi Arabia for covert operations that Congress had refused to finance. He oversaw a CIA plot that cost $10 million to overthrow the government of Jamaica, which included illegal arms shipments, inciting violent demonstrations and three assassination attempts on Prime Minister Michael Manley. Even the reggae-singer Bob Marley got caught up in the violence on December 3, 1976, when three men entered his house and shot him.

With Bush at the helm, CIA-backed operations against Cuba included supporting a Cuban exile terrorist group called CORU, which blew up Cubana de Aviación Flight 455 on October 6, 1976. After taking off from Barbados, a bomb exploded, killing all seventy-three people on-board, including the Cuban Olympic fencing team. Not quite as many as the 110 deaths due to the bomb aboard Avianca Airlines Flight 203 credited to Pablo, but Bush would far outshine Pablo in other murder methods, especially war.

For years, the CIA planned terrorist attacks in order to blame them on Cuba by manufacturing evidence. A US army memorandum dated March 1962 called *Possible Actions to Provoke, Harass or Disrupt Cuba*, included "downing a US plane and blaming it on Mr Castro," or demonstrating "convincingly that a Cuban aircraft has shot down a chartered civilian airliner." Sinking a warship "could be blamed on Cuba." Cuban exile terrorists could be used by the CIA to fly by the island to "distract local pilots with radio conversations with the aim of causing the crash." Another plan was to "sink a boatload of Cubans en route for Florida."

General Noriega accused CIA director Bush of sanctioning a bomb in Panama that destroyed a car owned by William Drummond, a prominent US resident of the American occupied Canal Zone. Drummond had been criticising the negotiations between the US and Panama. The CIA allegedly arranged the blast to pressurise US residents to end their resistance to the treaty.

"The US embassy in Panama didn't known about Bush's scheme and got nervous," Noriega said, "so Bush had to calm the embassy down: he created a problem to solve a problem." Noriega described Bush as "a cold-blooded killer."

After Jimmy Carter was elected in 1976, Bush asked to stay on as CIA director, but Carter replaced him.

Chapter 42

Vice President

Aiming to become the president, George HW Bush further ingratiated himself with the most powerful and wealthy entities: the banks, oil companies, pharmaceutical companies, intelligence community... He announced his candidacy on May 1, 1979.

He didn't consider his almost seventy-year-old opponent, Ronald Reagan, much of a threat. The two contenders had roughly equal support until Bush revealed his true colours at a debate. Originally, the debate was only supposed to include Reagan and Bush. With Bush refusing to contribute, Reagan ended up paying the costs of the debate. Having spent $3,500, Reagan decided to open the debate up to four more candidates.

Disgruntled by Reagan's initiative, Bush sat at the edge of the stage, refusing to talk to the other candidates. Attempting to get Bush to talk, a senator said, "If you don't come now, you'll be doing a disservice to party unity."

Bush replied, "Don't tell me about unifying the Republican Party. I've done more for this party than you'll ever do." He continued to rebuff the other candidates.

The audience yelled for all of the candidates to get the debate started. On the microphone, Reagan urged the same.

"Turn Mr Reagan's microphone off," a newspaper editor yelled.

"I'm paying for that microphone, Mr Green," Reagan said.

The audience applauded wildly, while Bush, according to William Loeb, "looked like a small boy who had been delivered to the wrong birthday party." Confronted with Reagan's action, Bush appeared weak.

By May 1980, Reagan had twenty-nine states and Bush only four, so he quit the race and handed his support to Reagan, convinced that Reagan would make him the vice president. Having being passed over for the vice presidency by Nixon once and twice by Ford, Bush figured that his birth-right was overdue. But instead, Reagan wanted Ford for vice president. Reagan and his wife, Nancy, disliked Bush.

"Why can't I pick someone I like?" Reagan told his aides. "I'm wary of a man who freezes under pressure. George froze that night. That haunts me."

After Ford declined the vice presidency, Reagan called Bush. "George, it seems to me that," Reagan said, grimacing, "the fellow who came the closest and got the most votes for president ought to be the logical choice for vice president. Will you take it?"

Reagan later wrote in his memoir, "He [Bush] didn't have a moment's hesitation."

When Reagan made the official announcement of Bush as vice president, everyone cheered, except for his wife, Nancy, who was standing next to him at the lectern.

After the media questioned Bush about his political differences with Reagan, he promptly changed his stance on abortion, the Equal Rights Amendment, school bussing and school prayer – as if to prove that he had a soul.

To help oust President Carter at the November election, the Reagan-Bush camp made a secret deal with Iran, whereby Iran agreed not to release fiftytwo American hostages being held at the US embassy since November 4, 1979. In the media, Bush railed against the lingering hostage crisis. As Carter had been promising their release by the election, his credibility was damaged when the hostages weren't freed. FBI and CIA documents released under the Freedom of Information Act showed that Bush played a major role in an arms deal worth $150 million. In return for not releasing the hostages, weapons were shipped to Iran illegally via Israel.

Reagan won the election. In his first inaugural address on January 20, 1981, he addressed the recession: "In this present crisis, government is not the solution to our problems; government is the problem."

However well-intentioned, Reagan was showing signs of fatigue. He napped for several hours a day and left matters of policy and control to Bush, who had planted numerous loyalists in the administration, many from the CIA. His CIA associates believed that if Bush were the president things would run more smoothly for them, but they knew that Bush only had a slim chance of becoming the president from the position of vice president.

Bush schemed to put Reagan's power in his own hands. An order was presented to Reagan for signing, which granted Bush powers over crisis management. Many of Reagan's advisers were opposed to the order, including Secretary of State Alexander Haig. Nevertheless, on March 25, 1981, Bush was named the leader of the US crisis management staff as part of the National Security Council system. It didn't take long for a crisis to occur.

On March 30, 1981, Ronald Reagan exited the Hilton Hotel in Washington DC, surrounded by Secret Service agents in grey suits and an outer circle of police in dark uniforms. People on the pavement yelled greetings at the president, who smiled and waved. When he was almost at his limo, a noise erupted that Reagan thought was firecrackers. Two people fell wounded to the ground. Others instinctively crouched.

A Secret Serviceman grabbed Reagan by the waist and threw him headfirst into the limo. Reagan landed on the seat. The Serviceman dived on top of him. Police and Secret Servicemen piled onto John Hinckley Jr, a twentytwo-year-old holding a .22 revolver.

As his limo took off for the White House, Reagan felt a pain in his chest. He told the Secret Serviceman on top of him to get up as he suspected he'd broken a rib. When the Serviceman moved, Reagan coughed bright-red frothy blood onto his hand.

"I guess the broken rib has pierced the lung." Reagan coughed blood into a handkerchief. The limo headed for George Washington Hospital. With his handkerchief soaked red, he used the Secret Serviceman's handkerchief, which quickly filled with blood.

At the hospital's emergency entrance, Reagan got out of the limo and walked in. "I'm having a little trouble breathing," he said to a nurse. His knees went out. He collapsed. They put him on a trolley and used scissors to cut his new suit off him.

Reagan prayed.

A bullet had entered Reagan's side, pierced his lung and was lodged near to his heart. He'd been hit while diving into the limo. The bullet had hit a rib, causing extreme pain. It had tumbled and stopped one inch away from his heart. He lost almost half of the blood in his body. The medical staff thought that he wasn't going to make it.

When informed about the shooter Hinckley, and Hinckley's mental condition, Reagan added Hinckley to his prayers.

As with the JFK assassination, all of the shots were immediately credited to a lone gunman, even though people reported shots coming from a position above and to the right of Hinckley. NBC correspondent Judy Woodruff said that at least one shot had been fired from an overhang above Reagan's limo. Most of the photos and footage of the shooting have disappeared, however one photo does show what appears to be a sniper on the balcony above and behind Reagan.

At the time of the assassination attempt, Bush had been at the Hyatt Regency in Fort Worth, delivering a plaque as part of the designation of a national historic site. After Secretary of State Alexander Haig informed the vice president about the assassination attempt, Bush flew to Washington to take control of the government.

In the Situation Room, Bush asked for a condition report on the president, any others wounded, the assailant and the international scene. The reports were handed over. Immediately, Bush announced that there had been no conspiracy. Just five hours after the attempt on Reagan, on the basis of fragmentary early reports, before the suspect had been properly questioned and before a full investigation had been carried out, Bush had declared that it was all the work of a lone gunman.

But the JFK-style assassination attempt failed by Reagan surviving.

Bush desperately didn't want anyone to know about his family's ten-year relationship with the Hinckley family.

On March 31 and April 1, 1981, newspapers started reporting that Bush's son, Neil Bush, had been scheduled to dine with Scott Hinckley, the brother of the lone gunman, at Neil's home on the day after the assassination attempt.

The *Houston Post* reported that Neil Bush "knew the Hinckley family because they had made large contributions to the Vice President's campaign." Neil said he "could not recall meeting John Hinckley Jr." Neil's wife Sharon said that the Hinckleys "are a nice family... and have given a lot of money to the Bush campaign."

The next day, Neil Bush hosted a press conference to correct inaccuracies reported in the *Houston Post* article. He claimed that the 1980 campaign records showed no contributions from the Hinckleys. The scheduled dinner with Scott Hinckley was downgraded to a dinner with a close female friend to whom Hinckley was only attending as a companion. Neil added that he'd only met Scott Hinckley once at a surprise party in 1981.

According to Charles Overbeck in his essay "Reagan, Hinckley, and the Bushy Knoll Conspiracy," the Hinckleys had been contributing to Bush as far back as 1970. John Hinckley Sr had raised money for Bush's campaign to get the presidential nomination from Reagan.

According to the author Barbara Honegger, the Secret Service had been warned about Hinckley's designs on Reagan two months before the shooting. In October 1980, Hinckley had flown to Nebraska to meet an American neoNazi and flown to Nashville to stalk President Carter, but was arrested at the airport with three handguns in his suitcase. He only spent five hours in custody. Mentally-unstable Hinckley had attempted to transport weapons over state lines and into a city visited by the president, yet had been released with a fine.

Just as LBJ stood to gain the most from the assassination of JFK, Bush stood to gain the most from the death of Ronald Reagan.

Following the shooting, Bush continued to expand his power. On May 14, 1982, a secret memorandum signed by Reagan formalised Bush as chief of all covert action and made him the de facto head of US intelligence. According to the memo, "National Security Decision Directive 3, Crisis Management, establishes the Special Situation Group (SSG), chaired by the Vice President. The SSG is charged... with formulating plans in anticipation of crises."

The memo also introduced the Standing Crisis Pre-Planning Group (CPPG), which funnelled intelligence to Bush and the SSG. Its members included representatives of Bush, the National Security Council (NSC), the CIA, the military and the State Department. It was to "meet periodically in the White House Situation Room." Its objective was to identify potential crises and present plans and policy options to resolve crises to the SSG under Chairman Bush. It was also to give Bush and his associates "recommended security, cover, and media plans that will enhance the likelihood of successful execution." CPPG members' names were to be provided to Oliver North, who operated as the middleman for Bush and Barry Seal.

In August 1982, Bush hired Donald Gregg and Felix Rodriguez from the CIA – both familiar faces to Barry Seal. When Bush had been the CIA director from 1976 onwards, Greg had worked under him. Another Bush loyalist, Rodriguez had been a CIA assassinations manager. Rodriguez operated out of the vice president's office.

The group Bush assembled included several of the co-conspirators in the death of Barry Seal.

Chapter 43

Gulf War

On the back of his campaign promise, "Read my lips. No new taxes," George HW Bush was elected president in November 1988. Within two years, he broke the promise. His popularity waned so much that at the mid-term elections the Republicans lost nine seats.

Prime Minister Margaret Thatcher reminded Bush that nothing works as well as war to boost ratings. According to Kitty Kelley, Thatcher told Bush that her popularity surged thanks to the invasion of the Falklands Islands in 1982. "I stayed in office for eight years after that," Thatcher said.

War would enable Bush to achieve the two things dearest to him: increase his approval rating and the profits of the companies run by his family and their associates, especially in the military and oil sectors.

In mid-1990, Saddam Hussein – a CIA-installed leader and a US ally – was amassing troops on Iraq's border with Kuwait, waiting for the green light from Bush to launch an invasion. On July 24, 1990, the State Department emphasised that the US had no commitment to defend Kuwait. On July 25, 1990, Saddam Hussein was told by Ambassador April Glaspie, acting on behalf of Bush, "We have no opinion on the Arab-Arab conflict like your border disagreement with Kuwait... I have direct instructions from the president to seek better relations with Iraq."

By July, 1990, Iraq had 100,000 troops on Kuwait's border. On August 2, Iraq invaded Kuwait with Bush's tacit approval.

The invasion couldn't have come at a better time for Bush. He just needed to stir things up a little more before he could take any action. In August, Bush told the Saudi ambassador, Prince Bandar, that he had satellite photos provided by the Pentagon showing Iraqi troops gathering on the Saudi border. Deceived by the fake photos, the Saudis permitted US troops on their soil, which was viewed by many in the Islamic world as infidels defiling holy territory. The Saudis also poured billions into the war effort.

The CIA-controlled media followed suit, drumming up hysteria against Saddam Hussein. Televised speaking to Congress, an innocent-looking fifteen-year-old Kuwaiti sobbed as she described witnessing Saddam Hussein's soldiers snatching babies from their incubators in a hospital in Kuwait City and tossing them on the floor to die. She was known only by Nayirah as her full name had to be kept confidential to prevent reprisals against her family in occupied Kuwait. Her testimony was circulated in a media kit prepared by Citizens for a Free Kuwait. It made headlines worldwide. In November, Bush repeated the story to US troops to motivate them to slaughter Iraqis. The PR exercise was highly successful. The sobbing teenager hadn't even been in Kuwait at the time of the invasion. She was the daughter of the Kuwaiti ambassador in Washington. The firm Hill and Knowlton had coached her on what to say.

The University of Massachusetts conducted research useful to Bush. They surveyed public opinion and correlated it with the public's knowledge of the basic facts about US policy in the Middle East. They concluded that the more television people watched, the fewer facts they knew. The less people knew in terms of facts, the more likely they were to back the Bush administration. Dee Alsop of the Within Group bragged that his job was to "identify the messages that really resonate emotionally with the American people." Alsop found the biggest emotional reaction came from emphasising "the fact that Saddam Hussein was a madman who had committed atrocities even against his own people and had tremendous power to do further damage and he needed to be stopped." Alsop even used audience surveys to adapt the clothing and hairstyle of the Kuwait ambassador, so he'd be more likeable to TV viewers.

The Gulf War began with an extensive bombing campaign on 17 January, 1991. The Coalition flew over 100,000 sorties and dropped 88,500 tons of bombs, far exceeding Pablo's bombing capabilities. News stations such as CNN showed the precision bombing of military infrastructure, while dismissing civilian casualties as collateral damage. An investigation by Beth Osborne Daponte estimated total civilian fatalities at about 3,500 from bombing and 100,000 from the war's other effects.

The US claimed that only 148 troops were killed in action, but a multiple of that died slowly and agonisingly from a group of mysterious illnesses that has become known as Gulf War Syndrome. One of those affected was Joyce Riley – the spokesperson for the American Veterans Gulf War Association – who has campaigned tirelessly on the issue.

Joyce Riley came from a military family. Her father had been a belly gunner on a B-17. Every night before she went to bed, he played the US Air Force song:

Off we go into the wild blue yonder,
Climbing high into the sun
Here they come zooming to meet our thunder
At 'em boys, Give 'er the gun!
Down we dive, spouting our flame from under
Off with one helluva roar!

We live in fame or go down in flame. Hey!
Nothing can stop the US Air Force!

Wanting to improve the world by helping the sick, Joyce studied nursing at the University of Kansas and graduated with a Bachelor of Science. As a director of nursing in four institutions, she specialised in medical surgical nursing and organ transplantation. She assisted in heart, lung, liver and kidney transplants and helped cancer patients. She flew around the US transporting organs to operating rooms.

By 1990, the year of Bush's Gulf War, Joyce was in the military serving as a flight nurse, but she wasn't dispatched to the Middle East. In one day, she received ten injections and wrote in her journal, "I would have taken a hundred shots today just to save my country." She knew about people passing out receiving shots, but she didn't know what it meant.

Six months after the vaccinations, Joyce became so ill that she could barely walk or function. After the Gulf War ended in February 1991, Joyce was hospitalised in Houston and told that she had an illness like MS. As she hadn't been deployed to the Middle East and therefore hadn't been exposed to oil-well fires or chemical or biological weapons, she suspected that her illness might be related to the vaccines. She decided never to take a vaccine again as long as she lived or to give any vaccines.

Within six months of taking their vaccines, other nurses became sick. When Joyce told her superiors, she was told she had a mental problem. "There are so many of us who are sick here," Joyce said. "So many! What are we gonna do?"

"They're not sick," said Colonel Mountain, the commander of the unit. "You're not sick. Nobody's sick."

Joyce and the sick nurses went to the US Department of Veterans Affairs (VA). The VA told them that because they were in the reserves, they were ineligible for treatment. Joyce was shocked, not because of the lack of treatment, but because she wanted to find out why they were all sick.

Further research led her to discover that the Reagan-Bush administration had sold chemical and biological weapons worth billions to Iraq before the Gulf War. Aware that Saddam Hussein had repeatedly used chemical weapons on Iranian soldiers and Iraq's Kurdish minority, the Reagan-Bush administration helped Iraq develop its chemical, biological and nuclear weapons programs. Joyce even obtained the batch numbers and dates that the weapons were sold. With billions from oil revenues and loans from its Arab neighbors, Iraq became one of the biggest arms importers in the world. Countries competed to sell arms to Saddam Hussain as he built a million-man army and spent over $50 billion on military hardware.

By attacking Iraq, a country that Bush had helped to arm – a manoeuvre that probably made Prescott Bush smirk in his grave – US weapons manufacturers reaped billions of dollars from US taxpayers and money staked by Saudi Arabia and Kuwait. Destabilising the Middle East made the price of a barrel of oil soar from $15 to $42, generating billions in revenue for the multinational oil companies controlling the oilfields in which the Bush family and their associates held investments.

Joyce also discovered that huge profits were being made from the Gulf War by pharmaceutical companies – another fertile area of Bush family investments and directorships. She found out about secret vaccine trials undertaken by the Tri-Service Vaccine Task Force, and that the Bush government was doing experiments with the same chemical and biological weapons they'd sold to Iraq in order to develop a vaccine that would be effective against what they knew the troops would be exposed to.

Joyce believes that anthrax, hepatitis B and experimental vaccines made numerous soldiers sick, a situation that was exacerbated in cases were the shots had been administered on the same day. The military introduced a new policy. You could get compensation for MS if you reported it within one year of leaving the military. MS is rarely seen in the male population from seventeen to twenty, but numerous Gulf War veterans in that age bracket started to have symptoms of a demyelinating disease – a disease in which the myelin sheath comes off the nerve ending and it misfires horribly. It's like having a seizure where you're awake and alert, but your body can't stop doing the things it's doing.

Joyce took all of the documents to her attorney and spread them out on a big table.

Examining the documents, he turned pale. "I'm no longer your attorney. I will not watch after you. I cannot do anything for you. I couldn't handle the tax audit that I'd get if I helped you." She never saw him again.

Joyce travelled across the country speaking at veterans' groups such as the American Legions and the Veterans of Foreign Wars. Her tour infuriated Bush's Department of Defense. The commander of the American Legion in

Washington DC issued a memo banning Joyce from any American Legion venue on the grounds that she was falsely trying to make veterans think that they were sick. They ejected her from their facilities. Other organisations tried to destroy her credibility. She had a sign on her car: American Veterans Gulf War Association. She got stopped by the police so much that she had to remove the sign.

In one state, a highway-patrol pulled her over.

"What's wrong, officer?" she said.

"Ma'am, I could get fired for what I'm doing," the policeman said. "I'm not supposed to stop you. I don't have a reason to stop you."

"What's the matter?"

"Ma'am, I think I've heard you. Are you the nurse on Art Bell [a radio show]?"

"Yes."

"I just had a baby born that's deaf. I wanna know have you heard about any other babies that have been born deaf because their parents had served in the Gulf War?"

"Yes, I'm sorry to tell you."

The officer's eyes filled with shock and sadness. "Because I called the DOD and the VA, and they told me that no other babies had been born deaf." "They're lying to you." He began to cry.

She received a letter from a veteran, who'd been a highway patrolman for twenty-nine years. Never in his career had he felt the need to shoot anybody. After Desert Storm, he had an urge to kill himself or someone else. Thinking he was crazy, his wife left him after over twenty years of marriage. He felt his life was ruined and wanted to die. Joyce offered to contact his wife. She explained about the prevalence of Gulf War syndrome. It wasn't her husband's fault. He needed help. They reconciled and sent Joyce a thank-you letter with a picture of them.

In California, Joyce was speaking at a Veterans auditorium about the large amount of veterans coming home from the Gulf War with herpes, yet they hadn't been unfaithful. The audience was shocked. A couple on the third row began to cry and hold each other. Joyce stopped the meeting. "Can I help you? What's going on?"

"I'm a pastor of my local church here," the man said. "I was a chaplain in the Gulf War. I came home from the Gulf War with herpes and I was never unfaithful to my wife. My wife and I have gone through hell because she could never trust me. She never believed me."

"Now we have a marriage again," his wife said, in-between sobbing. "If only I would have known this."

In Indiana, Joyce was talking to a group about veterans' children who had been affected by Gulf War illness. Uniforms brought home from the Gulf War were contaminating kids. The uniforms contain depleted uranium and traces of chemical and biological weapons, none of which washed out.

"If anybody brought home uniforms," Joyce said, "be very careful of the equipment that you have and where you store it. The chemicals in the uniforms and equipment can affect your family members, and make them ill."

At the back of the room, a lady started crying. Joyce called a break and approached the lady. "What's going on?"

"When my husband came back from the war," she said, "shortly after that, my son started behaving really bizarre and started throwing up and being sick. They told me he was just imagining it and acting out. He was really sick and he's only four, but they put him in a psychiatric facility and started giving him all these drugs. He got worse and worse on the drugs and he's in that psych facility now. He's been there for two months and they're saying that it's just because he wants to be sick for whatever reason. Now I know why my son is really sick, but I can't get him out of there."

"Do you have any of your husband's equipment?" The woman began to get hysterical and couldn't talk. "What's the matter?"

"All of my husband's uniforms and all of his equipment are stored under my boy's bed."

"Oh dear God! You've got to get that out of there."

"I'm going to the hospital right now. I'm going to tell them what you just told me and I'm going to get my son out of the hospital." The mother was able to retrieve her son.

A US representative sent his team to see her talk. During the meeting, five team members furiously scribbled notes. At the half-time break, they called her over. "The representative has a message for you." "Really," Joyce said.

"The representative wants you to know that he's not gonna support you."

"Well, nobody else has either... But why is he not gonna support this?"

"He says you know a lot about this, but you don't know it all. If you knew the rest of the story and the public knew, it would bring down this country as we know it. His message to you is, 'Keep doing what you're doing. Don't stop.'"

Joyce helped make a documentary, *Beyond Treason*, about Gulf War illness. It included testimony from Lieutenant Doug Rokke, a US Army Health Physicist Nuclear Medicine Sciences Officer with expertise in nuclear, biological and chemical warfare operations. He stated that exposure to depleted uranium was a major cause of his Gulf War illness. The US military granted him disabled status due to depleted uranium and other exposures. "All of the Iraqi equipment and a lot of the US equipment contained radiological components. When that equipment was blown up, the radiological materials were released into the environment, exposing and contaminating. And then to top it all off, we used uranium munitions known as depleted uranium. They've been used back in 1973 by the Israelis against the Egyptians, but during Gulf War One, Desert Shield and Desert Storm, we took it to a totally new level. The use of radioactive materials on the battlefield. Deliberately taking tons and tons, actually taking over 350 tons of solid radioactive materials and dispersed it across Kuwait, Saudi Arabia and Iraq. Taking our radioactive waste and throwing it in somebody else's backyard."

Depleted uranium has a half-life of 4.468 billion years. Iraq and all of the countries contaminated with it since the Gulf War will be toxic for a while – exacerbated by Bush's son who employed the same war strategies as his father. Dust storms recycle the DU onto civilian populations. DU is invisible and the particles are so small that they get through the protective masks and clothing issued by the military.

Birth defects and cancer rates, including leukaemia, have skyrocketed in Iraq. In 2004, Fallujah was bombarded, causing cancer and infant mortality rates to exceed those reported after atomic bombs were dropped on Hiroshima and Nagasaki. Babies have been born with organs outside their bodies, one eye on the forehead, known as Cyclops babies, limbs growing out of heads, multiple heads, spina bifida, brain dysfunction, spinal conditions, unformed limbs and cleft palate... The first question parents in Iraq have started asking isn't about the sex of their baby, but rather, whether it's normal. Many mothers have watched their babies die shortly after birth. Some women in Fallujah have avoided pregnancy.

Joyce got a call from a navy commander at the Pentagon about her documentary, *Gulf War Illness Fact or Fiction*. "I want you to know that you are not to give out that documentary to anyone in the military."

"Pardon," Joyce said. "What's inaccurate in it?"

"It's not that. It's that you are one of us. It's not allowed to be given out."

"No, sir. If you think I'm going to participate in the wholesale manslaughter of our military, you're wrong. Until you can show me what's inaccurate, I'm going to continue to give it out." Immediately, Joyce had a thousand extra DVDs made because she feared her home would be raided and her inventory seized.

Bush's Department of Defense tried to sabotage her talks. Joyce was asked to speak at a college in Michigan. The night before, Joyce received a call from the college: "Joyce, we've got a problem. The DOD has called here three times. They don't want you to speak and they told us not to allow you to speak."

"Really! What are you going to do?"

"We've decided that if they would call three times to tell us that we shouldn't hear it, we probably need to hear it."

"Great. I'll be there."

Joyce arrived at the college at 4 pm for dinner with the PR people and the alumni. The PR director was summoned to the phone. When he returned, he told Joyce, "We've got a problem. The DOD just landed at the airport in a DOD plane. They're coming to the meeting."

"Fantastic. That is the best thing that I could imagine."

Before the talk, he said, "Are you sure you want to do this? Three people from the DOD are here."

"Absolutely! Everything I have to say is true and accurate or I wouldn't be saying it."

Joyce entered a full auditorium. After introducing herself, she said, "How many of you are students?" Numerous hands shot up. "How many of you are professors?" They raised their hands. "How many of you all were paid to be here tonight?" Not one hand went up. "I understand there are three people from the DOD here, from the Secretary of Defense's Office and I'd like to have them recognised." No hands went up. "Since I'm only a captain and I understand that Lieutenant Colonel Thompson is here, I defer the rank. I'd like for you to be recognised, sir. I don't want to continue until you're recognised." For a few seconds, it remained quiet until suddenly, three people stood up on the back row. "I want to welcome you here tonight and I want you to know that I'm going to say some of the most damning evidence ever against the Department of Defense and I'm going to prove it with your own documents. But before I begin, I want you to agree that if there is anything that I say that's inaccurate here tonight, I want you to stop me or it will stand as accurate." Joyce began to speak and go through all of the documents. Not once did any of the men stand. At the end of the three hours, they scurried away.

Upset by Joyce, the DOD called a press conference. They invited media people who'd attended Joyce's talk. In a light blue uniform, Colonel Thompson did a PowerPoint on the magnificence of the military and how wrong Joyce Riley was.

After ten minutes, an investigative reporter stood up. "Colonel Thompson, I think I need to stop you and tell you that I don't think there's one person in this audience who believes a word that you're saying. Is it true, like Captain Riley said, that the US sold weapons to Iraq before the Gulf War. Is that accurate?"

"There's no way that we could possibly know that because that's all compartmentalised information. I'm sure Joyce doesn't have anything that could prove that."

"You saw her show the evidence of the sale of those biologicals to Iraq last night. There's not a person believing anything that you are saying here."

An aide emerged from the side of the curtain. "Colonel Thompson, you're needed in Washington immediately. Your plane is ready to leave." The colonel abandoned the press conference.

As an increasing amount of troops got sick from Bush's Gulf War, Joyce refused to shut up. She started her own radio show, *The Power Hour*, talking about Gulf War illness. She received letters from thousands of ill people, who were being told there was nothing wrong with them. The government had lied to them so continuously that they didn't understand their situations. They'd served their country their whole lives. They were told to obey and take orders and if they got sick they'd be taken care of. After registering as sick, they were told they had mental problems and placed on psychotropic drugs manufactured by companies that had contributed to Bush's election campaign. This didn't make any sense to them. It made financial sense to the companies supplying vaccines and drugs. SSRI drugs were being used to keep veterans quiet and so their illnesses could be classified as mental. The abandonment by the military is one of the causes of so many veterans committing suicide.

"They're just writing me off," a veteran said on a call to Joyce. "I'm noncommissioned. I've been in the military for twenty-seven years and they won't take care of me. I'm going to be going over to the VA one last time because now I'm in a wheelchair. I cannot walk. So now they're gonna have to listen to me. My wife is gonna take me over there and our children are gonna go over there and we're gonna get an answer today regardless."

"Great. Call me after you go the meeting with them and let me know."

He went to the meeting. "I'm in a wheelchair. Now will you guys believe me that I am sick and I don't have a mental problem?"

The doctor went over to the veteran's wife. "Look, I hate to have to tell you this, but we gave your husband a psych evaluation and we think he's a latent homosexual and that's why he's doing this to himself."

Angry, the veteran's wife grabbed the physician's white jacket. "How dare you say that to my husband in front of his family! You know that is so far from being true!" The family was ejected from the VA hospital.

Joyce became familiar with the tricks of the medical staff who'd stop at nothing to convince veterans that their problems were psychological. The first thing they did was to give psych evaluations, so they could always find a fall-back reason for the illness. If that didn't work, they humiliated or embarrassed them.

While the Bush dynasty fortune increased from war profiteering, officials continued to tell veterans that the government had played no role in their Gulf War illness, even though the government knew it was a lie. In Senate Report 103-97 chaired by John D. Rockefeller IV in 1994, the government acknowledged that soldiers are routinely experimented on without prior knowledge or consent and lasting harm was caused to many veterans:

During the last 50 years, hundreds of thousands of military personnel have been involved in human experimentation and other intentional exposures conducted by the Department of Defense (DOD), often without a servicemember's knowledge or consent. In some cases, soldiers who consented to serve as human subjects found themselves participating in experiments quite different from those described at the time they volunteered. For example, thousands of World War II veterans who originally volunteered to "test summer clothing" in exchange for extra leave time, found themselves in gas chambers testing the effects of mustard gas and lewisite [an organoarsenic compound that causes blisters]. (Note 1)

Additionally, soldiers were sometimes ordered by commanding officers to "volunteer" to participate in research or face dire consequences. For example, several Persian Gulf War veterans interviewed by Committee staff reported that they were ordered to take experimental vaccines during Operation Desert Shield or face prison. (Note 2)

The goals of many of the military experiments and exposures were very appropriate. For example, some experiments were intended to provide important information about how to protect US troops from nuclear, biological, and chemical weapons or other dangerous substances during wartime. In the Persian Gulf War, US troops were intentionally exposed to an investigational vaccine that was intended to protect them against biological warfare, and they were given pyridostigmine bromide pills in an experimental protocol intended to protect them against chemical warfare.

However, some of the studies that have been conducted had more questionable motives. For example, the Department of Defense (DOD) conducted numerous "man-break" tests, exposing soldiers to chemical weapons in order to determine the exposure level that would cause a casualty, i.e., "break a man." (Note 3) Similarly, hundreds of soldiers were subjected to hallucinogens in experimental programs conducted by the DOD in participation with, or sponsored by, the CIA. (Note 4), (Note 5) These servicemembers often unwittingly participated as human subjects in tests for drugs intended for mind-control or behavior modification, often without their knowledge or consent. Although the ultimate goal of those experiments was to provide information that would help US military and intelligence efforts, most Americans would agree that the use of soldiers as unwitting guinea pigs in experiments that were designed to harm them, at least temporarily, is not ethical.

Whether the goals of these experiments and exposures were worthy or not, these experiences put hundreds of thousands of U.S. servicemembers at risk, and may have caused lasting harm to many individuals.

Despite the low battlefield casualty figures touted by the media during the Gulf War, Joyce calculated that hundreds of thousands of service-people became ill and six thousand have died so far as a result of Gulf War illness. She estimated that more than fifty percent of the military was experimented on. Joyce estimated civilian deaths to be 300,000 worldwide from millions infected.

These figures push the total deaths attributable to decisions made by Bush into the hundreds of thousands.

The deaths were kept off Bush's balance sheet by his administration paying millions to organisations such as the Rand Corporation to do research that concluded there is no evidence that Gulf War illness exists. When confronted with over 100,000 sick veterans, the government was able to say that they went to the Rand Corporation, an independent organisation, who found no link.

The Department of Defense became the biggest purchaser of SSRI drugs in the world. Medicated to the hilt, troops still died at record levels due to suicides and homicides. Presently, veterans from the recent wars in the Middle East are committing suicide at the rate of over twenty per day. The government continues to pretend that the causes are unknown.

After years of campaigning, on the day before Thanksgiving, Joyce went into an emergency room. They did an MRI and CT scan. She was told, "You have spinal cancer, really, really badly." They began emergency radiation on Thanksgiving Day.

"This must be bad if you're doing it on Thanksgiving," she told the oncologist.

"If we didn't do it today, you probably wouldn't be here."

Even cancer didn't deter Joyce from exposing the crimes committed on the service-people during Bush's Gulf War.

The only country to indict Bush as an alleged war criminal was Japan in 1997, after sixteen Japanese citizens were barred from the US due to alleged war crimes during World War II. Due to his attacks on Iraq and Panama, Bush was at the top of the list of ten Americans – including Reagan and Oliver North – banned from Japan for "war crimes, crimes against humanity and violations of human rights."

The first Gulf War resulted in over 100,000 deaths, eclipsing Pablo's 4,000. In this context, the death of Barry Seal would have been insignificant to a master of wholesale slaughter such as Bush.

Chapter 44

Protecting Paedophiles

Waging war and dropping bombs can boost a leader's ratings – as Margaret Thatcher pointed out to Bush – but protecting paedophiles has never been popular with the public. It has been alleged that Bush did so during his presidency, putting more children at risk. One victim claimed that Bush engaged in paedophilia, and allegations have been made about some of his inner circle.

The brave and tireless campaigning of Noreen Gosch – whose son was snatched from a street – helped to expose the Franklin paedophile ring, but agencies under President Bush obstructed any form of justice for the victims.

In 1982, Noreen was living the normal life of housewife with three kids in West Des Moines, Iowa. She enjoyed baking cookies and going to ball games.

On September 5, her twelve-year-old, Johnny, left the house at about 5:45 am to deliver Sunday newspapers. He headed down the street, pulling a little wagon with his dog riding along with him. When he got to the street corner, a man in a car stopped him and asked for directions. Having been instructed not to talk to strangers, Johnny didn't engage with the man. Other kids on the corner saw Johnny walk away from the stranger.

The stranger did a U-turn, sped back up the street and stopped where the boys were gathering their papers. The stranger turned off his engine, opened the passenger door, put his feet on the curb and chatted in slurred speech to the boys.

Johnny turned towards sixteen-year-old Mike. "This man is nuts. There's something wrong with him. I'm scared and I'm leaving." Johnny threw his papers into the wagon and took off down the street.

The other boys left. A forty-four-year-old lawyer had parked his car to get his son's papers. He saw the stranger and the licence plate. Unaware of what was going on, he departed.

Mike heard Johnny's dog growl. The stranger got back in his car, slammed the door, started the engine, raised his hand and clicked the dome light three times. Mike saw Johnny walking along, and another stranger, about 6-foot-3, emerge from in-between two houses. The second stranger started following Johnny, who went around the corner, out of Mike's sight. A few seconds later, a car door slammed, tyres screeched, and the original stranger's car ran a stop sign, turned left and headed out of town. During the twelve minutes that Johnny was absent from his home, Noreen and her husband, John, had been sleeping. For thirteen months, Johnny had always woken his dad up before going on his newspaper round, but that day he hadn't. It was the only day that he'd gone out alone.

The phone started to ring because neighbours hadn't got their papers.

Assuming Johnny was running late, John told Noreen that he'd go out and help him. John left, only to screech back onto the drive a few minutes later. "Call the police immediately! Johnny's gone! Somebody took him! His wagon is up on the street corner full of papers! Not even the bundle ties have been cut!"

Noreen called the police to report a missing child. Awaiting the police, Noreen called her other two children and asked them to come home. One was working at Pancake House; the other was at a college in a nearby town. She asked her friends to help her search for her son. She called the *Des Moines Register* district manager of her area, Johnny's boss at the newspaper, who brought a register of the names of all of the boys who had been delivering newspapers that morning. Noreen called them all.

The police arrived forty-five minutes after she had called them. By then, she had a description of the stranger and his car, a partial licence plate number and every detail that every witness could remember. She filled out and signed a missing person's report.

"Did your son ever run away before?" a policeman asked.

"He's never run away, period. Why would you say such a thing? Didn't you just listen to me? What I told you! What the witnesses had said."

The policeman recoiled as if to say, *How dare you talk to me like that!* "I have to go back to the station." He left at about 8:30 am.

Noreen organised search parties and contacted the media. Thousands of people searched for Johnny in the state parks, cornfields and anywhere a body could have been dumped.

Twenty of the searchers showed up at Noreen's house, furious. "I thought you wanted help," one said.

"I do want help," Joyce said, confused. "What's wrong?"

"The police chief just showed up at one of the state parks, drunk, and got on top of a picnic table and shouted through a bullhorn, 'Everyone go home!

Johnny Gosch is nothing but a damn runaway!'" Much later, that police chief was shamed and lost his job. Eventually, he was arrested for shoplifting.

Realising that the police weren't going to help her, Noreen called the FBI. Two agents arrived at her home. Sitting at a table, they explained, in-between slurping coffee, that they couldn't investigate the case because there was no crime.

"I have no son," Noreen said. "What are you going to do about it?"

"The police chief told us that this case does not require the FBI, so we will not be in the case."

For the next few days, Noreen suffered from confusion and turmoil. Every fifteen minutes, her phone rang, day and night. Local TV stations began to show Johnny's picture. The news spread throughout Iowa and other states that a young boy had been snatched off the street.

The local police did nothing. Noreen walked into the police station and demanded to speak to the chief. "If there had been a bank robbery, would you have called it runaway money for the first seventy-two hours or would you have begun to work on it?" she said. The chief told her to leave the station.

At least now she knew she was on her own. Within a week, she was interviewing private investigators. The investigator she chose set up surveillance at the location of the kidnapping, and began to monitor cars at the same early time at which Johnny had been taken. Two squad cars showed up and arrested the investigator for vagrancy.

Noreen returned to the police chief. "If you aren't going to work on my son's case that's your choice, but step aside 'cause I am. I don't want to see or hear again that my private investigators have been disturbed or arrested. They're licensed in Iowa to operate, so you need to back off if you're not going to do your job."

The investigators gathered information. One did house-to-house interviews, during which a neighbour described seeing a van parked in the wrong direction on the street with its motor running. Its loud engine had drawn his attention, so he'd watched it through his window. He saw a car pull up next to the van, and two men load something long wrapped in a blanket from the car to the van. Then they all left. Unaware a kidnapping had occurred, he just thought it odd at the time. Noreen decided not to share the information with law enforcement because she believed that somebody would come forward with that piece of information. If it hadn't been broadcast by the media, she'd know that the person was authentic.

Six months after Johnny's disappearance, another boy was kidnapped. The parents received a call on their son's cell phone demanding a ransom. The FBI sent numerous agents to Des Moines. They found the child within thirtysix hours.

The next day, a special agent led his FBI team into Noreen's home. "We really had to work on that case because there was a human life at stake," he said.

Noreen was shocked. "Well, what do you think my son is? Don't you think his life matters?"

"Mrs Gosch, there's something you don't understand. The other family are very wealthy. They're very prominent in Des Moines. We had to search for their son because they are more prominent people than you are."

Noreen picked up a cup of hot coffee and threw it across the room. It just missed the agent's face.

"I can see that you're distraught. Is there anything I can do for you?"

"Yes. You can get the hell out of my house! Don't ever come back! If you're not going to investigate my son's case, then step aside because I'm coming through. I'll find out what happened to my son, regardless of whether you accept the information or whether you don't. I will at least know before I die."

Reflecting on what he'd said, Noreen realised he'd done her a favour. He'd told her the bottom line.

Over the years, Noreen received leads that raised her hopes, but went nowhere.

Nine long years later, Paul came forward. He'd been tortured and sexually abused as part of a pornography and prostitution ring. In jail, accused of perjury and sex crimes, he had told his lawyer that he'd participated in Johnny's kidnapping.

The lawyer tried to call Noreen, but Johnny's dad, John, answered because Noreen wasn't home. John didn't tell Noreen. She only found out about Paul two years later.

Noreen met Paul and read his diaries, including the entry about Johnny's kidnapping. Paul said they had a van parked a couple of blocks from the kidnapping site. Johnny had been loaded from a car into the van, which had transported Johnny to a location in Iowa. As the information matched what Noreen's witness had seen, she knew Paul was authentic.

Noreen took Paul's information to the police and the FBI, who refused to act because Paul was "a nut" with no credibility. They said he had multiple personalities due to the abuse and programming he'd suffered, and not one word of his statement could be taken as fact.

Noreen noticed that Paul had never wavered from his story under questioning over the years. After eleven years, what Paul had said about Johnny remained the same, verbatim. When asked about something he had no knowledge of, Paul had always said, "I'm sorry. I don't know about that." He never made up stories or changed any words, which impressed. Noreen.

From Paul's statement, Noreen concluded Johnny's kidnapping was highly organised. Two weeks before the kidnapping, a neighbour had seen Johnny being photographed on his way home from school. The car had out-of-state plates. The photographer had leaned out of the window and used a camera with a long telephoto lens. The neighbour had reported it to the police, who said it wasn't a crime to take photos.

The morning of the kidnapping, the kidnappers had those photos. About four years older than Johnny, Paul had been in the back seat. They'd used a child to lure a child. Johnny had come close enough to the car for them to pull him in.

Paul revealed that the two vehicles involved in Johnny's kidnapping had rendezvoused at a farmhouse outside of Sioux City, Iowa. For two weeks, Johnny was kept in the basement of the old farmhouse. On film and at gunpoint, Paul and another young man sexually abused Johnny. After two weeks, a man called the Colonel arrived and paid a lot of cash to the kidnappers. Paul was under the impression that the Colonel was taking Johnny back to Colorado and the West Coast.

Paul didn't see Johnny again until 1986, during an orgy at a ranch belonging to the Colonel. It was in a remote area in the mountains. Adults were having sex with kids. Johnny's hair had been dyed black. They'd switched his name to Mark. Paul said kids were flown all over the country to wealthy paedophiles, who requested kids by description. The kids were constantly moved around.

Noreen complained bitterly to her state senators that the FBI had continued to refuse to investigate the case. Her senators got in touch with the FBI office in Washington. The FBI was forced to do a house-to-house search. A neighbour reported that the FBI agents were disgruntled and mouthing off about Mrs Gosch for having forced the search upon them. They hadn't intended to search at all.

Why, Noreen wondered, *would a police chief not investigate and try to find Johnny, and why would the FBI refuse to investigate a bona fide kidnapping case with multiple eyewitnesses? Why do they keep saying we have no crimes?* Noreen was sick of hearing that phrase. *Are they stupid? Do they not know how to investigate a case like this? Are they naïve? Are they compliant in protecting a bigwig that is a paedophile? Or are they involved in it themselves?*

Noreen recalled that shortly after Johnny had been kidnapped, there'd been an article in the *Des Moines Register* about the kidnapping of two girls, thirteen and fourteen, who'd been taken to Omaha and put into a pornography ring. They were returned and the kidnappers were arrested. Noreen took the clipping to the police chief and asked him to investigate the lead.

"I don't have a feel for that, so I'm not going to do anything," he said.

"Can you call the police chief of Omaha just to ask about it? Omaha is only two hours away. If they came here for the girls, they could have come here for my son, too." The police chief and the FBI refused her request.

Noreen hosted a press conference. She read the clipping from the paper and recited the reaction from the police chief and the FBI. Four days later, she received the first of many death threats. "If you don't stop rocking the boat and making waves, you're going to die."

What boat did I rock? Noreen thought. *What wave did I make?* She realised the wave was asking about Omaha. She was knocking on the back door of the Franklin Credit Union scandal, years before the story erupted. The authorities in Des Moines were not going to let the story break by solving Johnny's case.

Noreen found out that the police chief she'd been dealing with was good friends with the police chief in Omaha, Nebraska. They both had allegedly attended orgies in Omaha together, where they used young boys and girls. The police chief of Omaha had been accused of impregnating an underage girl at a party. It finally made sense to Noreen why the police chief had told everybody searching for Johnny to go home and why he wouldn't investigate the Omaha connection. Noreen felt sick, but also thankful that she finally knew what she was dealing with and what the obstacles were.

She pledged to keep Johnny's story alive and let as many people as possible know that children were being abducted from the streets for sex rings. She started the Johnny Gosch Foundation to help raise money for private investigators to keep searching for Johnny. She developed a program: In Defense of Children. She gave up her life to go on the road, speaking in schools, churches, civic organisations and network TV shows. In five years, she did 700 speeches.

She wrote legislation for the State of Iowa. The Johnny Gosch Bill provided for any family with a missing child to have an immediate investigation started. No more waiting seventy-two hours. The FBI would be called in to start work immediately. Her second bill provided for victims of sexual abuse to testify via video camera, rather than having to recount everything in open court in front of their assailant. She introduced a children's Bill of Rights to help protect sexually-abused children. Her laws were passed in other states bordering Iowa, codifying procedures for missing and abused children.

Around this time in Washington DC, the National Center For Missing Children was being formed. Parents of missing children, including Noreen, were flown to Texas to testify before the Justice Department on video, explaining what went wrong in their cases, who was responsible and why they hadn't done their jobs. Noreen related the mistakes on Johnny's case. She ended her speech with, "If the FBI was not going to investigate missing children's cases, then the Justice Department should cut their funding. They should take that amount of money and give it to an organisation to start a missing children's centre, so that those of us who have missing children will have some government agency to turn to for assistance."

The room fell silent. John Walsh, the grieving parent who hosted *America's Most Wanted*, rushed over to Noreen. "I can't believe you said that. I can't believe you said to cut their funding."

"John, I meant it. If they're not going to do their job, cut their funding and give it to someone who will. I'm very serious about it. Why does everybody think the FBI is a sacred cow that you can't challenge? They didn't do their job for my son. They didn't follow their own code of ethics for the criteria of a kidnapping case. Perhaps if they would have moved a little swifter, Johnny would be with me today."

She wanted Johnny's kidnapping to stand for something and progress to be made in the system, so other parents wouldn't have to suffer. Every time she did a TV show or a speech, leads and information trickled in. With the help of her investigators, she slowly assembled the jigsaw. She discovered what had happened to Johnny, why, who was responsible and how they profited from children.

"Kiddie porn is a multi-billion dollar business in this country," Noreen said. "The only reason it is is because of supply and demand... Somebody has to supply the children to the paedophiles who have this thing for young children and the money to pay for it. My son just happened to be one of them." Noreen concluded that the police didn't investigate Johnny's kidnapping because of their involvement in the paedophile ring.

In December 1996, Noreen was invited to a talk show in LA with other mothers who'd lost their children. They were asked to give a Christmas message to their missing children.

"Johnny, if you're still out there and if you're alive and you're getting this message, I'll help you in any way I possibly can. I still live in West Des Moines. I've divorced your father. My name and address are listed in the phone book, so you can find me. Contact me and I'll help you." Noreen flew home.

In March 1997 in the middle of the night, someone knocked continuously on Noreen's door. Noreen got up. Living alone, she wouldn't normally have opened the door at that time. The peephole revealed two young men in the doorway with the hall lights illuminating the face of a man resembling Johnny. "Who's there?"

"It's me, mom. It's Johnny."

Overwhelmed by emotion, she opened the door and let them in. "You're gonna have to have a safe place to stay," Noreen said, thinking Johnny was back for good. "Let me call someone who can come here tonight and give us some legal advice and help."

"I can't stay. You don't understand. It's not safe. You wouldn't be safe if I stayed here. They'll kill me." Johnny said he'd been abducted into a highlevel pornography and prostitution ring that was also involved in drug running. They catered to people across the country at the top of politics from senators all the way to the White House. In shock, Noreen listened as Johnny said he wanted her to get his story out in the hope of making arrests happen, so that he and the other kids could be free to safely reunite with their families.

Johnny said that a few years ago, he and another boy had stolen a car and escaped from the kidnappers, who stored the kids across the country in safe houses. He'd sought sanctuary on an Indian reservation, which he considered safe from the authorities because reservations are classified as a sovereign state. But he was tracked down and brought back into the ring.

Johnny said that it was too dangerous for him to stay. He said goodbye.

After they left, Noreen ran outside in a daze and saw them disappear into the night on foot. She never saw Johnny again.

The witness who'd come forward, Paul, who said he'd helped to lure Johnny into the car, had been involved in the Franklin paedophile network. It had been run by Larry King – a personal friend of Bush – and Craig Spence, a lobbyist, CIA asset and blackmail artist.

A rising star in the Republican Party, King had operated in Franklin, where he was the vice chairman for finance of the National Black Republican Council. King had campaigned for Bush to become president and had hosted a $100,000 gala for Bush at the 1998 Republican Convention in New Orleans. He also had an appetite for sex with boys. He'd operated a welltuned pornography and prostitution ring, using kids from foster homes and Boys Town: a Catholic orphanage for troubled boys.

Craig Spence threw sex and drug parties at his home, which had been bugged by the CIA to facilitate blackmail. While Bush was president, Spence took call boys on midnight tours of the White House. Some of the children King flew around the country ended up in Spence's home in Washington DC, where orgies were filmed.

The first victim to speak out was Eulice Washington, a sixteen-year-old who'd been placed in a foster home run by one of Larry King's cousins, where children were whipped and beaten. She'd arrived at age eight, and had eventually been transferred to a different foster home. She told her new foster mother that her adopted father at the previous foster home had molested her. She passed a polygraph, but her adopted father was never prosecuted.

In March 1986, Eulice told a Boys Town youth worker that Larry King had flown her and other kids from Boys Town to orgies in New York and Chicago. She added that she had seen Bush at one of the orgies. The FBI was informed, but no action was ever taken. A social worker investigating the abuse at Eulice's previous foster home was threatened by the FBI.

In 1988, the Omaha police started investigating King and a photographer for child pornography. They gathered evidence, but the investigation was shut down.

A fifteen-year-old victim in a psychiatric hospital told the staff that she had been in a prostitution and pornography ring since age nine. She told Omaha police about Larry King's involvement. The police report said that the victim had been credible, but she was never interviewed again and no investigation happened.

On July 20, 1988, a supervisor of the Nebraska foster care system reported the existence of a child exploitation ring to the Attorney General. The investigator assigned to the case didn't interview any victims.

On November 4, 1988 – four days before Bush was elected president – federal agents raided Larry King's Franklin Credit Union, from which King had allegedly embezzled $39.4 million. Researchers have speculated that Bush was getting rid of King because his paedophile ring was attracting too much attention.

Senator Schmit, who'd drafted a resolution to form the Franklin Committee to investigate the failure of King's credit union, received a call warning him not to investigate because it would "reach to the highest levels of the Republican Party." Disregarding the warning, the committee uncovered accounts of child trafficking and abuse that had occurred without the authorities acting even though they knew about it.

After receiving more threats, Schmit said, "I've been told to leave it alone or my kids were going to be orphans."

A group of Nebraskans who'd heard about children such as Johnny getting snatched from the streets formed Concerned Parents. At one of their meetings, a woman stood up and said, "I think George Bush is involved in this child-abuse case and that is why all these people have been dying."

An ex-CIA employee, a psychologist in Omaha, came to the attention of Concerned Parents, after he claimed that rumours of Bush engaging in paedophilia were rampant when Bush was running the CIA.

The Franklin Committee assigned Gary Caradori – an ace private investigator with a background in the military and the police – to investigate the allegations of paedophilia. From the outset, his efforts were blocked. Witnesses and victims were too fearful to talk to him. FBI agents were waiting at places he went to as if they knew his movements in advance. A phone-company employee confirmed Caradori's phones had been tapped.

Caradori learned that Larry King had been taking almost weekly chartered flights across the country without listing the names of the kids accompanying him.

Over time, Caradori found four victims willing to go on the record. He videotaped them describing their abuse at the hands of prominent people.

Their statements all matched up. Caradori took the tapes to the Franklin Committee, who didn't know what to do with them because of their mistrust of the state and federal authorities who'd previously failed to act on the earliest victims' testimonies. In December, 1989, the Franklin Committee sent twenty-one hours of videotaped testimony to the Nebraska attorney general and Nebraska's US attorney, forcing the state and federal authorities to act.

A grand jury was formed to investigate the allegations the same week that President Bush arrived in Omaha for the Nebraska governor's fundraiser. King had purchased a ticket for the fundraiser, but the Secret Service whisked him off to an Omaha federal courthouse, where he appeared on February 7, 1990. The magistrate ordered King to undergo an immediate mental-health evaluation at the US Medical Center for Federal Prisoners in Springfield, Missouri. Federal marshals escorted King to Springfield, where a US District Court judge assigned him to a psychiatric hospital, safely away from the grand-jury investigation into his paedophile ring.

Over a year, despite obstacles placed in his way by the authorities and the media, Caradori gathered more evidence and testimonies about child-sex crimes. He was tipped-off about a plot to implicate him in scripting the allegations that would have led to his arrest. He wrote to a lawyer that the paedophile ring reached "to the highest levels of the United States."

As the case revolved around child pornography, Caradori set about obtaining some as evidence. He tracked down one of King's pornographers. He called a *Washington Times* reporter from a payphone to say that he was on the verge of acquiring photos. He also told another person "we got them by the shorthairs." Five sources claimed that Caradori had obtained pictures.

The next day, July 11, at approximately 2 am, his single-engine plane crashed in a cornfield, killing Caradori and his eight-year-old son. According to the National Transportation Safety Board, his plane had broken up in flight, but no mechanism by which it had happened was ever discovered.

Caradori had been working closely with Paul Rodriguez, a reporter for the *Washington Times*, whose first article on the subject was titled, "Homosexual prostitution inquiry ensnares VIPs with Reagan, Bush 'Call Boys' took midnight tour of White House." The next story was titled, "Power Broker Served Drugs, Sex At Parties Bugged For Blackmail."

Six victims, including Eulice Washington, agreed to testify to the Franklin Committee and the police. Despite receiving threats, Eulice maintained her story, including that she had seen Bush at a paedophilic orgy in Chicago in

1984. FBI intimidation saw off two of the witnesses, who recanted their testimony.

With Caradori out of the way, a special prosecutor presented evidence and witnesses in such a way that the state grand jury concluded that the child-sex allegations were a "carefully crafted hoax." The grand jury concluded that no children had been trafficked across state lines for immoral purposes. Two of the brave victims who'd testified about the sexually horrific things that had happened to them at the hands of the paedophile ring were charged by the state with perjury, and told they were facing hundreds of years of imprisonment if convicted. Eulice Washington wasn't charged. The media backed up the grand-jury verdicts and called the Franklin Committee a disgrace. Even Larry King's partner in crime, Spence, was exonerated of all of his crimes.

One of the victims, twenty-one-year-old Alicia Owen, was told that she was facing over three-hundred years in prison. If she was convicted, the paedophile ring would be protected. Before the trial, her brother died in strange circumstances. The vast resources of the state were used against her in the longest trial in Nebraska history. After deliberating for three days, the jurors found her guilty. She was sentenced to between nine and fifteen years. She spent the first two in solitary confinement. All of the members of the judicial system who'd facilitated the cover-up were promoted. Some became judges.

The Bush administration's FBI and Secret Service helped to suppress any exposure of the Franklin paedophile network. Author Roger Stone believes that was coordinated from the top. The end result was that the victims ended up in prison, not the perpetrators.

Throughout his years in politics, Bush feigned having a heart, while protecting associates engaged in paedophilia. Someone willing to stoop to that level would have had no twinge of conscience when it came to ordering the assassination of Barry Seal.

Chapter 45

War on Drugs and CIA Drug Trafficking

Throughout the 1980s, the Reagan-Bush administration launched an expansion of the War on Drugs. The "Just say no" campaign was funded largely by tobacco, alcohol and pharmaceutical companies. The government claimed that the war was necessary to take down drug lords such as Pablo Escobar, but its burden fell mostly on hundreds of thousands of non-violent marijuana users, many of whom were SWAT-team raided and dragged off to jail.

Reagan's wife, Nancy, was a leading spokesperson: "If you're a casual drug user, you're an accomplice to murder." The campaign, in combination with sensational headlines about rabid black crack users murdering white people, prostituting themselves for a pittance and giving birth to malnourished alien-like babies, caused public opinion about drugs to swing in favour of the zero-tolerance policies that filled prisons with non-violent drug users from the poorest neighbourhoods. Private prisons and all of the industries that grew up around them became a massive source of profit for the politicians taking contributions from them.

In 1982, Ronald Regan created the South Florida Task Force, headed by Bush. It combined elements of the FBI, army and Navy to fight traffickers who weren't working with the CIA. The media published images of soldiers, surveillance planes and helicopter gunships off the coast of Florida, waging war with Pablo's smugglers. As drug seizures rose, Reagan and Bush posed for photos amid tons of confiscated cocaine, and proclaimed their success in the War on Drugs. They never mentioned that the price of cocaine in America was falling despite the gunboats, a sure sign that the supply into America was increasing. Even DEA agents complained that the War on Drugs was just a handover of money to the military.

In 1983, a program called Drug Abuse Resistance Education (DARE) started in American schools. Students were encouraged to let the police know about their friends' and families' drug habits, so they could swiftly be incarcerated. The Reagan-Bush administration doubled the federal prison population. Young offenders and non-violent drug users were sent to Special Alternative Incarceration boot camps to have their rebellious attitudes demolished. They often emerged traumatised and more inclined to take drugs.

Simultaneously, the Reagan-Bush administration quietly instructed American universities to destroy all of the research into marijuana undertaken between 1966 and 1976, which could have benefited people with a range of ailments, including cancer patients at risk of death because they couldn't eat, and children born with rare conditions who had hundreds of seizures a week and were at risk of entering comas and dying.

The federal government used planes to illegally spray marijuana fields in Kentucky, Georgia and Tennessee with the toxic weed-killer Paraquat, risking the lives of marijuana smokers. Banned in several European countries, Paraquat is highly toxic to animals and has serious and irreversible delayed effects if absorbed. As little as one teaspoonful of the active ingredient is fatal. Death occurs up to thirty days after ingestion. It's also toxic if absorbed through the skin, and can cause nose bleeding if inhaled. No antidote for poisoning exists although it is recommended that hospitalisation is sought without delay. The government was able to use it by classifying it as having low acute toxicity when sprayed.

Reagan's Drugs Czar, Carlton Turner, said that kids deserved to die as a punishment for smoking poisoned weed, to teach them a lesson. Two years later, he called for the death penalty for all drug users. On one occasion, the DEA had been ordered to spray Paraquat on a marijuana plantation in Georgia, but the Forest Service had miscalculated the location. The Paraquat ended up on a corn crop. Drugs Czar Turner was a co-owner of a patent, along with the University of Mississippi, on a chemical test that detected the presence of Paraquat on crops. Although he stood to earn royalties from the patent, he denied any conflict of interest.

Extending the War on Drugs into Colombia included dropping chemical poisons on peasants and their crops. Many had to leave the little pieces of land they owned, and they were reduced to begging. Their land often ended up in the hands of the wealthy and foreign corporations.

By 1986, officials in Florida acknowledged that the amount of drugs entering the US had skyrocketed. The Government Accounting Office stated that cocaine imports had doubled in one year.

In the summer of 1989, the Commissioner of US Customs resigned because he believed that the only real battles were being fought against minorities and the downtrodden, while those in authority were protecting the government's monopoly in the trade. "The War on Drugs is a war of words," he said.

While the international narcotics trade thrived, Reagan declared the War on Drugs to be one of his best achievements. But in 1989, the Iran-Contra scandal revealed that the US government – via the CIA – had been trafficking in hard drugs for military weapons. During the investigation, the increasingly frail and senile Reagan feigned ignorance and most people believed him. Throughout Reagan's term, ex-CIA-director Bush had really been calling the shots.

On September 5, 1989, President Bush outlined his strategy for eradicating drug use. He asked Congress for $7.9 billion, 70 percent for law enforcement, including $1.6 billion for prisons. "This scourge will stop." His focus was on reducing demand, meaning arresting more drug users, rather than prevention, education and medical treatment. He increased the repressive measures against marijuana users. "Our nation has zero tolerance for casual drug use... You do drugs, you will be caught, and when you're caught, you will be punished. Some think there won't be room for them in jail. We'll make room."

The story of Keith Jackson illustrates Bush's duplicity in the War on Drugs. On September 5, 1989, President Bush appeared on TV. "This is the first time since taking the oath of office that I've felt an issue was so important, so threatening, that it warranted talking directly with you, the American people. All of us agree that the gravest domestic threat facing our nation today is drugs. Drugs have strained our faith in our system of justice. Our courts, our prisons, our legal system, are stretched to breaking point. The social costs of drugs are mounting. In short, drugs are sapping our strength as a nation. Turn on the evening news or pick up the morning paper and you'll see what some Americans know just by stepping out their front door: Our most serious problem today is cocaine, and in particular, crack..." Reaching to his side, Bush produced a bag labelled EVIDENCE with chalky rocks in it. "This is crack cocaine seized a few days ago by Drug Enforcement agents in a park just across the street from the White House. It could easily have been heroin or PCP. It's as innocent-looking as candy, but it's turning our cities into battle zones and it's murdering our children. Let there be no mistake: this stuff is poison. Some used to call drugs harmless recreation; they're not. Drugs are a real and terribly dangerous threat to our neighbourhoods, our friends and our families..."

Bush's claim aroused suspicion in Michael Isikoff, an NBC correspondent, who doubted that crack was being sold in Lafayette Square, an urban park north of the White House. Through contacts at the DEA, Isikoff learned the truth. Bush's speech writers had decided that a prop would enhance the president's rhetoric, so they wrote the Lafayette Square crack story into the script before it had happened. After Bush approved the idea, the DEA was told to make a drug purchase near the White House in order to fit the script.

The assignment ended up with Special Agent Sam Gaye, who was asked by his boss, "Can you make a drug buy around 1600 Pennsylvania Avenue? Can you call any defendants you've been buying from?" In court, Gaye testified, "I had twenty-four hours to buy three ounces of crack."

Using informers, Gaye set up a purchase, which fell through after the dealer didn't show up in the park. During the second attempt, the agent's body microphone malfunctioned, and the cameraman about to film the transaction was assaulted by a homeless person.

Finally, an informant contacted an amenable low-level dealer, Keith Jackson, an eighteen-year-old high-school student who lived across town. Gaye asked Keith to meet him in the park.

"Where's Lafayette Park?" Keith said.

"It's across the street from the White House."

"Where the fuck is the White House?" Keith said.

"We had to manipulate him to get him down there," said William McMullan, assistant special agent in charge of the DEA's Washington field office. "It wasn't easy."

When the DEA video tape was played in court, the jury laughed. It showed Gaye waiting on Pennsylvania Avenue with the White House and tourists behind him. Before Jackson and an informant arrived by car, an irate woman sprung up from below the camera's vision, and yelling was heard as an altercation unfolded.

"There was this lady," Gaye said, "who got up off the ground and said, 'Don't take my photo! Don't take my photo!'"

For the White House transaction, as well as three earlier sales, Keith ended up facing ten years to life without parole even though he had no previous convictions. The first trial was a mistrial, but on retrial he was convicted of three counts with two being dropped, including the Lafayette Park sale. The judge sentenced him to ten years due to the mandatory minimums for selling crack near a school, but suggested that he seek clemency, which was never granted.

A teenager had been sacrificed to improve Bush's ratings.

After the fall of the Berlin Wall in 1989 and with the Soviet Union contracting, the US was rapidly running out of Communists to fight. Bush needed enemies to maintain his popularity at the voting booths and to keep the war machine in business. Pablo was ideal.

In November 1990, Bush signed a bill that coerced the states into suspending the driver's licences and revoking government permits and benefits (including college loans) of those convicted of drug crimes. He advocated the heavy use of forfeiture or confiscation of property that the government believed to be drug related. It was primarily used to take cars and currency, and the money was recycled back into the state and federal government. These laws operated under presumed guilt, which did not require a trial or even a conviction.

By 1992, there were more people in federal prisons for drug charges than there were for all crimes in 1980, with the burden overwhelmingly falling on black people. Twice as many people were arrested for possession than supplying. Chief Justice of the Supreme Court, William Rehnquist, said there were too many arrests. New York City jails filled to breaking point, and jail boats had to be opened. Bush's policies did nothing to stop people from buying and selling drugs.

That Bush was simultaneously waging a War on Drugs while facilitating their importation via the CIA is hard for some people to swallow. But it must be probed further to understand Bush's ability to deceive.

In 1985, Retired US Navy Lieutenant Commander Al Martin had dinner with George HW Bush, Jeb Bush and a CIA veteran Felix Rodriguez, who'd taken $10 million from the Medellín Cartel for Nicaraguan rebels involved in trafficking cocaine. Over food, George HW Bush boasted that he operated on the Big Lie principle, whereby big lies would be believed because the public couldn't conceive that their leader was capable of bending the truth that far, such as a president railing against drugs while overseeing drug trafficking worth billions.

Anyone who tried to blow the whistle on Bush's phoney War on Drugs ended up paying a price. Former DEA agent Cele Castillo wrote *Powderburns: Cocaine, Contras & the Drug War* (1998), in which he detailed a meeting with Bush. Assigned to El Salvador in 1986 to investigate a pilot who stored his plane at the Ilopango airbase, Castillo had discovered that the Nicaraguan rebels were smuggling cocaine to the US, using the same pilots, planes and hangers as the CIA and NSC (National Security Council), under the direction of Bush's frontman Oliver North. At Ilopango, he often saw Bush's buddy, Felix Rodriguez, whom Castillo described as an American terrorist. Bewildered, he told his bosses about the cocaine smuggling. They instructed him to use the word "alleged" in his reports instead of stating things as factual.

Castillo reported that a CIA agent was requesting a US Visa for a Nicaraguan-rebel drug smuggler who was flying cocaine from Costa Rica to anti-Castro Cubans in Miami. The cocaine in Costa Rica was picked up from the ranch of an American, John Hull, who, by the admission of the CIA's station chief in Costa Rica, was working with the CIA on military supply and other operations on behalf of the Nicaraguan rebels, and was being paid $110,000 a month by Oliver North.

After Castillo blew the whistle, Vice President Bush met him briefly during a visit to Guatemala City on January 14, 1986, at a cocktail party at the ambassador's residence. Protected by a retinue of Secret Service agents, Bush was talking to embassy personnel and Guatemalan dignitaries. Bush approached Castillo and read the tag on his lapel, which identified him as a member of the US embassy. Shaking hands, Bush asked what he did.

"I'm a DEA agent assigned to Guatemala."

"Well, what do you do?"

"There's some funny things going on with the Contras in El Salvador."

Without uttering a response, Bush smiled and walked away. Castillo realised that Bush was in on the drug trafficking.

Following the party at the ambassador's house, the US Ambassador to El Salvador sent a back-channel cable to the State Department. A few days later, the DEA closed down Castillo's investigation. The reports he'd filed disappeared into what Castillo called a black hole at DEA headquarters. In February 1987, DEA investigators found "no credible information" to indicate that traffickers were part of any political organisation, including the Nicaraguan rebels and the government of Nicaragua. Castillo received so much harassment that he ended up quitting the DEA in 1990.

Presidential candidate and billionaire Ross Perot hired Bo Gritz, a Green Beret who'd earned multiple medals for bravery, to find American POWs imprisoned in Asia decades after the Vietnam War. While on his mission, Gritz came across General Khun Sa, a Burmese drug lord who offered to identify US government officials he claimed had been trafficking in heroin for over twenty years. Having uncovered CIA drug trafficking in Asia, Perot and Gritz were shocked.

Perot requested a meeting with Bush, so that he could present his evidence. Bush told Perot to go to the proper authorities and refused to help any further. Here are extracts from a letter Gritz wrote to Bush:

Sir:

Why does it seem that you are saying "YES" to illegal narcotics in America?

I turned over video tapes to your NSC staff assistant, Tom Harvey, January 1987, wherein General KHUN SA, overlord of Asia's "Golden Triangle" offered to stop 900 tons of heroin/opium from entering the free world in 1987. Harvey told me, "...there is no interest here in doing that."

Unfortunately, Khun Sa knew nothing about US POWs. He did, however, offer to trade his nation's poppy dependence for a legitimate economy.

Instead of receiving an "Atta Boy" for bringing back video tape showing Khun Sa's offer to stop 900 tons of illegal narcotics and expose dirty USG officials, Scott was jailed and I was threatened. I was told that if I didn't "erase and forget" all that we had discovered, I would, "hurt the government." Further, I was promised a prison sentence of "15 years."

I returned to Burma with two other American witnesses, Lance Trimmer, a private detective from San Francisco, and Barry Flynn from Boston. Gen Khun Sa identified some of those in government service he says were dealing in heroin and arms sales. We video-taped this second interview and I turned copies over in June 1987, to the Chairman of the Select Committee on Intelligence; Chairman of the House on Foreign Affairs Task Force on Narcotics Control; Co-Chairman, Senate Narcotics Committee; Senator Harry Reid, NV; Representative James Bilbray, NV; and other Congressional members. Mister Richard Armitage, Assistant Secretary of Defense for International Security Affairs, is one of those USG officials implicated by Khun Sa. Nothing was done with this evidence that indicated that anyone of authority, including yourself, had intended to do anything more than protect Mr Armitage. I was charged with "Misuse of Passport." Seems that it is alright for Oliver North and Robert MacFarlane to go into Iran on Irish Passports to negotiate an illegal arms deal that neither you nor anyone else admits condoning, but I can't use a passport that brings back drug information against your friends.

Lance Trimmer and I submitted a "Citizen Complaint of Wrongdoing by Federal Officers" to Attorney General Edwin Meese, III on 17 September 1987. Continuous private and Legislative inquiries to date indicate that the Attorney General's Office has "lost" the document. Congressional requests to the Government Accounting Office have resulted in additional government snares and stalls.

January 20, 1988, I talked before your Breakfast Club in Houston, Texas. A distinguished group of approximately 125 associates of yours, including the Chief Justice of the Texas Supreme Court, expressed assurance that you are a righteous man. Almost all of them raised their hand when I asked how many of them know you personally. If you are a man with good intent, I pray you will do more than respond to this letter. I ask that you seriously look into the possibility that political appointees close to you are guilty of by-passing our Constitutional process, and for purposes of promoting illegal covert operations, conspired in the trafficking of narcotics and arms.

Please answer why a respected American Citizen like Mister H Ross Perot can bring you a pile of evidence of wrongdoing by Armitage and others, and you, according to *TIME magazine* (May 4, page 18), not only offer him no support, but have your Secretary of Defense, Frank Carlucci tell Mr. Perot to "stop pursuing Mr Armitage." Why Sir, will you not look into affidavits gathered by The Christic Institute (Washington, D.C.), which testify that Armitage not only trafficked in heroin, but did so under the guise of an officer charged with bringing home our POWs. If the charges are true, Armitage, who is still responsible for POW recovery as your Assistant Secretary of Defense ISA, has every reason not to want these heroes returned to us alive. Clearly, follow-on investigations would illuminate the collective crimes of Armitage and others.

...in May 1987, Gen Khun Sa, in his jungle headquarters, named Richard Armitage as a key connection in a ring of heroin trafficking mobsters and USG officials. A US agent I have known for many years stopped by my home last month en route to his next overseas assignment. He remarked that he had worked for those CIA chiefs named by Khun Sa, and that by his own personal knowledge, he knew what Khun Sa said was true. He was surprised it had taken so long to surface.

I am a registered Republican. I voted for you twice. I will not do so again. If you have any love or loyalty in your heart for this nation; if you have not completely sold out, then do something positive to determine the truth of these most serious allegations. You were Director of the CIA in 1975, during a time Khun Sa says Armitage and CIA officials were trafficking in heroin. As Director of Intelligence you were responsible to the American people for the activities of your assistant – even as you should know what some of these same people are doing who are close to you now as our Vice President because I feel these "parallel government" types will only be promoted by you, giving them more reason to bury our POWs.

Parting shot Mr Vice President: On 28 January 1988, General Khun Sa tendered an offer to turn over to me one metric ton (2,200 pounds) of heroin.

He says this is a good faith gesture to the American people that he is serious about stopping all drugs coming from the infamous Golden Triangle. If you and Nancy Reagan are really serious about saying "NO" to drugs, why not test Gen Khun Sa? I challenge you to allow me in the company of agents of your choice to arrange to receive this token offer worth over $4 billion on the streets of New York City. It will represent the largest "legal" seizure of heroin on record. You can personally torch it, dump it in the ocean, or turn it into legal medication; as I understand there is a great shortage of legal opiates available to our doctors. I think Gen Khun Sa's offer is most interesting. If you say "YES" then the ever increasing flow of heroin from Southeast Asia (600 tons—'86, 900 tons—'87, 1200 tons—'88) may dry up – not good for business in the parallel government and super CIA circles Oliver North mentioned. If you say "NO" to Khun Sa, you are showing colors not fit for a man who would be President.

Respecting Your Office,

James "Bo" Gritz, Concerned American, Box 472 HCR-31 Sandy Valley, NV 89019, Tel: (702) 723-5266

Further investigation of the CIA drug trafficking led Ross Perot to Mena and Bush's involvement.

"When you look into the [Vietnam POW] cover-up," Perot said, "you find government officials in the drug trade who can't break themselves of the habit. What I have found is a snake pit [CIA drug trafficking] without a bottom. They will do anything to keep this covered up."

Unable to get Bush to acknowledge the trafficking, Perot ran against Bush in the 1992 election.

Chip Tatum was a CIA deep-cover agent for twenty-five years. Like Barry, he flew cocaine into Arkansas for the CIA. Realising he was expendable, Chip filed away documents and conversations he'd recorded that would incriminate the CIA and government officials such as George HW Bush and Bill Clinton. When he refused to surrender the documents to the CIA, he was imprisoned for embezzlement and so was his wife. In jail, he broke the leg of a debt collector working for the Mexican Mafia, who subsequently put a hit out on him. Realising that if he died, the documents would be released, the CIA secured his release.

Chip Tatum stated that Bush was so terrified of Perot becoming president and prosecuting Bush for drug crimes that Bush made plans to assassinate him. When Perot ran again in 1996, Tatum wrote him a letter:

Dear Mr Perot:

As you prepare your part for the 1996 election, there is a matter of grave importance of which you should be aware.

In 1992, as the commander of a Black Operations Unit called Pegasus, I was ordered to neutralize you. Our unit was directed by President George Bush. It was determined, at some point, that the party you formed was counter to the American system of democracy. In his attempt to justify your neutralization, Mr Bush expressed not only his concerns of the existence of your party and the threat which you posed to free America, but also the positions of other US and world leaders.

I had been associated with Pegasus since its creation in 1985. The original mission of our unit was to align world leaders and financiers with the United States. I was personally responsible for the neutralization of one Mossad agent, an army Chief of Staff of a foreign government, a rebel leader and the president of a foreign government.

However, all of these missions were directed toward enemies of the United States as determined by our President. And because of this, I did not hesitate to successfully neutralize these enemies.

The order to neutralize you, however, went against all that I believed in. It was obvious to me that his order was predicated on a desire to remain as President rather than a matter of enemy alignment. I refused the order. I further advised the President and others that if you or members of your organization or family were threatened or harmed in any way, I would cause information, which includes certain documents, to be disseminated from their six locations in various areas of the world, to various media and political destinations. I walked away from Special Operations that day with the knowledge that you don't just quit! I felt, however, that the time capsules protected my interests.

In September of 1994, I received a telephone call demanding the information "or else!" It was obvious from the day that I walked out of Pegasus that to turn this information over would be terminal. In the spring of 1995, I was arrested by the FBI for wire fraud. Although innocent of the allegations, I found it necessary to plead guilty in an attempt to tarnish my credibility. It was my opinion, as I expressed it to [Felix] Rodriguez when he called and threatened me, that if I were of questionable credibility, the documents, if ever made public, may not stand on their merits.

With this arrest, I seized upon the opportunity to effect this theory. I have since been indicted on a second fraud charge, this time involving my wife. I will not allow this prosecution of my family. I have notified the authorities that I intend to put my case to a jury. While awaiting the trial, I wrote a book involving my first experience in the Special Operations arena. Since then, I have found that the US Marshals have instructed the Hillsborough County jail to hold me, regardless of the outcome of the instant trial charge.

The new charge is treason. For over twenty years I have dedicated my skills, time, and health to my country. I have been shot, tortured, and beaten, fighting to protect our right to form and run our government as determined by the Constitution. I am not aware of an active Pegasus unit. I had assumed it was disbanded with the new President... Someone had to orchestrate this. So, be aware and alert!

Good luck and good fortune in 1996.

In 1996, Perot's strategy to take votes from Bush worked, and Bill Clinton won – a president involving in drug trafficking was replaced by another involved in trafficking.

On YouTube, Chip Tatum stated that Bush had direct knowledge of the drug operation coming out of Central and South America. Tatum saw Bush at a drugs camp, standing by a cocaine press. Thanks to YouTube, the testimonies of numerous US pilots who flew drugs into America for the CIA are available: Google Beau Abbott, Tosh Plumlee or Terry Reed.

In April 1989, Senator John Kerry's Subcommittee on Terrorism Narcotics and International Operations released its report, "Drugs, Law Enforcement and Foreign Policy." It included diary entries from Bush's frontman Oliver North. In July 1984, North wrote that he wanted "aircraft to go to Bolivia to pick up paste, want aircraft to pick up 1,500 kilos." On July 12, 1985, he wrote, "$14 million to finance [arms] Supermarket came from drugs."

While others took the fall for trafficking, the DEA never investigated North. Even though he'd kept his hands clean by not actually flying the drugs himself, he was guilty of conspiracy under statutes passed by Congress in 1953, concerning anyone committing any act, no matter how small, in the furtherance of a crime. The DEA had stood down, even though North had used international traffickers on the DEA's most wanted list.

One example in the Kerry Report was the airline SETCO, described as "the principal company used by the Contras in Honduras to transport supplies and personnel," in 1986. As early as 1983, US Customs had told the DEA that the owner of the airline was Juan Matta Ballesteros, one of the biggest cocaine traffickers in the world. By 1980, the DEA was aware that Matta and his coconspirators were estimated to be trafficking one-third of the cocaine used in America. Oliver North had obtained funding from the State Department for Matta's SETCO and three other airlines, all established and run by traffickers. The DEA's response was to close their office in Honduras and to have their officials lie to the public. The difficulty of this deceit was compounded after Matta and his accomplices conspired to kidnap, torture and murder a DEA agent in Mexico in 1985. As they'd all been contributing drug money and weapons to the Nicaraguan rebels, Matta wasn't arrested until 1988, as part of a strategy for Bush's run for the presidency.

Born into a CIA family, Mike Ruppert rose up the ranks as an LA police officer. After witnessing huge CIA shipments of cocaine into California, he blew the whistle and was forced to quit amid death threats. After the journalist Gary Webb detailed the CIA cocaine trafficking that Bush had overseen, people were so outraged that the CIA director appeared at a townhall meeting at a high school in LA – an epicentre of the crack epidemic that CIA cocaine had helped to fuel. Mike Ruppert decided to attend.

A Congresswoman approached the microphone. "It's not up to us to prove the CIA was involved in drug trafficking in South Central Los Angeles. Rather, it's up to them to prove they were not."

As CIA director Deutch got up to speak, the crowd booed and jeered. "I'm going to be brief," he said. "I want to make four points, and only four points. First, the people of the CIA and I understand the tremendous horror that drugs have been to Americans, what drugs do to families and communities, and the way drugs kill babies. We understand how ravaging drugs are in this country. CIA employees and I share your anger at the injustice and lack of compassion that drug victims encounter."

"He sounds just like Clinton!" someone yelled.

"During the past two years," Deutch said, "while I have been director of Central Intelligence, our case officers' intelligence operations have directly worked to capture all of the Cali Cartel drug lords. We have seriously disrupted the flow of coca paste between the growing areas of Peru and Bolivia to the cocaine processing facilities in Colombia. We have seized huge amounts of heroin grown in the poppy fields of Southwest Asia. Our purpose is to stop drugs from coming into the US. So my second point is that the CIA is fighting against drugs." The audience grumbled.

"Our activities are secret. Accordingly, there's not a lot of public understanding of what we do. I understand that people are suspicious of the CIA, and in the course of recruiting agents to break up those groups that bring drugs into the US, our case officers, our men and women deal with bad people, very bad people, sometimes at great risk to their lives. These are criminals with which we must deal, if we are going to stop drugs from coming to the country. They frequently lie about their relationships with us for their own purpose. So it is hard for members of the public to know what is true and what is not true...

"Now we all know that the US government and the CIA supported the Contras [Nicaraguan rebels] in their efforts to overthrow the Sandinista government in Nicaragua in the mid-80s. It is alleged that the CIA also helped the Contras raise money for arms by introducing crack cocaine into California. It is an appalling charge that goes to the heart of this country. It is a charge that cannot go unanswered," Deutch said, pounding on the table.

"It says that the CIA, an agency of the United States government founded to protect Americans, helped introduce drugs and poison into our children and helped kill their future. No one who heads a government agency – not myself or anyone else – can let such an allegation stand. I will get to the bottom of it and I will let you know the results of what I have found.

"I've ordered an independent investigation of these charges. The third point I want to make to you is to explain the nature of the investigation. I've ordered the CIA Inspector General to undertake a full investigation." The crowd yelled their discontent so loudly that Deutch had to wait a minute before continuing. "Let me tell you why he's the right official to do the job. First, the IG is established by law of Congress to be independent, to carry out activities, to look for fraud and crimes within the CIA. Secondly, the inspector general has access to all CIA records and documents, no matter how secret. Third, the IG has the authority to interview the right people. Fourth, he is able to cooperate with other government departments. For example, the Department of Justice, the DEA, the Department of Defense, all of which had operations on-going in Nicaragua at the time. Finally, the IG has a good track record of being a whistle-blower on past misdeeds of the CIA. For example, just last month he uncovered that some CIA employees were misusing credit cards and they are now in jail."

"What about Guatemala? What about those murders?" a heckler yelled, referring to CIA-sponsored military regimes in Guatemala murdering thousands of civilians.

"Most importantly, when this investigation is complete, I intend to make the results public, so that any person can judge the adequacy of the investigation. Anyone in the public who has a wish to look at the report will be able to do so. I want to stress that I am not the only person in the CIA who wants any American to believe that the CIA was responsible for this kind of disgusting charge. Finally, I want to say to you that as of today, we have no evidence of conspiracy by the CIA to engage in encouraging drug traffickers in Nicaragua or elsewhere in Latin America during this or any other period."

A question came from a graduate student of the Tuskegee Institute in Alabama: "I'd like to know how this incident differs from what happened at my school, where, for forty years, the government denied inflicting syphilis on African-American men?"

Deutch conceded that what had happened at Tuskegee was terrible. "Let me say something else. There was no one who came forward forty years ago and said they were going to investigate."

"Where I live there are no jobs for the children and our kids are just seen as commodities," a woman said. "They are being cycled through the prisons. They come back to the street and are marked and scarred for the rest of their life. You, the President and everybody else should be highly upset. You should be saying, how did this cancer get here?"

A man stood up. "And now we are supposed to trust the CIA to investigate itself?"

Deutch tried to quell the malcontents by overemphasising the Inspector General's independence, which incensed the crowd.

"Why don't you turn it over to an independent counsel? Someone who has the power to issue subpoenas. It would have more credibility."

Deutch responded that no independent counsel was possible because no criminal complaint had been filed.

It was Mike Ruppert's turn to speak. For years, he'd been waiting for such an opportunity. The rowdy audience hushed as Mike said, "I will tell you, director Deutch, as a former Los Angeles Police narcotics detective, that your agency has dealt drugs throughout this country for a long time."

There was a standing ovation. The audience went wild. It took a few minutes to calm everybody down.

"Director Deutch, I will refer you to three specific agency operations known as Amadeus, Pegasus and Watchtower. I have Watchtower documents heavily redacted by the Agency [CIA]. I was personally exposed to CIA operations and recruited by CIA personnel who attempted to recruit me in the late 70s to become involved in protecting Agency drug operations in this country. I have been trying to get this out for eighteen years, and I have the evidence. My question for you is very specific, sir. If in the course of the IG's [CIA Inspector General's] investigations... you come across evidence of severely criminal activity, and it's classified, will you use that classification to hide the criminal activity or will you tell the American people the truth?"

There was more applause and cheering as Deutch wrung his hands and clasped them together as if praying.

"If you have information," Deutch said, "about CIA illegal activity in drugs, you should immediately bring that information to wherever you want, but let me suggest three places: the Los Angeles Police Department—" "No! No!" the crowd yelled.

"It is your choice: the Los Angeles Police Department, the Inspector General or the office of one of your congresspersons..."

The audience started chanting, "He told you!"

"If this information turns up wrongdoing," Deutch said, growing exasperated, "we will bring the people to justice and make them accountable."

"For the record..." Mike said, "I did bring this information out eighteen years ago and I got shot at and forced out of LAPD because of it." Mike finished to massive applause.

"My question to you is," a spectator said to Deutch, "if you know all this stuff that the Agency has done historically, then why should we believe you today, when you say certainly this could never happen in Los Angeles, when the CIA's done this stuff all over the world?"

"I didn't come here thinking everyone was going to believe me," Deutch said. "I came here for a much simpler task. I came here to stand up on my legs and tell you I was going to investigate these horrible allegations. All you can do is listen to what I have to say and wait to see the results."

"But how can we know how many documents have been shredded and how can we be certain that more documents won't be shredded?"

"I don't know that anybody has found any lost documents in the operational files," Deutch said. "I know of nobody who has found any gaps in sequences, any missing files, any missing papers for any period of that time. That may come up."

"Hey, do you know Walter Pincus?" a man asked, referring to a journalist who spied on American students abroad for the CIA.

"Yes," Deutch said. "Why?"

"Is he an asset of the CIA?"

As if he'd had enough, Deutch clasped his head and shook it.

The crowd vented on the lady who'd invited Deutch to the meeting. "I don't know why this lady is saluting Deutch's courage for coming here today, when everybody knows this building has got hundreds of pigs in it. There's pigs behind those curtains. There's pigs on the roof. We're not going to get no ghetto justice today." The crowd murmured its approval.

A man stood and pointed at Deutch. "To see you coming in this community today in this way is nothing more than a public-relations move for the white people of this country. So you are going to come into this community today and insult us, and tell us you're going to investigate yourself. You've got to be crazy."

Refusing to take any more questions, Deutch concluded with, "You know, I've learned how important it is for our government and our agency to get on top of this problem and stop it. I came today to try and describe the approach and have left with a better appreciation of what is on your mind." Immediately, the media tried to spin the meeting in a way favourable to the CIA. Via satellite, Ted Koppel of *Nightline* interviewed members of the audience, trying to extract a positive testimony, only to find himself rebuffed by questions such as, "You come down here and talk about solutions. We have kids that are dying. We have hospitals for babies born drug addicted. When are you guys going to come down and bring cameras to our neighbourhood?"

"I'm not sure that anybody even thought that was why Director Deutch came there today," Koppel said. "He's come here because a lot of you are in anguish. A lot of you are angry. A lot of you are frustrated by what you believe to be the CIA's involvement in bringing drugs to South Central LA. Now, I want to hear from someone who thought it did some good."

"Well, I am glad Mr Deutch was here today," said Marcine Shaw, the mayor pro tem of Compton. "I'm glad Congresswoman Macdonald had him here because that's what it took to get your cameras here, Mr Koppel."

Koppel shook his head. "Yes, but that's not the question." Koppel finished his broadcast with, "If any suspicions were put to rest or minds changed, there was no evidence of it in South Central this evening."

Originally, Pablo Escobar was in bed with the CIA through the Medellín Cartel's contributions to the Nicaraguan rebels. Traffickers who made such payments to the CIA were allowed to operate. Testifying as a US government witness at the Noriega trial, the Medellín Cartel's Carlos Lehder admitted contributing millions to the Nicaraguan rebels.

The CIA had helped to overthrow the government of Bolivia in 1980, and put cocaine traffickers in charge – detailed in my book, *We Are Being Lied To: The War on Drugs*. In the name of fighting Communism, the CIA had put Klaus Barbi – a Nazi war criminal responsible for the deaths of up to 14,000 people – in charge of the coup in Bolivia. His Argentine death squad had massacred numerous civilians.

After the coup, the CIA-backed Bolivian government exported raw coca. One of its customers was the Medellín Cartel. As the anti-Communist cause was being advanced, the CIA protected this activity by obstructing investigations by other law-enforcement agencies. In doing so, it created a secure route for coca paste to go from Bolivia to Colombia. In Medellín, the Bolivian paste was processed and distributed to the US.

The Argentine intelligence services made a fortune from selling Bolivian paste. Some of the money was laundered in Miami and recycled into other anti-Communist causes, which included buying massive amounts of weapons from US manufacturers, which Bush represented, along with banking interests. That's how Bush used drug money to finance the Nicaraguan rebels.

Prompted by the journalism of Gary Webb, the CIA and Justice Department investigations confirmed that the Nicaraguan rebels had been involved in the cocaine trade throughout the 1980s. The CIA had been aware of it, and they'd steered other agencies, such as DEA investigators, away from the truth.

Despite Bush holding Pablo accountable for nearly all of the cocaine entering America, CIA-protected cocaine wasn't only coming from Colombia. Pablo was used as a smokescreen for cocaine coming from various routes originating in South America. In El Salvador, the military were involved. Honduras was a major transiting point. Anti-Castro Cubans active in Costa Rica sent boatloads of cocaine to Miami. As usual, the CIA stopped all of the investigations into these areas. The mainstream media avoided it. Long after Pablo's demise, the tangled roots of this infrastructure keep the cocaine flowing to this day.

Part 3 The
Verdict

Chapter 46

Verdict

Pablo Escobar ordered approximately 4,000 deaths, but he was an amateur in the murder leagues in comparison to George HW Bush, whose proclivity for taking America to war and to drop bombs on impoverished populations caused well over 100,000 deaths and the poisoning of hundreds of thousands of US troops and personnel. Backed up by presidential pomp and circumstance, video-casts of precision bombing and an ability to write off the mass murder of civilians as collateral damage, Bush committed murder with panache. With God and the media on his side, he acted out his capacity for violence and never suffered any consequences.

The analysis of Bush's character suggests that someone who initiated wars for personal gain, protected political paedophiles and was the head of the CIA would easily have ordered the elimination of Barry Seal, who had threatened Bush in various ways.

To reach a verdict, it's necessary to go beyond a character analysis. It's time to examine the clues that arose in the aftermath of the murder.

After shooting Barry Seal, Quintero Cruz sprinted to the getaway car and handed his MAC-10 to Cumbamba, who was wearing green surgical trousers. Speeding away, the Buick almost hit a bystander. Roughly a quarter of a mile away, the car was abandoned – with its engine still running and the MAC-10 inside – at a children's activity centre parking lot. The Colombians dashed to a red Cadillac. Two sheriff's deputies providing security at a bingo game noticed the Colombians laughing as they switched cars.

Hunting for the killers, FBI agents poured into the airport. Some checked hotels for Colombian names.

At 7:30 pm, two of the Colombians checked out of the New Orleans Hilton. At New Orleans International Airport, they abandoned the red Cadillac shortly after 8:36 pm.

At 8:45 pm, two FBI agents grew suspicious of a nervous sweaty man at an Eastern Airlines ticket counter attempting to get a direct flight to Miami. When questioned, Cumbamba claimed to be a lost traveller and provided a passport for Miguel Velez. With no probable cause or description, the agents released him. He said he intended to return to his hotel and get a taxi to another airport. Fifteen minutes later, descriptions of the hit men were broadcast. The FBI realised that Velez was one of them. Agents found out that he had taken a taxi.

But for a deer running onto a highway, Cumbamba might have escaped. At 2:20 am, in Meridian, Mississippi, the police spotted a broken-down taxi that had collided with a deer. They pulled over and questioned the passenger in green trousers. Upon finding $3,270 and the keys to the red getaway car on Cumbamba, they arrested him. Cumbamba had made the mistake of changing his green surgical trousers for another pair of green trousers. Upset with losing his fare, the taxi driver couldn't understand why the police were so concerned about a dead deer.

Vasquez had made a few errors, too. He'd used his true identity, including his American Express card, to hire the getaway car. He managed to ensconce himself in a friend's house in Algiers, New Orleans, unaware that his friend was an FBI informant. The next day, the FBI captured him with $860 in cash and $9,800 in cashier's checks. Quintero Cruz suffered a similar fate, busted in a safe house in Marrero, Louisiana with $3,127.

It seems that the Colombians were meant to be captured quickly, so that the case could be closed.

Cumbamba's lawyer, Richard Sharpstein, told author Daniel Hopsiker that representing Cumbamba was one of the most amazing experiences of his life. Sharpstein said that the three Colombians who'd been arrested all told their lawyers the same thing: after they'd arrived in America, their mission to assassinate Barry Seal was directed by an anonymous gringo, a US military officer, who they figured out was Oliver North. After they'd rendezvoused together in America, they received instructions over the phone from a man who insisted on remaining anonymous, but identified himself as an American military officer. They'd been put in touch with the officer through Rafa.

Numerous sources confirmed to Hopsiker that Oliver North was running assassinations from his White House office. North had also drawn up contingency plans, including implementing martial law if the drug-trafficking facilitated by the CIA were ever exposed to the public.

The official story is that a three-man hit team assassinated Barry Seal. Yet six Colombians were arrested fleeing the scene. A seventh, Rafa was charged in absentia for organising the hit, but was shot to death at his antique car dealership in Colombia, thus eliminating the contact between the arrestees and Oliver North.

The eighth co-conspirator was the supplier of the MAC-10, Jose Coutin. He owned Broadway Boutique, which stocked ladies' clothes in the front of the shop and military supplies in the back. Being a CIA asset, an FBI informant and a weapons supplier for the Nicaraguan rebels, Coutin wasn't charged with the hit even though he was guilty of conspiracy to commit murder by supplying the MAC-10. Coutin testified against the three Colombians. When asked about his connections to the CIA and the Nicaraguan rebels, he lost his cool on the stand.

Three of the six Colombians originally arrested included Rafa's brother, John Cordona who was busted at a safe house; Eliberto Sanchez, who was caught at New Orleans International Airport; and Jose Renteria, who was arrested at Miami Airport about to board a plane. Sanchez and Cordona were deported without any charges being filed.

Renteria had picked up the weapons from Coutin and delivered them to the three Colombians. On the basis that he wasn't at the murder scene, Renteria's trial was severed from the trial of the three Colombians, which Cumbamba's lawyer, Sharpstein, found highly suspicious. Sharpstein said that Renteria had offered to cooperate, but the federal government was not keen on that happening. According to witness testimony, Renteria had photographed the murder scene. At New Orleans Airport, an FBI agent had confiscated his camera and exposed the film inside. In record time, Renteria received a plea bargain for minor charges and was deported, to avoid, according to Sharpstein, his testimony ever being heard.

The trial of the three was structured to create an official version of events that precluded any involvement of George HW Bush's proxy Oliver North. As the residents of Baton Rouge had heard so much about Barry Seal, the trial was moved to Lake Charles, Louisiana, an oil-refinery town near the Texas border, 170 miles away from the tainted jury pool. Hoping to boost its local economy, Lake Charles had launched a campaign to host the trial.

The trial started on April 6, 1987, over a year after Barry's death. With none of the Colombians willing to cooperate against their co-defendants, the prosecutor sought the death penalty for all three.

Protected by federal marshals, Max Mermelstein – whose half-hearted attempt to assassinate Barry Seal on behalf the Medellín Cartel had failed – was handed a MAC-10 by the prosecutor, while in the witness box.

"Mr Mermelstein, would you look at these two exhibits before you mark State's 14 [the MAC-10] and State's 15 [a silencer for the MAC-10], please?" said the prosecutor, a short no-nonsense woman with dark hair. "Have you ever seen previously either Exhibit 14 or 15?"

"Yes, I have," said Max, overweight with grey hair and a beard, wearing a colourful shirt and a blue blazer. With the three Colombians gazing at him, he spoke slowly and with little emotion.

"Would you tell the jury the circumstances under which you first saw that?"

"Sometime in April or May of 1984, they were brought to my residence," Max said.

"By whom were they brought?"

"By Rafael Cardona," Max said, referring to Rafa, a link to Oliver North who was silenced by assassination.

"And why did he have that weapon with him?"

"To show me what he had just gotten..."

"Was anything done with that weapon when it got to your residence?"

"He showed me the weapon and told me he wanted to test-fire it by the pool." Max admitted organising the logistics for thirty-eight 450-kilo airshipments of cocaine, and for being responsible for 50,000 kilos of cocaine entering America. As well as providing compelling testimony, Max identified Cumbamba.

"How much cash did you arrange to be taken out of the United States?" said Sharpstein, the tanned and well-dressed Miami lawyer defending the Colombians.

"Approximately three-hundred million."

The jury gasped.

"You yourself arranged for approximately $300 million in illegal money to be taken out of the country?"

"That is correct, sir."

Addressing the jury, ten women and two men, Sharpstein said, "Max Mermelstein is a man who would make Barry Seal look like a midget... [Max was] another Barry Seal, a clone, maybe even worse than Seal..."

Physical evidence presented by the prosecutor included the fingerprints of the three Colombians found in the murder vehicle, chemical evidence on Cumbamba's hand indicating that he'd handled a recently fired weapon, and car keys found in Cumbamba's pocket. A car salesman described selling the murder vehicle to Vasquez for $6,500. Two witnesses placed Quintero Cruz at the murder scene. It took five weeks and 118 witnesses for the prosecution's case to be presented.

"Why did they use a machine gun instead of walking up to Barry Seal and shooting him?" the prosecutor said, brandishing the MAC-10. "Because this weapon was used to teach a lesson – gangland style – to deter other snitches."

Sharpstein called no witnesses. He attacked Barry Seal's character. "The man was too complex. The man had many sides, not just two sides, right and wrong. Adler Barry Seal was a drug smuggler. He was a soldier of fortune. He was a mercenary. He was a man who would do what benefited Barry Seal. He was a man who understood the system… He always found a back door out and he always used it to benefit Barry Seal. He put bullets in his own head. I tell you the tale of Barry Seal will point in the direction of that because he himself is responsible for where he is."

After deliberating for thirty minutes, the jury found the three Colombians guilty with a penalty of life imprisonment.

After the trial, when asked why Barry was murdered, Sharpstein recounted the various times that Barry had telephoned George HW Bush for help. Barry had been moved to the halfway house and stripped of carrying weapons just one week after he had asked Bush to get the tax authorities off his back. Although Cumbamba had pulled the trigger, the Colombians, according to Sharpstein, had received orders from government officials who wanted him dead.

Sharpstein's conclusion was backed up by Red Hall, a CIA electronics expert. Hall told author Hopsiker that the CIA had a lot to do with it, and that Oliver North had directed the assassins. Hall added that North had previously tried to eliminate Barry much earlier by blowing the whistle on Barry's sting operation while Barry was in Nicaragua.

Ex-CIA deep-cover agent Chip Tatum told Hopsiker that Oliver North's role in the death of Barry Seal wasn't exactly the secret of the century.

The night Barry died, federal agents swarmed the state police headquarters at Baton Rouge, and demanded all of the evidence from the homicide detectives in charge of preserving it. They physically seized Barry's belongings from the boot of his Cadillac, including files on important people that he had kept as leverage.

By law, the state police should have prevented the FBI from confiscating the evidence. A lawyer for one of the Colombian hit men stated that the state police would have had to draw their guns on the federal agents to prevent them from taking the evidence. Some of the things accounted for in the trunk were never returned. Barry was known to have kept three boxes of precious documents, including the encrypted numbers of Swiss bank accounts, where senior politicians stashed money. One account under the encrypted code KPFBMMBODB with over $10 million belonged to the Secretary of Defense, Caspar Weinberger, who'd allegedly received kickbacks on drugs and arms sales.

On March 16, 1986, four months after Barry's death, Ronald Reagan appeared on TV, hoping to gain support for his request for $100 million in aid for the Nicaraguan rebels. Brandishing one of the grainy photos Barry had snapped during the Nicaraguan sting, Reagan said, "I know every American parent concerned about the drug problem will be outraged to learn that top Nicaraguan government officials are deeply involved in drug trafficking. There is no crime to which the Sandinistas will not stoop. This is an outlaw regime."

The War on Drugs is about spending money, but in this case, the public wasn't swayed. Even the DEA knew that Reagan had lied. The DEA stated that it had no information implicating "the Minister of Interior or other Nicaraguan officials."

The Nicaraguan rebels were allowed to finance their war through the importation of cocaine to America with the help of the CIA. Business continued as usual after Barry's death. Weapons out and drugs in. Even though Barry couldn't talk from the grave, the Fat Lady almost revealed all.

On October 5th, 1986, the Fat Lady was shot down over Nicaragua. After Barry's death, she had reverted to the CIA's Southern Air Transport and had continued to smuggle weapons illegally to the Nicaraguan rebels.

Only one crew member survived, Eugene Hasenfus. The fatalities included the pilot who'd replaced Emile Camp at Mena, Bill Cooper, and Wallace Sawyer Jr, who was in possession of a notebook with the names of thirty-four CIA operatives and a card with a number on its back, pertaining to a Swiss bank account with a balance of $12 million – profits from arms sales. Other records on-board linked the Fat Lady to Barry and Area 51: a CIA base in Nevada and a nuclear weapons facility.

Under interrogation by the Nicaraguans, Hasenfus revealed details about the operation. He identified two of his commanders as Ramon Medina and

Max Gomez [Felix Rodriguez], both heavy hitters in the CIA and close friends of George HW Bush. Hasenfus identified the operation's safe house in El Salvador, from which telephone records showed numerous calls to Oliver North at the White House (202-395-3345), to Southern Air Transport and to the Stanford Technology Trading Corp, a Virginia front run by retired Air Force General Richard Secord, who was involved in US assistance to Southeast Asian heroin operations during the Vietnam War.

In response to the downing of the Fat Lady, Oliver North embarked on a document- shredding binge that lasted for three days. Among the names shredded was Barry Seal's. Plenty of incriminating documents survived. Investigators found over 500 references to drugs in North's notebooks.

The co-conspirators in Barry's death allowed the media to run with stories of illegal arms shipments, but stories of CIA drug trafficking were off-limits. Due to the CIA's relationships with the media, the strategy worked.

"After the Hasenfus plane was shot down, you couldn't find a soul around Mena," said William Holmes, an Arkansas gun manufacturer, who'd supplied Barry and the CIA.

But business quickly resumed. In early 1987, an Arkansas state police investigator wrote, "New activity at the [Mena] airport," involving C-130s and an Australian company linked to the CIA. Under oath, the investigator said that two FBI agents warned him that the CIA had something going on at the Mena airport involving Southern Air Transport, and they didn't want him to screw it up.

In 1991, an IRS investigative memorandum stated that "the CIA still has ongoing operations out of the Mena, AR airport… and that one of the operations at the airport is laundering money."

In 1985, when confronted with accusations of participating in activity at Mena, the CIA blamed Mena on "a rogue DEA operation." The DEA's response was "no comment."

A few weeks before Barry's death, state authorities were monitoring a cocaine shipment on one of Barry's boats, Captain Wonderful. When they tried to get on board, they were prevented by DEA and CIA agents.

The same day that Barry was killed, three senior members of the Medellín Cartel were assassinated: Pablo Ochilla, Pablo Carrera and a brother-in-law of Jorge Ochoa. Author Hopsicker believes that these murders and Barry's were parts of a co-ordinated black op and that all along the CIA had been using the war against the Medellín Cartel as cover, while they worked with the Cali

Cartel. Hopsicker goes so far as to claim that the CIA, with Barry's help, had created the Medellín Cartel by encouraging the different factions to work together, a claim that was backed up by Paul Etzel, a Colombian accountant who interpreted for Barry during the Panamanian meeting with Pablo Escobar. Journalist Alexander Cockburn has claimed that in the beginning, the Medellín Cartel was working with the CIA. After the demise of the Medellín Cartel, cocaine continued to pour into America on planes used in CIA covert operations.

None of Barry's fleet of planes, including the Fat Lady, were seized following his assassination because they were still being used in black ops.

In August, 1987, two teenagers, Kevin Ives and Don Henry, witnessed a CIA drug drop at Mena and were killed. Their bodies were put on a railroad track. The medical expert appointed by Bill Clinton ruled that they'd gotten stoned on marijuana, fallen asleep side-by-side and were run over by a train. All of the family's attempts to get to the truth were blocked. I detail their story and Linda Ives struggle to get justice for her son in the third part of this trilogy: *We Are Being Lied To: The War on Drugs*.

A decade later, journalist Gary Webb exposed the CIA drug trafficking in the 1980s, which had helped to spawn the crack epidemic. The story caused a sensation, but the propaganda machine responded quickly. Hounded out of his job, Webb eventually committed suicide by shooting himself in the head – twice. Webb's revelations forced the CIA to announce that it was investigating itself. In a 1998 CIA Inspector General's report, the CIA admitted "briefing" Vice President Bush on how it had lied to Congress about cocaine trafficking by its agents.

The CIA continues to deny that it facilitated the arms-for-cocaine trafficking performed by Barry Seal. Authors and journalists investigating the paper trail of federal aircraft registrations and outfittings have discovered that many of the aircraft that Barry used were previously owned by Air America, a CIA proprietary company. The transportation service that Barry provided was part of a government operation that expanded way beyond Colombia and Nicaragua to include the provision of arms to Bolivia, Argentina, Peru and Brazil, an area known as the Southern Tier. The multi millions that were made financed black ops, and was used to pay off politicians such as Bill Clinton who played along with the CIA. Mena was a part of a network of rural airports in states such as Arizona, Alabama, Florida, Louisiana, Mississippi and Kentucky used by the CIA; all afforded the same protection – under the guise of national security – from conventional law enforcement.

Two law enforcement officials investigating Mena documented the crimes they'd discovered in a thirty-five volume 3,000-page Arkansas State Police archive. Not only were they never asked to testify, their investigation and careers were destroyed.

One wrote in his diary on November 17, 1987, "Should a cop cross over the line and dare to investigate the rich and powerful, he might well prepare himself to become the victim of his own government… The cops are all afraid to tell what they know for fear that they will lose their jobs."

After 1987, nine more investigations into Mena were suppressed. In December 1988, a US Senate subcommittee report stated that a Mena investigation had been dropped even though there was enough evidence "sufficient for an indictment on money laundering charges," because "the prosecution might have revealed national security information, even though all the crimes which were the focus of the investigation occurred before Seal became a federal informant [in 1984]."

In 1996, one of Barry's former associates testified that Barry's flights had been provided CIA security, including the installation of highly classified encoding devices that thwarted air defence and surveillance.

After Barry's death, Terry Reed continued to work for the CIA in Mexico, where he witnessed first-hand the CIA's involvement in drugs. He attempted to quit the business, so the CIA tried to assassinate him. With his family, he went on the run. Arrested on bogus charges, he and his wife ended up in prison and were ruined financially. By saddling him with a criminal record, the feds destroyed Terry's whistle-blower potential – all documented in his book, *Compromised: Clinton, Bush and the CIA.*

In 1991, a month before announcing his candidacy for president, Bill Clinton made his only statement as governor about the crimes of Mena. Continuing the cover-up, he claimed that the state had done all it possibly could have to investigate allegations about drugs and weapons smuggling through Mena airport. "I've always felt we never got the whole story there, and obviously if the story was that the DEA was using Barry Seal as a drug informant… then they ought to come out and say that because he's dead."

The state police had conducted a "very vigorous" investigation several years ago, and the enquiry had raised questions "that involved linkages to the federal government." A file had been turned over to the US attorney, who convened a grand jury that returned no indictments, which was not the state's fault.

He blamed Barry's murder on inadequate security. "[The Seal case] raised all kinds of questions about whether he had any links to the CIA and if he was involved with the Contras... and if that backed into the Iran-Contra deal."

The next day, the *Gazette* reported: "CLINTON: STATE DID ALL IT COULD IN MENA CASE."

It is the verdict of this book that George HW Bush sanctioned the hit on Barry Seal in response to threats by an increasingly desperate Barry to expose the drugs side of the operation. Barry also antagonised Bush by claiming that he had evidence that Bush's sons had been caught in a drug sting operation – an allegation that still remains unproved.

According to Hopsicker, there was a persistent rumour that Barry had organised a DEA sting on the Bush brothers because George HW Bush wasn't helping him. With the Bush brothers ensnared by videotape evidence, Barry supposedly posed as a saviour by using his influence to make their problem go away. Now they owed Barry a favour, but just in case they didn't follow through, Barry had kept a copy of the videotape. It had been in one of the boxes of the precious documents in his car that had been confiscated by the FBI, who arrived ten minutes after Barry's death.

A lawman told Hopsicker that he'd found a drilling rig moored in Mexican waters that served as a safe harbour for drug smuggling. A sting operation had been set up at a Florida airport, but cancelled at the last minute by someone high up after it was discovered that the Bush Brothers – George W and Jeb – were flying in on a King Air the lawman was tracking.

In *Blue Thunder*, authors Burdick and Mitchell quote an imprisoned drug smuggler called Teagle, who claimed that Jeb Bush and Donald Aronow – who built speedboats for George HW Bush – had been partners in a cocainetrafficking operation, and they owed Colombians $2.5 million. In his car on February 2, 1987, Aronow was assassinated.

After his death, Barry became a fall guy for the orchestrators of the Mena activity. The importation of tons of cocaine on CIA planes was blamed on a renegade smuggler. Those in charge of Mena had the most to gain from Barry's death. So who was running things? Certainly not Bill Clinton, who, as a mere governor, could only provide legal and police protection for the bigger players. Under the provisions of Executive Order 12333 and National Security

Decision Directives Number 2 and Number 3, George HW Bush was in charge of all intelligence operations, including Mena.

Barry died with George HW Bush's telephone number in his possession. Their relationship had soured after Bush reneged on what Barry had perceived as their agreement. Barry had worked diligently for Bush at Mena in the expectation of Bush using his power to squash any unforeseen legal difficulties. But by mid-1985, Barry was more valuable to Bush as a scapegoat. When Bush failed to provide protection, Barry must have realised – based on the pattern of his deceased associates, including Lee Harvey Oswald, David Ferrie and Emile Camp – that his end was near.

Barry had spearheaded Mena for Bush, but, after his death, the smuggling flights continued, proving not only that Barry hadn't been a rogue smuggler, but also that he was no longer needed to keep the operation going. Any doubts as to whom Barry was working for were laid to rest by the IRS in a posthumous tax assessment, which cited his "CIA-DEA employment," and claimed that Barry owed $86 million in back taxes on earnings from Mena in 1982 and 1983.

Killers sometimes keep trophies of their crimes. After Barry's death, his 1982 Beechcraft King Air 200 (FAA registration number N6308F and Serial Number BB-1014) ended up becoming one of George W Bush's favourite methods of transportation.

On March 30, 1985, Chip Tatum took notes while conversing with Oliver North as they inspected cocaine factories at villages on Nicaragua's border with Honduras. North said that they were making so much money from drugs and arms that they'd be able to retire after a year if they could keep the Arkansas hicks in line. He was referring to Clinton and his cronies stealing cash that Barry had been assigned to launder through Arkansas. He said Bush was so concerned about the missing money that he was going to have Jeb Bush arrange something out of Colombia, which Chip later understood to be the assassination of Barry, whom they also suspected of stealing money.

Rather than help Barry, Bush had him killed. All Mafia dons have underlings who carry out their orders, so that there is no trail of evidence linking directly to them. Oliver North performed this function for Bush. With the threat from the Medellín Cartel, North's work was easy and he had the perfect smokescreen.

"All the federal government had to do to kill Barry Seal was to do nothing. Then let mischief work its will," said Barry's Baton Rouge lawyer.

But just in case mischief didn't work, George HW Bush and Oliver North helped it along.

In Baton Rouge, Barry was buried in a sky-blue casket with a Snickers bar, his telephone pager and a bunch of twenty-five cent coins. He had written his own epitaph in his personal Bible which was etched onto his grave marker and read at the funeral: "A rebel adventurer the likes of whom in previous days made America great."